Savings
for the Poor

BROOKINGS METRO SERIES

The Center on Urban and Metropolitan Policy of the Brookings Institution is integrating research and practical experience into a policy agenda for cities and metropolitan areas. By bringing fresh analyses and policy ideas to the public debate, the center hopes to inform key decisionmakers and civic leaders in ways that will spur meaningful change in our nation's communities.

As part of this effort, the Center on Urban and Metropolitan Policy has established the Brookings Metro Series to introduce new perspectives and policy thinking on current issues and attempt to lay the foundation for longer-term policy reforms. The series will examine traditional urban issues, such as neighborhood assets and central city competitiveness, as well as larger metropolitan concerns, such as regional growth, development, and employment patterns. The Metro Series will consist of concise studies and collections of essays designed to appeal to a broad audience. While these studies are formally reviewed, some will not be verified like other Brookings research publications. As with all Brookings publications, the judgments, conclusions, and recommendations presented in the studies are solely those of the authors and should not be attributed to the trustees, officers, or other staff members of the institution.

Also in the Brookings Metro Series

Laws of the Landscape:
How Policies Shape Cities in Europe and America
Pietro S. Nivola

Reflections on Regionalism
Bruce J. Katz, editor
(forthcoming)

BROOKINGS
METRO
SERIES

Savings for the Poor

The Hidden Benefits
of Electronic Banking

Michael A. Stegman

BROOKINGS INSTITUTION PRESS
Washington, D.C.

BNV1477-7/3

Copyright © 1999
THE BROOKINGS INSTITUTION
1775 Massachusetts Avenue, N.W., Washington, D.C. 20036
www.brookings.edu

Library of Congress Cataloging-in-Publication data

Stegman, Michael A.
  Savings for the poor : the hidden benefits of electronic
banking / Michael A. Stegman.
  p. cm.
  Includes bibliographical references and index.
  ISBN 0-8157-8093-1 (paper)
  1. Electronic funds transfer—United States. 2. Electronic
benefits transfers—United States. 3. Public welfare—United
States—Data processing. I. Title.
  HG1710 .S82   1999   99-6678
  332.1'0285—dc21   CIP

9 8 7 6 5 4 3 2 1

The paper used in this publication meets minimum require-
ments of the American National Standard for Information
Sciences—Permanence of Paper for Printed Library Materials:
ANSI Z39.48-1984.

Typeset in New Baskerville and Myriad

Composition by Cynthia Stock
Silver Spring, Maryland

Printed by Automated Graphic Systems
White Plains, Maryland

ⒷＴＨＥ ＢＲＯＯＫＩＮＧＳ ＩＮＳＴＩＴＵＴＩＯＮ

The Brookings Institution is an independent organization devoted to nonpartisan research, education, and publication in economics, government, foreign policy, and the social sciences generally. Its principal purposes are to aid in the development of sound public policies and to promote public understanding of issues of national importance.

The Institution was founded on December 8, 1927, to merge the activities of the Institute for Government Research, founded in 1916, the Institute of Economics, founded in 1922, and the Robert Brookings Graduate School of Economics and Government, founded in 1924.

The Board of Trustees is responsible for the general administration of the Institution, while the immediate direction of the policies, program, and staff is vested in the President, assisted by an advisory committee of the officers and staff. The by-laws of the Institution state: It is the function of the Trustees to make possible the conduct of scientific research, and publication, under the most favorable conditions, and to safeguard the independence of the research staff in pursuit of their studies and in the publication of the result of such studies. It is not a part of their function to determine, control, or influence the conduct of particular investigations or the conclusions reached.

The President bears final responsibility for the decision to publish a manuscript as a Brookings book. In reaching his judgment on competence, accuracy, and objectivity of each study, the President is advised by the director of the appropriate research program and weighs the views of a panel of expert outside readers who report to him in confidence on the quality of the work. Publication of a work signifies that it is deemed a competent treatment worthy of public consideration but does not imply endorsement of conclusions or recommendations.

The Institution maintains its position of neutrality on issues of public policy in order to safeguard the intellectual freedom of the staff. Hence interpretations or conclusions in Brookings publications should be understood to be solely those of the authors and should not be attributed to the Institution, to its trustees, officers, or other staff members, or to the organizations that support its research.

Contents

Foreword

Basic bank accounts are something that most middle-class Americans take for granted. We use our savings accounts to put aside money in case of an emergency, or to invest one day in a house or an education. Our checking accounts relieve us of the worry of carrying large amounts of cash. By contrast, an estimated 13 percent of U.S. families, including 10 million people who receive federal benefits, do not have bank accounts and the security that they provide. One-third of all minority households are "unbanked," as are one out of four renters, one out of six people under the age of 35, and 15 percent of families earning between $10,000 and $25,000 annually.

To be unbanked is to be under an economic disadvantage. It means that many people have to rely on fringe banking services, such as check-cashing outlets with high fees. But what is worse is the savings deficit that it creates for many working-class, and minority, and young citizens, who have a much harder time acquiring and building assets. These families and individuals are missing out on a critical component of economic opportunity. After all, building a nest egg is difficult to do if you do not have a nest.

In the past few years, in recognition of this savings deficit, the impetus of social policy has moved from that of entitlement to that of empowerment. Saving is empowering. It allows families to live without public aid, and provides them with a ladder into the middle class. It can actually change a family's economic station and set a better course for future generations. Electronic Funds Transfers (EFTs), which are essentially the direct deposit of federal benefit checks, add to that effect. It may seem like a small thing, but it can have an enormous impact by encouraging federal benefit recipients to establish bank accounts, often their very first. It also encourages mainstream financial institutions to offer low-fee accounts to attract this customer pool. This changes the relationship between many low-income people and banks, ultimately to the benefit of both. The 104th Congress expressed its support for EFTs when it added an EFT amendment to the Debt Collection Improvement Act, and the Treasury Department is in the midst of shifting to an EFT system for all federal benefit checks.

When combined with Individual Development Accounts (IDAs), EFT becomes even more powerful. IDAs are dedicated savings accounts for working poor people that can be used for purchasing a first home, acquiring more education or job training, or starting a small business. When individuals deposit a portion of their earnings, private or public partners match that money, dollar for dollar—or even more generously in some cases. Essentially, EFT will bring people into the banking system, and IDAs will give them an incentive to use the system to its fullest in order to make their money work for them and their children. A national IDA initiative, which would match those saved dollars, could contribute to the success of EFT by increasing the likelihood that people would save. This would help benefit recipients accumulate wealth, and make EFT a better deal for banks. In other words, this would be a classic win-win situation.

This work by Michael Stegman, the director of the Center for Community Capitalism at the University of North Carolina, and former assistant secretary for policy development and research at the Department of Housing and Urban Development, cogently explains the thinking behind the shift to EFT and the implementation of the program this year, known as EFT'99. It provides an insightful analysis of why low-income people and banks have not established relationships with one another, and how EFT's implementation must take this into account. Professor Stegman also argues that EFT and IDAs are natural complements. For example, financial literacy efforts are a critical and common link between EFT and IDAs, as are getting people more comfortable with mainstream banking services and giving people a clearer understanding of the benefits of saving.

This book is a valuable guide to the myriad aspects of EFT and IDAs. I recommend it to anyone interested in helping federal benefit recipients become self-sufficient. Professor Stegman makes a powerful argument that the advantages of a bank account, and especially of savings, should not be reserved for the rich and middle class, but rather should be easily available for anyone trying to move from welfare to work, to save her money, increase her assets, and improve her life or her children's chances. Electronic Funds Transfer, especially when combined with a national, permanent IDA program, can put these opportunities within reach of people who need them most.

JOSEPH I. LIEBERMAN
U.S. Senate

Preface

Just about the time that I resigned my position as assistant secretary for policy development and research at the U.S. Department of Housing and Urban Development to return to academic life as a professor of public policy analysis and business in July 1997, I ran across a speech by Treasury Secretary Robert Rubin on "Making Welfare-to-Work Work," which inspired this book. As he had done so many times before in more places than he probably cared to remember, Rubin ticked off in priority order an eight-point program that the Treasury Department was pursuing to bring "its broad-based experience in capital markets and financial services to bear on the inner city." Not ranking high enough to make the list, and almost as an afterthought, Rubin mentioned "EFT'99," the name that Treasury had given to a recent amendment of an obscure law mandating the delivery of federal benefits by electronic funds transfer beginning in 1999. The initiative, he said, "has not attracted any attention, but could have significant economic and social effects."

EFT'99 is potentially so powerful because there are millions of lower-income people who receive government benefits who do not have bank accounts, and the law gave Treasury the responsibility of figuring out how to get these unbanked recipients into the mainstream banking system—possibly for the first time in their lives. If this works, said Rubin, it "will not only give them a more efficient way to cash checks and access to other financial services, but it may also encourage people to save, to plan financially, and therefore, to improve their economic life over time."

Savings for the Poor: The Hidden Benefits of Electronic Banking chronicles the evolution of EFT'99 from an obscure exercise in technology transfer to a nationwide movement that has the potential to help millions of working families join the financial mainstream. Part of the story, not incidentally, is how the U.S. Treasury Department has become a major force in shaping Clinton administration social policy.

I believe that if all the pieces come together, EFT'99 can do for the provision of affordable financial services what the Community Reinvestment Act has done for the provision of mortgage credit in underserved communities. Those pieces include a national financial education campaign and new savings initiatives for working families that do not benefit from existing tax-preferred savings incentives, such as individual retirement accounts.

An exploratory work like this book draws on many people. This project started with a conversation and initial support from a dear friend and colleague, Bruce Katz, director of the Center for Urban and Metropolitan Policy at the Brookings Institution. The Brookings working paper and policy briefs on EFT'99 that I prepared for the Center helped me test my ideas and get invaluable feedback that guided this effort.

I also want to thank Michael Barr, deputy assistant secretary for community development policy at Treasury, for his support and feedback during the course of this project. Because I worked with Michael when I was in the Clinton administration, I knew how smart and talented he is. But community development professionals across the country who have not had the privilege of working with him should know how important Michael has been in helping shape and carry out Treasury's impressive urban agenda.

Financial support and encouragement from Lisa Mensah, deputy director, economic development/asset building, at the Ford Foundation, has enabled me to devote more time to this enterprise than would otherwise have been possible. Through her efforts, I was able to meet and work with the leading scholars and practitioners who have pioneered the intellectual and operational development of Individual Development Accounts (IDAs). These included Professor Michael Sherraden, director of the Center for Social Development at the Washington University in St. Louis, and Robert Friedman, the founding chair of the Corporation for Enterprise Development (CFED), and his talented staff, who have long championed the cause of more asset-based social policies.

I owe an immense debt of gratitude to an extraordinary research associate, Kelly Thompson Cochran. Kelly—an accomplished journalist-turned-law-student at the University of North Carolina—played a critical role throughout the preparation of this book. Not only does chapter 4 draw upon her original research on state regulation of the check-cashing and payday loan industries, but her perceptive criticisms and recommendations sharpened the issues and strengthened the analysis, while her deft writing skills improved the flow of the entire manuscript. Kelly took on major project responsibilities while, at the same time competing for, and earning, a coveted position on *Law Review*.

Finally, I want to thank my editor, Eleanor Howes, and three peer reviewers, each of whom were generous with their time, as well as their criticisms and recommendations. Even if I have not been entirely successful, I know that this book is better because I tried to address their most serious concerns. Needless to say, I take full responsibility for all errors and omissions that remain.

MICHAEL A. STEGMAN
Chapel Hill, North Carolina

CHAPTER ONE

A Pathway to Empowerment: EFT'99

M illions of low-income, "bankless" Americans may soon become part of the financial mainstream, thanks to the recent amendment of an obscure law, advances in banking technology, and proposals to use supplemental savings programs to strengthen social security. If all goes according to plan, in coming years federal benefit recipients will join millions of private sector and federal workers and 90 percent of all federal retirees, in the system best known as *direct deposit*. In other words, they will receive their benefits through electronic funds transfer (EFT), rather than by paper check.

For as many as 10 million of these federal benefit recipients, the move to direct deposit will require opening bank accounts—perhaps for the first time in their lives—to receive their benefits electronically.[1] Like about 13 percent of U.S. families in general[2] and about 75 percent of families on welfare,[3] these recipients are often forced to pay extra for even the most basic financial services such as cashing checks and paying bills because they have no relationship with mainstream banking institutions. Without accounts, they also have a difficult time establishing credit histories and are denied many of the incentives to save for the future that middle- and upper-class Americans take for granted.

By promoting electronic delivery of benefits, the federal government's EFT'99 campaign and related efforts by state welfare and food stamp programs could change all this. By themselves, these campaigns can help provide inexpensive basic financial services to those who need them most. But if partnered with major financial education and savings initiatives like President Clinton's proposal to establish universal savings accounts (USAs) for working people,[4] these campaigns could become even more: a critical link in the nation's transition from entitlement programs to policies that promote work, self-sufficiency, and wealth accumulation. Direct deposit may be a matter of convenience for most people, but it could be the first step toward greater financial independence for millions of low-income Americans.

Upheaval in the Financial Services Industry

EFT'99 comes at a time when access to financial services for low-income families has become increasingly problematic. The interplay of many factors—among them the deregulation of interest rate ceilings in the 1980s, new technology, and growing competition from nondepository institutions—has led to a significant decline in the number of financial institutions in the United States and has driven banks to charge for services that they formerly subsidized with cheap, regulated deposits. "After fluctuating between 13,000 and 15,000 since the 1930s, a wave of bank failures and mergers caused the number of commercial banks insured by the FDIC to decline from 14,434 in 1980 to 12,343 in 1990 to 9,143 in 1997."[5] Many economic studies predict further shrinkage in the number of banks by the year 2000 by anywhere from 2,000 to 6,000 institutions.[6]

At the same time, the banking industry is restructuring to focus on higher-income markets. The recent wave of mergers and closings has sparked a small wave of new banks established by bankers who have been laid off or chose to leave their former positions. However, most of these new players are focusing on serving affluent professional or middle market businesses, or both.[7] In 1998, 216 new banks were chartered, up from just 53 three years before.[8] While the total number of bank branch offices has increased by 29 percent during the last twenty years, nearly all of this growth has occurred in middle-income areas. In contrast, the number of branch facilities declined by 21 percent in low-income neighborhoods.[9] Between 1978 and 1995, for example, Brooklyn lost around 14 percent of its bank branches and the Bronx about 20 percent; a disproportionate share of closings occurred in the poorest neighborhoods.[10] A recent Deloitte & Touche study predicted that competition could force banks to close nearly half their branches over the next decade. With more branches being opened in affluent areas, the inevitable implication of this study is that low-income neighborhoods will continue to lose banking offices in significant numbers.[11]

Growing competition with nonbanks such as money market funds and mutual funds, along with technological advances, have also been important factors in both the recent wave of mergers and consolidations that has swept the financial services industry and in the move to fee-based banking. Between August 1997 and April 1998, the five largest bank mergers of all time took place, causing the *Economist* to observe, "If there's a buzzword in banking right now, it's 'big.' The industry's future, goes an old mantra that is back in fashion, will belong to the super league of behemoths, with fingers in banking, broking, and insurance, that is emerging from the current wave of financial mergers. Some small banks may survive as niche operators. Middling ones, on the other hand, must either find partners or expect to be driven out of business."[12]

The growing competition with nonbanks has driven banks to charge for services that they used to subsidize.[13] In the twenty-first century, banks will meet their bottom lines more by charging fees for specific services than by living off the interest spread between taking deposits and making loans. This trend, which has important implications for lower-income consumers, is already discernible. For example, Wells Fargo, which recently merged with Norwest Bank, now gives checking account customers three free calls into its automated-voice-response telephone lines and then charges 50 cents for each additional call. To speak to an agent to shift funds or ask questions, customers are charged $1.50 per call.[14] "Some banks—mostly large, billion-dollar institutions—have even begun charging customers to close their accounts."[15] Two of the nation's giants—Charlotte-based NationsBank/Bank of America and First Union National Bank—charge a $10 fee if a checking account is closed within 180 days of opening.[16] By October 1997, some 35 percent of the total revenue for U.S. banks came from fees, the *Economist* noted. This was almost double the proportion in 1980.[17] In short, "at best, mega-mergers mean more ATMs, better technology for faster transactions, and computerized service and branches across the country. At worst, banks could close neighborhood branches and increase fees on everything from dealing with tellers to penalties for late payments."[18]

The Shrinking Community Reinvestment Act

The upheaval in the financial services industry has important implications for individual low-income customers who are being charged more for basic services and low-income communities, traditionally denied access to credit and capital needed for healthy development.

Federally regulated financial institutions are required to meet community credit needs under the Community Reinvestment Act (CRA).[19] Proponents of the act, which was passed in 1977, argued that "banks and other depositories were taking deposits from inner-city and other less affluent neighborhoods, while lending mostly in other areas and frequently overlooking qualified loan applications in the process."[20] According to Brookings Institution economist and banking scholar Robert Litan and his colleague Jonathan Rauch, providing for local community credit needs is a reasonable requirement in exchange for the special federal protections that banks receive: "This mandate was not imposed out of the blue: banks and thrifts, as the proponents noted (again with justice), enjoy federal charters, granted on the basis of a showing of need in a particular community, as well as recourse to a federal safety net in the form of deposit insurance. It was not illogical, therefore, to examine such institutions' community service records when considering whether to grant applications to merge with or acquire another institution, open or relocate a branch, seek a charter, obtain deposit insurance, or otherwise expand in ways requiring normal regulatory approvals."[21]

With respect to how well local community needs are being met, it is no small matter that when CRA took effect, roughly two-thirds of Americans' long-term savings were in CRA-covered institutions.[22] Today, less than 30 percent are, and this migration from the conventional banking system to mutual funds, money market accounts, and other savings vehicles outside CRA continues unabated. Technology will accelerate this phenomenon. Community advocates want Congress to extend community reinvestment requirements to nonbanks that control the vast majority of America's investable capital; however, they lack significant political support. This issue is part of the political debate surrounding financial modernization and looms large as the regulations that will govern the nation's transition to EFT are finalized by the Treasury.

Part of this debate involves disagreement over how federal regulators should define the assessment area—the geographic area within which the agencies evaluate an institution's CRA performance—for banks and thrifts that use alternative product delivery systems like the

Internet, rather than the traditional brick-and-mortar branch structure.[23] According to Office of Thrift Supervision Director Ellen Seidman,
"institutions that heavily use the Internet to deliver products may be
serving very few low- or moderate-income individuals or communities."[24]

The Impetus behind EFT'99: Saving Taxpayers Money

In the midst of this upheaval in the financial services industry, the push
to convert millions of federal benefit checks to electronic payment was
begun not out of concern for low-income families, but rather to save
the federal government money. Specifically, in 1996 Congress amended
the Financial Management Act, passed two years earlier in 1994, to
require electronic deposits not just for wages and salaries but also for
retirement benefits, programmatic benefits, vendor payments, and expense reimbursements to businesses.[25] Although 94 percent of federal
workers are now paid by direct deposit, the mandate represents a tremendous logistical challenge. About 390 million payments were disbursed by the U.S. Department of Treasury in the first five months of
fiscal 1999, and only 73 percent of those were made electronically.[26]
Nevertheless, the cost savings to the government—only 2 cents for an
EFT payment compared to 43 cents for a check payment—were deemed
substantial enough to justify the transition. Converting to an all-electronic payment system would save the government an estimated $100
million a year in postage and check production costs alone.[27]

Experience also suggested that direct deposit would be safer than
delivering checks by mail. Every year, the Treasury Department has to
replace more than 800,000 government checks that are lost, stolen,
delayed, or damaged during delivery, costing the government another
$65 million annually. In addition, an average of more than 75,000 Trea-
sury checks a year are forged and fraudulently negotiated.[28] With electronic funds transfer, forgeries, counterfeiting, and check alteration
are virtually nonexistent. According to the Treasury, "misrouted EFT
payments are never lost, and are typically routed to the correct bank
account within 24 hours."[29]

At the same time that the federal government decided to convert
to EFT, states also began taking advantage of its economies. In Ohio,
for example, two-thirds of the tax collections in fiscal 1996 were by
EFT. Of $10.1 billion in revenues, according to state Treasurer J. Ken-
neth Blackwell, $7.1 billion "were collected without a single piece of
paper."[30] Also, because the food stamp system is so labor-intensive—

food stamps cost federal and state governments $400 million a year[31] to print, ship, store, distribute, reconcile, and destroy—states will save millions when they convert to electronic delivery of food stamps, which they are required to do by 2002 under the national welfare reform law.[32]

According to one estimate, delivering food stamps by electronic benefits transfer (EBT) just in the eight states that compose the Southern Alliance of States would slash the U.S. Department of Agriculture's administrative costs by $22 million a year.[33] And while they are not mandated to do so, as of June 1999, forty states plus the District of Columbia were in the process of converting their emergency cash assistance programs (Temporary Assistance to Needy Families, or TANF) to electronic delivery in order to achieve even greater economies.[34] For example, New York State welfare officials expect to save at least $12 million a year in administrative costs once all welfare benefits are distributed through plastic debit cards.[35] Similarly, with 3 million Food Stamp clients, Texas has the country's largest EBT system. Now that it is fully installed, the state expects to save more than $1 million a year in processing costs alone.[36] Texas also found that "switching to electronic payment substantially reduced its food stamp rolls and wiped out the barter of food stamps for drugs."[37] While EBT advocates note that the EBT card is a more convenient and dignified way for clients to access their benefits, harnessing technology to reduce fraud in the $21 billion food stamp program was one of the policymakers' main motivations in mandating the change. Nationwide, $815 million, or about 4 percent of the face value of all food stamps, are exchanged illegally for cash by food retailers each year.[38]

At least forty states have already begun the transition to EBT. Most of them are embracing *Quest*, a plastic debit card delivery system whose goal is to develop a nationwide EBT system that will piggyback on existing debit card and automated teller machine (ATM) networks.[39] Some states have also added or are considering adding other state-delivered benefits to their EBT systems, including WIC (Women, Infants, and Children nutritional benefits), general assistance, childcare, and child support.[40] Perhaps the most ambitious effort now underway is to use EBT cards to improve information sharing and administrative efficiency among public and private health care providers in a state. The Health Passport pilot project in Bismarck, North Dakota, and Cheyenne, Wyoming is the first effort by states to develop a multipurpose, standard smart card that not only delivers food stamps, but is also designed "to streamline patient check-in, provide up-to-date health information, support referrals among providers, facilitate patient access to medical records, automate appointment reminders and promote access to preventative health information that can be used by many different programs within the state and, eventually, across state lines."[41]

While the technical distinctions between direct deposit (EFT) and EBT are discussed in chapter 5, the fundamental difference is that electronic funds transfer requires the recipient to have a bank account, while electronic benefits transfer does not. EBT provides remote access to benefits through debit card and ATM networks without establishing any banking relationship for or on behalf of the recipient. However, although EBT does not bring the unbanked directly into the financial services mainstream, it is a step in that direction, because it fosters the use of electronic banking technology by millions of Americans who may never have used an ATM. Moreover, many of the states that are converting their cash assistance programs to EBT are planning direct deposit campaigns as well, because direct deposit offers even greater cost savings and a chance to connect recipients with mainstream financial services.[42]

Federal direct deposit (EFT) and state EBT programs are both outstanding examples of how technological advances in the private sector can be adopted for the public sector to create a government that "works better and costs less," in the *reinventing government* vernacular. Though they operate under different timetables and separate rules, both EFT and EBT share the potential to connect unbanked individuals to the mainstream financial system. In the pages that follow, discussions of the opportunities and challenges of EFT'99 should be interpreted, in general, to include state-sponsored EBT programs.

As suggested above, however, economy and efficiency are not what gives these unheralded measures the potential "to pave the way for dramatic and far-reaching changes in our society," as Treasury Secretary Robert E. Rubin has argued. Instead, the real power of EFT and EBT is that they could "soon result in millions of Americans being brought into the banking system for the first time, and it will change dramatically the way in which they handle money,"[43] as Treasury Undersecretary John D. Hawke Jr. has noted.

The Unbanked

Nationwide, an estimated 13 percent of U.S. families—including up to 10 million federal benefit recipients—currently have no bank accounts.[44] Among federal benefit recipients, the unbanked are more likely to be people of color, younger, and poorer than are other benefit recipients. This distribution is partially explained by the fact that more than twice as many social security recipients than supplemental security income (SSI) recipients—75 percent compared to 46 percent–have their benefits deposited directly.[45] SSI recipients are much younger, more urban, less likely to have completed high school, and more likely to be of a racial or ethnic minority than people who receive retirement checks. Another reason for this large difference is that many banks reduce or waive fees for depositors who are over 65.[46] Typically, these low-cost services are not available to SSI recipients, or are not widely advertised by banks even when they do provide such accounts. Although seven states have enacted legislation creating lifeline banking accounts[47] and most banks offer some form of basic bank account, a recent study by the New York Public Interest Research Group found "that a third of bank employees did not mention low-cost account options when customers asked about checking accounts. And calls to banks show they frequently emphasize higher-fee accounts and are often slow to mention—and occasionally deny altogether—that they offer low-cost accounts."[48]

The universe of unbanked Americans, both recipients and non-recipients of federal benefits, represents one third of all minority households. One in four renters, one in six of those under 35 years of age, and 15 percent of the working poor—families earning between $10,000 and $25,000—do not have checking accounts.[49] Among welfare recipients, as many as three out of four are estimated to be without a bank account.[50]

The Policy Implications of EFT'99

To help the unbanked, EFT'99 is arriving on the scene at an especially auspicious time. As national social policy moves away from lifetime entitlements to time-limited emergency cash assistance and work-centered social policies, EFT'99 can help connect the dependent poor to the financial services system and enable them to begin saving money and building assets. From the outset, Treasury Secretary Rubin recognized the importance of this electronic initiative to the Clinton administration's urban strategy and especially to a more powerful welfare reform centered in economic development. Rubin saw EFT'99 as "a real opportunity to have an effect on a very large number of people in the inner city . . . If we can figure out a way to get them into the banking system for the first time, not only will it give them a more efficient way to cash checks and access to other financial services, but it may also encourage people to save, to plan financially, and therefore, to improve their economic life over time," he said. For millions of unbanked recipients, having to use "expensive check cashing services . . . is in itself a disadvantage."[51]

By connecting low-income people to the mainstream banking system, EFT'99 will enable them to build a credit history. It will also provide empirical data on their use of credit and their repayment practices, enabling mainstream financial services providers to create more appropriate methods for credit underwriting—methods that do not automatically assume that people with less income are necessarily higher risks.[52] And the power of EFT'99 will continue to grow as more and more welfare recipients start receiving their benefits electronically and become connected to the mainstream financial system. It is hard to imagine families successfully transitioning from welfare to work without having access to an affordable, secure bank account.

Understanding why so many Americans conduct their daily business without any formal relationship to the banking system is important for other reasons as well. Research suggests that the unbanked are less concerned about their credit ratings than are those who participate in the financial mainstream.[53] Knowing that minorities and immigrants are disproportionately likely to be unbanked, it is instructive that a recent Fannie Mae Foundation survey found significant percentages of African Americans and Hispanics who did not think that being late in paying their bills would reduce their chances of qualifying for a mortgage.[54] Along similar lines, housing economist George Galster found an inverse relationship between immigration rates (measured as people with poor English proficiency) and homeownership. "Cities with higher proportions of people who cannot speak English well," said Galster, "find housing demands skewed from owner to rental occupancy, greater demands for mortgage finance by those who do own, and a greater chance that their mortgage applications will be denied."[55] Thus connecting low-income families to mainstream banks can help educate them about the financial system and prepare them for homeownership.

The Purpose of This Book

With the aim of helping the unbanked and encouraging the transition to more asset-based social policies, I undertook this book. I wanted to chronicle the evolution of EFT'99 from an obscure exercise in technology transfer to a nationwide movement that has the potential to help millions of working families join the financial mainstream. If all the pieces come together, EFT'99 can do for the provision of affordable financial services what the Communty Reinvestment Act has done for the provision of mortgage credit in underserved communities. The CRA has proven to the financial community that low-income markets can be served profitably. We are at the front end of that same kind of discovery process for basic financial services. EFT and EBT are forcing policymakers to look at how technology and new delivery systems can be used to serve this community more effectively—*and* profitably. But achieving this goal will not be easy because EFT'99 raises many serious questions about consumer protection, access to technology and services, and costs. Because of these unresolved issues, the move to electronic benefits delivery is opposed by some powerful consumer groups and community development advocates, who believe EFT'99 "compels unbanked recipients into relationships that they have already determined are detrimental to themselves for the federal government's direct benefit."[56] I hope this book helps convince these advocates and others that this initiative can become a vehicle for building individual wealth in low-income communities and that they must work to secure the political support and resources EFT'99 needs to achieve its full potential.

The United States faces a very serious problem with under-saving. Despite blistering economic growth in 1998, Americans' personal savings rate fell to a post–World War II low of 0.5 percent of disposable income,[57] and declined still further to –1.2 percent in May 1999.[58] As Senator Bob Kerrey, D-Nebr., has said, "In a global economy, your economic health and security is measured by what you own, in addition to what you earn."[59] About 30 percent of U.S. households have no financial assets, and about half of all children in the United States are growing up in families that have no financial assets. Along racial lines, the difference in asset holdings between whites and African Americans is far greater than the difference in their incomes.[60] The household income of blacks is 61 percent that of whites, while black families possess only 12 cents for every dollar of wealth (median net worth) held by white families.[61] According to sociologist Thomas Shapiro, "the racial wealth gap is a very robust $48,817."[62] Under-saving for retirement is another big problem. As it has done for generations of middle- and upper-income Americans, the federal government should create policies that make compound interest work for the poor and help those with lower incomes join the asset-building classes. Thus my second goal in writing this book is to convince the administration and Congress to use EFT'99 as the vehicle for giving lower-income, low-wealth Americans—in Senator Kerrey's words—"a chance to own a piece of their country."

By bringing millions of unbanked people into the financial mainstream, EFT will facilitate savings by providing recipients with bank accounts. However, on its own, it will not provide them with a concrete incentive to save. We have a golden opportunity to expand EFT's impact by linking it with a national financial education campaign and a new savings initiative targeted at the working families of America who do not benefit from existing tax-preferred savings incentives such as individual retirement accounts.

The Clinton administration has made a commitment to share with benefit recipients the substantial cost savings made possible by EFT'99, and Treasury intends to meet part of this commitment by subsidizing recipients' electronic bank accounts. Subsidizing banks is not the best way to share savings with consumers; a better approach would be a major savings incentive for working families. This approach is explored in chapter 7.

How This Book Is Organized

The greatest challenge of the national move to electronic benefits transfer is in reaching the millions of benefit recipients without bank accounts, who have never used automated teller machines or plastic debit cards. Therefore, this book begins by examining the unbanked: who they are in the country as a whole and in Los Angeles, in particular. I have chosen Los Angeles because it is arguably the most diverse metropolis in the United States and a harbinger of America's urban future. Chapter 2 focuses on differences between the national and local perspective, a critical distinction because banking practices vary dramatically according to local demographics, racial differences, patterns and rates of immigration, the extent of concentrated poverty, and other local factors. To my knowledge, the Los Angeles analysis is one of the first local studies of the unbanked.

Chapters 3 and 4 address issues of electronic banking and the unbanked. A major focus is the digital divide. A July 1999 survey by the Commerce Department confirms that such a divide "still exists, and in many cases, is actually *widening* over time. Minorities, low-income persons, the less educated, and children of single-parent households, particularly when they reside in rural areas or central cities, are among the groups that lack access to information resources. Households with incomes of $75,000 and higher are more than twenty times more likely to have access to the Internet than those at the lowest income levels, and more than nine times as likely to have a computer at home."[63] Signs abound that the digital divide is fast becoming "a racial ravine," in the words of Commerce Assistant Secretary for Telecommunications Larry Irving.[64] "Between 1997 and 1998, the divide between those at the highest and lowest education levels increased by 25 percent, and the divide between those at the highest and lowest income levels grew by 29 percent."[65] This vast technology gap was recognized by Sun Microsystems CEO Scott McNealy when he said of the Internet: "It's equal opportunity if you're online, but if you're not, it isn't."[66] Recognizing this, chapters 3 and 4 pay special attention to how technology is shaping the banking industry's cost structure, opening up new delivery channels, and affecting access. Chapter 3 discusses the rise of electronic banking, its cost implications, and how technology is affecting the availability of banking services in low-income communities. Chapter 4 focuses on the rise of the fringe banking industry and how technology enables mainstream banks to partner with check cashers in order to improve their market penetration in lower income communities. Because they layer fees upon fees and can isolate the poor from the financial mainstream, it is these kinds of partnerships that have led the syndicated financial columnist Jane Bryant Quinn to believe that EFT'99 could end up hurting, not helping, the poor.[67] However, surveys suggest that fringe bankers—with their convenient locations, flexible hours, and bilingual services—have their fingers on the pulse of low-income communities, and that stopping them from playing a significant role in EFT'99, as many consumer advocates would like to do, will be no simple matter.

Chapter 5 is about EFT'99 and its transition from an exercise driven by economy to a new social policy built around financial inclusion and wealth accumulation. The chapter tracks the rulemaking process, from the inception of EFT'99 to Treasury's adoption of the final rule, and the struggle to engage the banking industry to use technology to create affordable products and services that a successful move to EFT/ EBT demands. The chapter concludes with a discussion of how some states are using their electronic benefits programs to bring welfare clients into the mainstream banking system.

The final two chapters deal with asset building, and why federal policy should link EFT'99 to a nationwide effort to help working poor begin to build wealth. Chapter 6 suggests that, contrary to popular belief, lower-income people do respond to well-conceived savings incentives; the chapter discusses the role of savings and asset building in state welfare reform plans. The concluding chapter presents four steps the president and Congress should take to make the transition to electronic benefit transfer all that it should be. The chapter starts with recommendations on how to maximize the potential of EFT'99 to connect the unbanked to the financial mainstream and ends with a proposal for creating a nationwide Individual Development Account (IDA) initiative.

One theme emerges above all others in this book. EFT'99 is not simply about the technology of electronic banking. It is, above all else, about financial inclusion, closing the opportunity gap, and building assets for the future.

CHAPTER TWO

The Impetus for EFT'99: The Unbanked

Before mainstream banks can design, price, and market new electronic banking products as part of EFT'99, the Treasury Department and the financial services industry need to know who the unbanked are, why they do not maintain deposit accounts, and what kind of accounts might appeal to them. Similarly, federal agencies like the Social Security and Veterans Administrations cannot effectively market direct deposit programs to the millions of recipients *with* bank accounts unless the agencies know why so many still prefer receiving their benefits by check. It is also impossible to design effective financial education programs to help people understand the cost advantages of mainstream financial services without knowing why so many of them have nothing to do with the formal banking system.

Gathering information about the unbanked is not easy. Substantially more is known about people who use electronic banking technologies than about those who avoid banks altogether. Because users of ATMs, debit cards, and similar technologies generally have substantially higher incomes than the general population, the financial services industry tracks their tastes, preferences, and consumption patterns closely in order to further develop and exploit this highly profitable market.[1] For instance, banks are keenly aware that customers who conduct bank transactions via their home computers carry larger balances, have lower attrition rates, and use more bank products and services.[2] Nationally, about 70 percent of online banking customers have annual incomes of more than $50,000, more than 80 percent have investments, and a large number run small businesses out of their homes.[3] More than half the customers of the first Internet-only bank in the United States, Security First Network Bank, earn more than $50,000 a year and own houses worth at least $100,000.[4] The typical Atlanta Internet Bank customer is a manager, professional, or technical person who has an annual income over $60,000 and owns a home.[5] Online customers also tend to be young—between 25 and 35 in the case of Security First Network Bank and 40 years old at Atlanta Internet Bank; and research shows that "people who bank with money-management software typically earn at least $150,000 a year."[6]

Moreover, the next wave of U.S. households to use electronic banking is not likely to look much different—what Norwalk (Conn.)-based INTECO Corp. calls "the early majority." These are "the select 10 percent of well-educated, higher-income households who will look to technology to overcome time constraints. Almost all households in this segment consist of married couples with incomes of nearly $90,000. Three-quarters are dual-income families. In 55 percent of these households, both adults have college-level education or beyond, compared to just 10 percent in all households."[7]

Until very recently, however, neither industry nor government made much of an effort to gather similarly detailed information on the millions of low-income consumers who not only do not use electronic banking but have no bank account of any kind. Even getting an accurate count of the "unbanked" has been difficult; estimates range from 6 to 22 percent of U.S. households, with the most frequently cited number as 13 percent.[8] This lack of information is finally beginning to change, however, because the move to electronic benefit delivery requires us to understand why millions of benefit recipients and other Americans operate outside the banking system, and how well they are being served by the fringe banking industry.

Recognizing the importance of understanding the unbanked better, the U.S. government has ratcheted up its funding for projects dealing with the unbanked. Recent and ongoing federal research includes a Treasury-sponsored study of the demographics of banked and unbanked federal benefit recipients; an analysis of the account features that might appeal to unbanked benefit recipients; focus groups of consumers, financial institutions, and third-party processors of electronic transactions to discuss the best way to resolve outstanding EFT'99 issues; and a grassroots information and education program to introduce benefit recipients to the advantages of direct deposit over mail delivery.[9] Also, the federal Office of the Comptroller of the Currency is surveying unbanked households in major U.S. cities to "better understand why millions of adults in the United States rarely, if ever, conduct their regular financial activities, particularly savings and transaction activities, through banks."[10]

Over the next several years, the outcome of this research will help move EFT'99 from a good cost-efficiency plan to a powerful new reality with the potential to connect millions of unbanked Americans to the financial mainstream. This, in turn, would enable them to participate more fully in retirement savings and other incentive programs that Congress might create to strengthen the social security system. Some social security reform proposals, for example, such as President Clinton's USA initiative, would provide federal funds for supplemental savings accounts, with which the unbanked have little experience.

This chapter focuses on what research reveals about the unbanked at every level: local, programmatic, and national. The first part of the chapter presents a national profile of unbanked households, drawn from EFT'99 research and the national Survey of Consumer Finances (SCF), which is conducted by the Federal Reserve every three years. The most recent survey for which data have been published was conducted in 1995. While these data already have been widely reported elsewhere, they nevertheless provide useful background on the unbanked, and a good comparison with the city-level analysis that follows later in the chapter.

The second half of the chapter contains an analysis of unbanked individuals in Los Angeles, the largest and arguably most diverse metropolitan area in the United States and one of the nation's top five cities in terms of the number of recipients who still receive their federal benefits by check rather than direct deposit.[11] Because the analysis is derived from one of the first statistically reliable surveys of unbanked individuals in a major U.S. city, it places the local situation in a national context. More important, it identifies other significant relationships that are not possible to explore using existing national data, including the roles of immigration and English proficiency in the banking equation and the importance of neighborhood geography—whether place matters—in determining one's banking status.

The data are from the Los Angeles component of a multi-city survey on urban inequality (the "LASUI") that was conducted in 1993–94 by the Center for the Study of Urban Poverty at the University of California at Los Angeles. The larger survey from which the Los Angeles data are derived was designed to determine the effect of labor market dynamics, racial attitudes and polarization, and residential segregation on the growing gap between "haves" and "have-nots" in urban America over the past two decades.[12] Thanks to additional funding by the banking industry, the Los Angeles component of the study was the only one to include specific questions on financial services.

A National Profile of Unbanked Households

If not steadily growing, the number of unbanked remains disturbingly high. According to the national Survey of Consumer Finances (SCF), the proportion of unbanked—those households that do not maintain a checking, savings, or other transaction account at a depository institution—grew from 9 to 17 percent from 1977 to 1989, or by 77 percent, and then leveled off at around 13 percent in both 1992 and 1995.[13] The 1995 results indicate that about 12 million U.S. households currently operate outside the financial mainstream.[14]

What accounts for this rise in the number of unbanked Americans? Deindustrialization and other macroeconomic forces that marginalized millions of blue-collar workers, deregulation of interest rates, changes in other bank regulations, technology, and inflation have all been implicated in this rise.[15] Forced to pay higher interest rates to compete with nonbank institutions such as mutual funds for large depositors, many banks in the 1980s stopped subsidizing low-balance accounts, eliminated money-losing services for small depositors, and increased fees. According to one estimate, the percentage of banks offering free checking accounts fell from 35 percent to just 5 percent between 1977 and 1991.[16] These changes, according to economist John Caskey, "encouraged many households with limited financial savings to abandon the banking system. . . . [which in turn helped] spur the demand for fringe banking services," such as check-cashing outlets.[17]

Although not derived from a nationally representative sample, Caskey's 1996 telephone survey of modest-income households in Georgia, Pennsylvania, and Oklahoma found that of those households without an account of any kind, 71 percent had previously had a checking or savings account at one time.[18] Changes in banking practices also had a dramatic impact on low-income families in California, where between 1986 and 1991, the percentage of households "with incomes between $30,000 and $50,000 who maintained bank accounts held steady at around 95 percent, while accountholders with incomes under $30,000 dropped from 89 percent to 78 percent."[19]

As indicated in chapter 1, consistent with the extensive body of research that shows significant racial differences in mortgage loan denial rates, there are also pronounced racial differences in the use of banks. Nationally, over one-third of African American households have no bank accounts. This compares with 29 percent of Hispanic households, 7 percent of non-Hispanic white households, and 10 percent of other households.[20] A higher proportion of females (20 percent) is unbanked than males (10 percent). Unbanked households are also younger, with a mean age of 43, than those with bank accounts, which average 49 years old. The unbanked are less educated, with a mean of 11 years of education compared to 13 years for households with bank accounts. They also have lower household incomes, with a mean of about $14,077 compared to $47,882 for households with bank accounts. Unmarried individuals are more likely to be unbanked than their married counterparts (19 percent versus 6 percent, respectively). And higher proportions of nonworking households—either laid-off/unemployed (42 percent) or not employed (30 percent)—have no bank accounts, compared to employed or retired households.

The SCF also asks respondents why they do not have checking accounts, but not why they do not have savings accounts.[21] While the SCF codes twelve different reasons why households do not have a checking account, they fall into four broad categories: economic, attitudinal, convenience, and physical. The SCF results are presented in table 2-1.

A survey sponsored by the Treasury Department asked a similar question of unbanked recipients of social security, supplemental security income, and smaller federal benefit programs to help guide the implementation of EFT'99.[22] Since the vast majority of those recipients are elderly and white, the survey population is significantly different from the respondents to the Survey of Consumer Finances.[23] Treasury's results (see table 2-2) showed marked differences as to the major reasons for not having bank accounts among respondents who were surveyed by telephone, who were mostly social security recipients, and those surveyed by mail. The mail population included more recipients of supplemental security income, who are more likely to be minorities

Table 2-1. *Why U.S. Families Do Not Have a Checking Account, 1995*

Reason	Percent of families
Economic	40.9
Do not have enough money	23.3
Minimum balance too high	8.8
Service charges too high	8.3
Not allowed to have an account because of welfare benefits	0.5
Attitudinal	33.0
Do not like dealing with banks	23.0
Cannot manage or balance a checking account	7.4
Have not got around to it	1.8
Do not need or want a checking account	0.5
Use alternative checking source	0.3
Convenience	24.2
Do not write enough checks	24.2
Physical	1.9
No bank with convenient hours or location	1.2
Checkbook has been lost or stolen	0.7

Source: Survey of Consumer Finances (SCF), 1995.

and to be younger than social security recipients, and recipients of all programs who were too poor to have telephones.

Not having a bank account, however, does not necessarily mean that all unbanked are estranged from the banking system. For example, the Treasury survey found that significant numbers of unbanked federal benefit recipients (63 percent of those surveyed by telephone and 42 percent of those surveyed by mail) regularly cash their benefit checks in a bank or other financial institution, followed by grocery stores (30 percent telephone, 24 percent mail), check-cashing outlets (10 percent telephone, 12 percent mail), and other retail stores (3 percent telephone, 10 percent mail).[24] This suggests that it would be a mistake to conclude that those without any formal banking relationships have no involvement with mainstream banks, although the gap in bank use between respondents in the telephone survey and those in the mail survey may indicate that the very poor are less comfortable using banks and look more toward retailers to meet their financial services needs. Recognizing the importance of retailers to many unbanked consum-

Table 2-2. *Why Federal Benefit Recipients Do Not Have a Bank Account, 1998*
Percent of respondents

	Survey	
Reason	Telephone	Mail
Do not have enough money	47	67
Do not need an account	21	27
Consider bank fees too high	6	24
Wish to avoid large fees, bounced checks, and overuse of ATMs	3	13
Have a bad credit history	1	10
Currently use another person's account	1	11
Generally distrust financial institutions	1	...
Difficult to get to a bank, banks are inaccessible	1	9
Desire to keep information about financial resources private	1	4
Do not like banks	1	...
Fear having assets frozen in the event of legal judgment	1	4
Other	2	13
Do not know	20	...
Total[a]	106	182

Source: Booz-Allen & Hamilton and Shugoll Research, *Mandatory EFT Demographic Study,* 1998.
a. Totals do not add up to 100 percent due to multiple responses.

ers, one entrepreneur has patented a system designed to convert discounts on grocery items from manufacturer- and store-promotions into personal savings. If it works as planned, the Amigo Card, which is scheduled for issuance in mid-2000, would be swiped at the checkout counter, and would deposit the value of a customer's coupon savings into her savings account at the bank of her choice.[25]

Based on these national sources, a general profile of the nation's unbanked population emerges, along with a sense of the magnitude of the problem. The SCF data suggest that financial education and inclusion campaigns will be most effective if targeted toward younger adults, low-income workers, minorities, and people without high school diplomas. The EFT'99 study also suggests that a large number of the unbanked are at least somewhat familiar with mainstream financial institutions and are comfortable with using them in a limited capacity.

However, these results should probably be interpreted with caution because they involve only the cashing of government benefit checks, which have a lower risk of bouncing than payroll and personal checks. Banks and retail stores are more reluctant to cash these latter types, so that the unbanked may have to turn to check-cashing outlets more frequently than the EFT'99 data suggest.

The SCF and EFT'99 surveys also suggest why some people choose not to open bank accounts. The results particularly from the SCF suggest that the unbanked are sensitive to the atmosphere of mainsteam financial institutions and that attitudinal issues might be more important than high fees and minimum balances per se. Both the SCF and EFT'99 data also suggest that a large segment of the unbanked feel that they simply do not have enough money or write enough checks to justify a traditional bank account, a sentiment that may be due in part to the rise in bounced check fees discussed in chapter 3. This suggests that developing new, streamlined banking products would be more appealing to this population than heavy marketing of traditional accounts.

Providing a Local Context for Understanding the Unbanked: The Case of Los Angeles

While national surveys can measure the magnitude of the problem and identify some of the reasons why so many households are unbanked, the reality is that individuals choose whether or not to open accounts at the local level based on their personal economic situations and their local banking and financial services options. Until more is known about what is going on in local communities, it will be difficult to identify and implement effective strategies to connect individual families to the financial mainstream. Unfortunately, however, there are even fewer data on the unbanked at the community level than there are at the national scale.

Thus the Los Angeles component of the survey on urban inequality is invaluable because it provides one of the first statistically reliable surveys of the unbanked in a major U.S. city. Its findings are of more than regional interest because Los Angeles has experienced many of the economic trends that are pushing more families into poverty and out of the mainstream financial system: the loss of well-paying manufacturing jobs in the 1980s, and economic growth limited to high-skill, high-wage jobs in producer services and to low-skill, low-wage jobs in personal services in the 1990s.[26] The Los Angeles data are also of particular interest because of the city's large number of recipients of federal benefits. Moreover, its multi-racial, multi-ethnic population foreshadows the kind of diversity that will characterize much of urban America in the twenty-first century.

The Local Context: Deindustrialization and Diversification

Over the course of the 1980s, California lost 700,000 jobs, including approximately 200,000 well-paying unionized manufacturing jobs in Los Angeles alone.[27] This loss is consistent with the experience of other major cities and the national trend toward deindustrialization. Northeastern and midwestern cities suffered similar debilitating losses.[28] During the same period, the percentage of the U.S. work force engaged in manufacturing fell from 27 percent to just 15 percent, while services industries grew rapidly, from 67 percent to 80 percent of nonfarm employment.[29]

Caskey identified economic restructuring, the increase in one-parent families, and other broad socioeconomic changes in the 1980s as factors not only in the rise of poverty and the number of unbanked, but also in a decline in wealth among the economically marginalized.[30] Since for the vast majority of families, the first financial asset to be acquired is a deposit account, Caskey concluded that the decline in account ownership probably also reflected a decline in household wealth.[31]

Although the national economy rebounded in the 1990s, the inequalities of income among racial and ethnic groups in urban areas continued to increase. Los Angeles' worsening imbalances in the regional labor market are a case in point. Major cuts in federal defense spending, corporate downsizing, and continued capital flight reduced the demand for labor, while at the same time aspiring job seekers poured into Los Angeles looking for work and a better life. Between 1990 and 1995, the population of Los Angeles increased by nearly 25 percent, primarily because of a steady stream of legal and illegal immigrants into the area.[32] This immigration pattern helped Los Angeles County maintain its position throughout the decade as the county in the United States with the highest number of Hispanics. By 1997, the county's Latino population had reached 4 million.[33]

Despite deindustrialization and rising inequality, however, a new economy and social fabric have emerged. Low-tech factories have replaced the big manufacturing plants as primary employers. There are now about 600 such new factories in East Los Angeles alone, where the workers receive about one-third of the wages that unionized employees used to make, with few or no health benefits.[34] New businesses have begun to fill abandoned buildings. The signs of this new vitality and hope are captured in a photo by the noted photographer Camilo Jose Vergara, in his dramatic photo essay "El Nuevo Mundo: The Landscape of Latino Los Angeles." In an old storefront on Alvarado Street in the Pico Union district, a pre-war building has been taken over by businesses offering passport applications, legal aid, work permit advice, insurance sales, instant photos, jewelry, wedding services, and the New Life Immigration Service.[35] Tens of thousands of unbanked Latinos will need jobs from such employers and support from such advocates if they are to be connected to the financial and economic mainstream.

The Los Angeles Survey on Urban Inequality

A detailed picture of Los Angeles' new economic reality and of residents' banking practices emerges from the LASUI. In addition to compiling information on employment, immigration status, and other factors, the survey questioned respondents on bank account status, borrowing behavior, and use of credit.[36] The survey is particularly useful because it not only was large and highly representative of the dominant ethnic groups—Asians, African Americans, Hispanics, and non-Hispanic whites—but of residents in both poor and nonpoor neighborhoods.[37]

This analysis of the banking relationships of Los Angeles residents is in two parts. The first section profiles the unbanked population as a whole and uses a bivariate analysis to compare various segments of the population, such as males versus females, rich versus poor. A multivariate analysis follows, which takes into account and statistically controls for the many factors that affect the likelihood of a person having a bank account (such as gender, race, marital and employment status, and income).

The reader is cautioned not to draw comparisons between this analysis of banking relationships in Los Angeles and national data on the unbanked. The LASUI is not compatible with the SCF data discussed above, even though many of the variables are the same, because the unit of analysis in the latter is the individual, while in the former, it is households.

Who Is Unbanked?

About one in five residents of Los Angeles is unbanked. Even accounting for sampling error, this still puts the number of unbanked at about 2 million people in Los Angeles County alone. About 30 percent of the unbanked come from the ranks of the working poor, while a slightly greater percentage of unbanked workers have an income between 100 percent and 150 percent of the poverty level (see table 2-3). While 80 percent of the unbanked are renters and most of them are poor, with an average income of just $7,400, the unbanked do not reside disproportionately in neighborhoods of high poverty, as one might expect. In fact, almost half live in neighborhoods with low poverty, where fewer than 20 percent of all people are poor. Another 43 percent live in neighborhoods with medium poverty. Just 8 percent live in neighborhoods where more than 40 percent of all residents are poor.

Three-quarters of all unbanked are either U.S. citizens or hold green cards and are therefore eligible for various federal and state-delivered benefits, such as supplemental security income, food stamps, and cash assistance. Welfare recipients account for 16 percent of all unbanked persons in Los Angeles, although the overall percentage of welfare recipients without bank accounts—55.8 percent—is lower than the statewide estimate of 75 percent.[38]

More than 70 percent of all unbanked individuals in Los Angeles are Hispanic. As more than 40 percent of the nearly 10 million people in Los Angeles County are Latino, this means there are about 1.4 million Hispanic residents who operate outside the mainstream financial system. The size of the unbanked Hispanic population is more than six times larger than the unbanked African American population (10.5 percent of the total unbanked) and about five times larger than the non-Hispanic white population (14.4 percent of the total). Among unbanked Hispanics, more than 60 percent have limited proficiency in reading or speaking English, or both.

A more complicated picture emerges when the proportions of unbanked within population groups are compared, rather than simply looking at raw numbers. Given the imbalances in the Los Angeles economy, it is logical to expect that the likelihood of being unbanked would be higher for individuals who are not well connected to the mainstream regional economy—especially those who are underemployed, minorities, or recent immigrants to Los Angeles. An analysis of the employment and income data from the LASUI, for instance, shows that Hispanics and workers with green cards or without any documentation earn only about one-quarter to one-half of what white male Angelenos earn.[39] With some important exceptions, the LASUI data reveal similar disparities in banking patterns among different demographic groups.

For instance, 37.1 percent of Hispanic residents of Los Angeles and 19 percent of African Americans are unbanked, compared with only 7 percent of the non-Hispanic white population and 8 percent of other ethnic groups (see table 2-4). The "other" category consists mostly of Asians, whose banking status varies with nationality. At 1.8 percent, Japanese residents of Los Angeles are about one-fifth as likely to be unbanked as those of Korean and Chinese ancestry. As is demonstrated shortly, the extremely high rate of unbanked among Hispanics is substantially accounted for by other factors. This is not true for African Americans.

The likelihood of being unbanked also varies inversely with age, education, and income. The percentage of Los Angeles residents ages 25 to 34 years old who are unbanked is about three times as high as the percentage of seniors ages 65 or older (24 percent versus 8 percent). Those without a high school diploma are almost five times as likely to be unbanked as those with a high school diploma (50 percent versus 11 percent). And those with an annual income under $10,000 are thirty-six times as likely to be unbanked as those with incomes between $25,000 and $50,000.

While significantly lower than the estimated statewide rate of 75 percent, the percentage of all welfare recipients in Los Angeles who are unbanked is still high: 56 percent. Thus, while it is hard to envision recipients moving from welfare to work without a bank account, this transition presents a daunting challenge. Even if Los Angeles can succeed in bringing the number of unbanked welfare recipients in line with the number of unbanked working poor—a change of about 20 percentage points—one-third of welfare recipients would still be operating outside the financial mainstream.

As might be expected, citizenship status and proficiency in English affect not only income and employment status, but also bank account

Table 2-3. *Characteristics of Unbanked Individuals, Los Angeles, 1992*

Variable	Percent	N[a]
Race or ethnicity		
Hispanic	72.2	449
African American	10.5	65
White	14.4	90
Asian	2.9	18
Total	100.0	622
Gender		
Male	41.5	258
Female	58.5	363
Total	100.0	621
Age[b]		
24 or less	21.2	132
25–34	34.0	211
35–44	22.2	138
45–59	15.6	97
60–64	3.0	18
65 or more	4.0	25
Total	100.0	621
Education[c]		
Less than 12 years	59.5	370
12 years or more	40.4	251
Total	99.9	621
Income[d]		
$9,999 or less	66.4	281
$10,000–$24,999	32.0	136
$25,000–$49,999	1.5	6
$50,000 or more	.1	1
	100.0	424
Marital status		
Married	48.4	301
Unmarried	51.6	321
Total	100.0	622
Employment status		
Employed	45.8	262
Retired	5.3	30
Laid off or unemployed	22.3	127
Other not employed	26.6	152
Total	100.0	571

Table 2-3 *(continued)*

Variable	Percent	N^a
Housing		
Owns	11.3	70
Rents	79.5	494
Other	9.2	57
Bank near home		
No	14.6	89
Yes	85.4	518
Neighborhood poverty		
Low (less than 20%)	49.2	306
Medium (20–39%)	42.7	265
High (40% or more)	8.1	50
English proficiency		
Speaks not at all/a little/just fair	62.5	389
Speaks well or very well	37.5	233
Reads poorly	61.8	384
Reads well	38.2	237
Citizenship status		
U.S. citizen	37.7	234
Green-card-holder	37.9	236
Other (undocumented)	24.4	152
Working poor	31.6	197
Nonworking poor	22.5	140
Moderate income, working [e]	34.7	216
Poor, not receiving AFDC	48.7	303
Receive AFDC	15.5	96
Information about bank services from		
Mail	32.0	190
TV	27.4	163
Radio	.8	5
Newspapers	6.6	39
Friends or relatives	18.1	108
Other	15.0	89
Total	99.9	594

Source: Author's calculations, based on Los Angeles Survey on Urban Inequality (LASUI), 1994.

a. Due to weighting, some *N*'s are inconsistent.

b. Average age, 36.1 years. Median, 33 years. Standard deviation, 13.5 years.

c. Average education, 9.3 years. Median, 11 years. Standard deviation, 3.9 years.

d. Average income, $7,419.70. Median income, $6,000. Standard deviation, $7,071.70.

e. 150 percent of poverty line.

Table 2-4. *Characteristics of Individuals by Bank Account Status, Los Angeles, 1992*
Percent, unless otherwise indicated

Variable	No checking account	No savings account	Neither	Have account
Overall	26.1	40.3	19.8	80.2
Race or ethnicity				
Hispanic	47.6	54.8	37.1	62.9
African American	27.6*	33.4	19.0*	81.0*
White	9.4	29.6	6.7	93.3
Other	9.7	37.1*	7.6	92.4
Gender				
Male	26.4*	40.2*	17.9+	82.1+
Female	25.9*	40.5*	21.4+	78.6+
Age				
24 or less	44.1	53.7	37.8	62.2
25–34	32.2	46.1	24.1	75.9
35–44	25.1*	39.4*	18.2*	81.8*
45–59	18.1	33.6	14.0	86.0
60–64	17.4+	35.7+	11.6+	88.4+
65 or more	13.3	28.4	8.3	91.7
Average age (years)	36.9	39.0	36.1	42.9
Education				
Less than 12 years	60.9	65.2	49.9	50.1
12 years or more	15.3	32.7	10.5	89.5
Average education (years)	9.6	11.2	9.3	13.3
Income				
$9,999 or less	44.4	54.3	36.2	63.8
$10,000–$24,999	28.0	43.5	18.4*	81.6*
$25,000–$49,999	3.4	25.7	1.0	99.0
$50,000 or more	3.1	11.1	.4	99.6
Average income (dollars)	9,162	14,648	7,419	26,903
Marital status				
Married	22.5	37.8	17.1	82.9
Unmarried	30.8	43.4	23.4	76.6
Employment status				
Employed	19.2	34.0	13.8	86.2
Retired	13.0	30.6	8.9	91.1
Laid off or unemployed	49.7	56.8	34.3	65.7
Other not employed	44.4	59.2	39.7	60.3

Table 2-4 *(continued)*

Variable	No checking account	No savings account	Neither	Have account
Housing				
Owns	7.4	20.0	4.4	95.6
Rents	43.8	55.9	34.8	65.2
Other	47.6	44.3	33.1	66.9
Bank near home				
No	37.9	50.6	31.4	68.6
Yes	29.2	40.6	21.9	78.1
Neighborhood poverty				
Low (less than 20%)	18.1	34.5	13.0	87.0
Medium (20–39%)	48.1	56.3	38.2	61.8
High (40% or more)	70.7	72.0	61.0	39.0
English proficiency				
Speaks not at all/a little/just fair	46.3	59.7	38.7	61.3
Speaks well or very well	23.7	34.4	16.9	83.1
Reads poorly	47.9	61.1	39.9	60.1
Reads well	23.6	34.4	16.8	83.2
Citizenship status				
U.S. citizen	23.8	35.6	17.8	82.2
Green-card-holder	37.6	47.2	27.2	72.8
Undocumented	60.4	75.0	54.9	45.1
Working poor	43.3	50.7	33.6	66.4
Nonworking poor	54.6	56.8	39.2	60.8
Moderate income, working [a]	37.0	47.9	28.3	71.7
Poor, not receiving AFDC	43.0	49.1	31.3	68.7
Receive AFDC	61.3	72.8	55.8	44.2
Information about bank services from				
Mail	34.8	41.2	32.0	50.4
TV	24.3	17.8	27.4	9.2
Radio	.6	1.5	.8	1.6
Newspapers	6.1	5.7	6.6	6.4
Friends or relatives	17.2	13.5	18.2	8.1
Other	17.1	20.3	15.0	24.3
Total	100.1	100.0	100.0	100.0

Source: Author's calculations, based on Los Angeles Survey of Urban Inequality, 1994.

χ^2 significance: *insignificant, +significant at 0.05 level, otherwise significant at 0.001 or beyond. N (weighted/unweighted) = 3,143/4,025.

a. 150 percent of poverty line.

use. Undocumented immigrants are twice as likely to be unbanked as those with green cards (55 percent versus 27 percent), and are more likely to be unbanked than U.S. citizens (18 percent). Those who speak and read English poorly are also twice as likely to be unbanked as those who speak and read English well (39 to 40 percent versus 17 percent).

Finally, housing and neighborhood characteristics affect the likelihood of being unbanked. Renters are almost nine times more likely to be unbanked than homeowners. The likelihood of being unbanked also increases with the extent of poverty in a neighborhood. Despite the raw numbers, a comparison of percentages within each population group reveals that an Angeleno living in a neighborhood where more than 40 percent of all residents are poor is almost five times more likely to be unbanked as someone living in a neighborhood that is less than 20 percent poor.

Multivariate Analysis

To get a more complete picture of how changes in particular variables such as race or education will affect the chances that a given individual will be unbanked when all other variables are held constant, I used a multivariate statistical technique called logistical regression (logit) analysis. The first step was to construct a base case as a benchmark using mean values of important population charcteristics: a non-Hispanic white male, age 39, with 12.73 years of education and $22,000 in annual income, who is a renter and a U.S. citizen, is unmarried, reads and speaks English well, works either full- or part-time, lives in a low-poverty neighborhood, and lives or works near a bank.[40] The likelihood that this individual would be unbanked is just 6 percent, which is substantially below the overall population average of 20 percent (see table 2-5).

By holding constant all but one or a few of the above characteristics, it is possible to estimate the incremental impact of race, citizenship, earnings, or other variables on the likelihood of being unbanked. Thus, for example, if the base case were an Asian male, rather than a non-Hispanic white male, but all other characteristics were the same, the probability of the individual being unbanked would fall by half, to 3 percent. Similarly, if Hispanic is substituted for non-Hispanic white, and all other variables are held constant, the probability of the individual being unbanked increases from 6 to 7 percent, a statistically insignificant change. In contrast to the bivariate analysis—which showed 37 percent of all Hispanics in Los Angeles to be unbanked, compared with 7 percent of all non-Hispanic whites—the logit analysis indicates that, by itself, being Hispanic makes no difference in the chances of being unbanked. Between Hispanics and non-Hispanic whites, the big difference in their chances of being unbanked lies in other variables, such as education, income, citizenship, and English proficiency. When race is changed to black, however, the logit analysis indicates that the probability of being unbanked increases to 11 percent even when other variables are controlled for. Thus, blacks are almost twice as likely as whites to be unbanked and are the least likely to be connected to the mainstream banking system of any of the racial or ethnic groups included in the LASUI. The implications of this finding will be discussed in more depth below.

The importance of education on the chances of being unbanked can be seen by changing years of education in the base case model while holding all other variables constant. Recall that in the base case, with 12.73 years of education, the chance of being unbanked was 6 out of 100. The probability increases to 10 percent for an individual with eight years of education and falls steadily as the education level rises— to 7 percent with eleven years of education, 5 percent with fourteen years of education, and to 4 percent for college graduates.

The probability of being unbanked also varies inversely with income. Holding all other variables unchanged, when the base case individual's income is $4,000 instead of the sample mean of $22,000, the probability of being unbanked more than doubles, from 6 to 13 percent. Other things being equal, the probability of being unbanked also varies inversely with age. The likelihood that a 25-year-old will be unbanked is more than four times greater (9 percent versus 2 percent) than it is for someone over 65.

By changing the base case gender from male to female, employment status from working to not working, and income from $22,000 to $4,800, the mean for all benefit recipients, the probability of a woman who receives welfare being unbanked is 43 percent.

Interestingly, our evidence is mixed as to whether the rise in the number of unbanked is related to the closing of bank branches in low-income neighborhoods. For example, a 1991 study by the Los Angeles City Council found that "in a 409-square-mile region of South Central Los Angeles, 133 check-cashers and only 19 banks served 587,000

Table 2-5. *Predicted Probabilities of Being Unbanked, Los Angeles, 1992* [a]

Variable	Probability
Hispanic	0.07
Black**	0.11
Asian*	0.03
White	0.06
Female***	0.04
Male	0.06
Female and black	0.07
Age (years)***	0.09 @ 25 years
	0.04 @ 50 years
	0.02 @ 65 years
Education (years)***	0.10 @ 8 years
	0.07 @ 11
	0.05 @ 14
	0.04 @ 16
Annual income (in $1,000 units)***	0.13 @ 4
	0.10 @ 10
	0.02 @ 50
Married*	0.04
Unmarried	0.06
Owner***	0.02
Renter	0.06
Undocumented*	0.11

people. Nearby Gardena boasted 21 banks for 49,800 residents."[41] Our analysis confirms what others have found—the likelihood of being unbanked is not affected by whether one lives or works near a bank.[42] The LASUI does suggest, however, that the *extent* of neighborhood poverty is strongly correlated with one's banking status. While residing in a medium-poverty neighborhood has no statistically significant effect on whether one has a bank account, living in a high-poverty neighborhood significantly increases the likelihood of being unbanked. Other things being equal, the probability that a resident of a high-poverty neighborhood will be unbanked is twice as great as if that same individual lives in a low-poverty neighborhood (12 percent versus 6 percent).

The multivariate analysis also confirms that immigration status and English proficiency are highly correlated with bank account use. Un-

Table 2-5 *(continued)*

Variable	Probability
Green-card-holder	0.06
Speaks English well	0.06
Speaks English poorly, and undocumented	0.12
Reads English well[+]	0.06
Reads English poorly	0.11
Working (part or full time)***	0.06
Not working	0.18
AFDC (all values for women)***	0.09
AFDC = income set to mean for group (.48)	0.43
AFDC = income set to sample mean	0.18
Lives in medium-poverty neighborhood	0.07
Lives in high-poverty neighborhood***	0.12
Working and poor	0.08
Working and poor, income set to mean for group (7.22)	0.15
Working and income at 150 percent of poverty	0.07
Working and income at 150 percent of poverty, income set to mean for group (10.02)	0.12
Bank located near home or work	0.06
No bank near home or work	0.07
Constant	

Source: Author's calculations, based on Los Angeles Survey of Urban Inequality (LASUI) data, 1994, and logit model.

a. Sample means: age, 39; years of education, 12.73; annual income, $22,000. The base case has a 6 percent probability of being unbanked. Two-tailed significance levels: +0.10, *0.05, **0.01, ***0.001.

documented Hispanic males with poor English skills who earn the mean income for all working poor, $4,481, and live in high-poverty neighborhoods have a 71 percent chance of being unbanked. For undocumented Hispanic females with otherwise identical characteristics, the probability of being unbanked is a somewhat lower but still substantial 66 percent.

Implications for EFT, EBT, and Broader Financial Initiatives

The LASUI data have important implications for EFT'99 and related state efforts as well as for broader initiatives that attempt to connect unbanked individuals to the financial mainstream. To start with, a comparison of banked and unbanked respondents reveals significant differences in the principal source(s) of information on financial services. Among people with bank accounts, 50 percent reported that they received most of their banking information by mail, while this is the case for only about one-third of the unbanked (see table 2.4). Moreover, the unbanked are about three times more likely than those with an account to receive most of their banking information via TV (27 percent versus 9 percent). The unbanked are also more than twice as likely to get their banking information from friends or relatives (18 percent versus 8 percent.) This strongly suggests that bank marketing and financial inclusion campaigns may need to target television and personal networks to be successful. The current lack of such efforts by mainstream banks is giving fringe bankers free reign to capture this market. Western Union, which has found a niche market with money transfer services, money orders, and utility payments for people that banks do not serve, specifically targets the unbanked.

"We do quite a bit of marketing on TV and radio for our services, and we go into Hispanic communities and African American communities and specifically target people who may not have bank accounts," Peter Ziverts, Western Union's vice president for corporation communications, has said. "We feel we are successfully reaching those who have no relationships with banks, and it works for us."[43]

The LASUI data also underscore the critical importance of tailoring new initiatives to specific demographic groups. Bilingual materials are obviously critical for Los Angeles, given that that 70 percent of all unbanked individuals are Hispanic. The difference in banking rates among citizens, green-card-holders, and undocumented workers may also indicate that cultural differences influence the way recent immigrants from other countries view banks. For instance, some marketing specialists suggest that many working class Hispanics do not bother opening bank accounts in the United States because in their homelands, in Mexico and other Latin American countries, banks generally cater only to the wealthy.[44]

Ethnographic studies on home purchase and financing not only confirm the influence of race and culture, but suggest that immigrants and minority group members feel distanced from mainstream realtors, banks, and mortgage lenders in different ways. According to ethnographer Mitchell Ratner, for non-English speakers, the estrangement may be due to a language gap, or to cultural differences in the way debts are

repaid, or whether assets are publicly declared.[45] In their study of Hispanic and African American home buyers in Syracuse, New York,
Hamilton and Cogswell speak of the important role played by "cultural
brokers," such as a Peruvian woman loan officer at a local bank who
helped Hispanics understand the requirements for getting a mortgage,
and helped bank underwriters understand the Hispanic custom of
pooling money for a down payment.[46]

After some reluctance, mainstream banks are now beginning to
cultivate the Hispanic market for financial and account services other
than mortgage loans by "trying to reach out to all consumers in a language they understand," as a Texas Commerce Bank official once put
it.[47] Texas Commerce's Lyons & Lockwood branch, which is located in
a modest Houston neighborhood with a mostly African American and
Hispanic population, exceeded all expectations by becoming profitable within sixteen months of its 1993 opening.[48] Understanding the
language and the culture, and having minority bankers who "look like"
their customers, enhances market appeal. This is a big part of the reason why Texas Commerce was able to draw as much as 60 percent of its
customers away from check cashers and other fringe banking outlets.[49]

Cultural sensitivity and a decision to specifically target Hispanics
in the six states with the biggest Hispanic populations—California,
Florida, Illinois, New Jersey, New York, and Texas—accounts for much
of the early growth of Banco Popular, the largest bank and credit card
issuer in Puerto Rico, which recently entered the U.S. mainland market. "We have an understanding of the language and culture, and targeting the Hispanic consumer is what we do for a living," said Donald
R. Simanoff, president of the bank's Orlando-based U.S. credit card
division.[50] In June 1998, Banco Popular hired a Spanish-language television personality to market its credit cards, and then signed a
cobranding deal with Dallas-based Heftel Broadcasting Co., which owns
39 broadcasting Spanish-language programs. While most of the bank's
customer service staff, statements, and promotional material are bilingual, officials have found that many Hispanic customers read English
better than Spanish and that 40 percent of people who call the bank
prefer to speak English.[51]

The fact that most of Banco Popular's U.S. credit card portfolio is
unsecured puts to lie the common belief that the Hispanic market consists mostly of high-risk subprime customers.[52] Recognizing the potential of this market, and knowing that Hispanics are growing more rapidly

than just about any other population group in North Carolina, NationsBank (now Bank of America) has launched special advertising campaigns targeting Spanish-speaking customers. In Charlotte, its head-quarters city, NationsBank has created a Hispanic banking center staffed completely with bilingual associates and has launched a pilot loan pro-gram, the Hispanic Money Management Program, to give people with no credit history an opportunity to build credit. The program includes classes offered by the bank's bilingual associates on budgeting, manag-ing a checking account, and understanding the importance of credit history. After completing the classes, participants with green cards may apply for either a $1,000 unsecured line of credit or a $15,000 secured auto loan, using nontraditional verification of credit history, such as rent and utility payments.[53]

However, relatively little attention is being paid to why so many blacks are outside the financial mainstream—a problem that cannot be so easily explained by language and citizenship issues. As discussed above, blacks are the least likely to be connected to the mainstream banking system of any of the racial or ethnic groups included in the LASUI. This finding is consistent with social science research pertain-ing to racial and ethnic differences in wealth, which suggests that con-tinuing segregation and lingering discrimination in both residential and lending markets hinders the accumulation of housing assets by blacks.[54] The lack of full explanation for this racial effect on banking relationships is an important finding and a critical area for future re-search because it will be extremely difficult to design effective financial education and inclusion programs without understanding whether the root of the problem is systemic racial discrimination in the banking sector, as some advocates allege and empirical research seems to sug-gest, or whether the unexplainably high rate of black estrangement from the mainstream banking system is due to more benign reasons.

Conclusion

With a strong assist from government and community partners, the transition to EFT provides banks, thrifts, and credit unions an oppor-tunity to help bring millions of unbanked Americans into the financial mainstream. For EFT to succeed will require more than product devel-opment; it will also require new marketing strategies. More than half of all commercial banks probably offer some sort of low-cost basic or lifeline accounts, primarily for low- to moderate-income households, but they are neither heavily marketed nor utilized.[55] A big challenge of EFT is learning to use technology to lower the costs of serving, first, unbanked benefit recipients and finally, all unbanked individuals. This includes blacks who, our analysis shows, are least likely to be connected to the financial mainstream, even after controlling for other factors. This finding reinforces the idea that, despite legal gains, powerful forms of racial discrimination remain that disadvantage blacks relative to other racial and ethnic groups. The next chapter discusses how technology is changing the face of the banking industry in ways that, if left to pure market forces, could deepen the racial divide. "There is," says Ohio State Treasurer Kenneth Blackwell, "a dangerous disconnect when we provide service around the world, but not around the corner. There is a price, and it is levied in crime, arson, strife, stress, and general discontent."[56]

CHAPTER THREE

How Technology Is Changing the Organization and Delivery of Financial Services

Recent advances in communications technology, including the development of more powerful computers, are paving the way for new banking products and services and are changing the way traditional banking is done. The resulting changes will have great impact on the cost, availability, and accessibility of financial services for the unbanked and the poor. This chapter explores those possibilities.

The new world of electronic banking is ever-changing. Electronic banking, or electronic money, as former Comptroller of the Currency Eugene Ludwig prefers to call it, "covers some activities that have been with us for some time now—such as the use of personal computers or telephones to pay bills, transfer funds and obtain account information—and others that we're just beginning to consider—such as electronic commerce on the Internet, stored value cards in lieu of cash, and using technology to dispense federal and state benefits."[1]

This technology has added a new dimension to the competitive pressures that are already reshaping the financial services industry. While technology often offers banks substantial savings, it also puts new pressures on them to keep up with current competitors, such as mutual funds, and potential new ones. Charles Rice, chairman of Barnett Banks, which was acquired by NationsBank in 1997 (which subsequently merged with BankAmerica), sees banks "evolving from being oriented around geography to being oriented around lines of business. . . . You need to provide services at the lowest possible cost, with technology driving change."[2]

Other observers predict that banks that are unable or unwilling to use technology to transform themselves will open the door to powerful third parties led by software firms like Microsoft and Intuit, which have set out to give "investors subatomic-level control over their finances with sophisticated products that balance risk and reward, cost and value."[3] William M. Randle, senior vice president for strategic planning at Huntington Bancshares, blames banks' inherent conservatism for allowing new competitors to redefine the industry and for losing market share: "Existing branch delivery systems, which absorb more than half of the operating capital and define the organizational structures of most banks, represent an important incentive to maintain the status quo. As a result, despite major financial investments in technology, banks have avoided the strategic restructuring needed to establish less costly, more customer-friendly distribution channels, leaving non-bank financial services companies to establish leadership in the electronic delivery of financial information."[4]

More customer-friendly distribution channels lie at the heart of Citicorp's strategy. Citicorp, which became part of Citigroup with its merger with Travelers, is banking on technology to grow its customer base from its current 100 million to 1 billion by 2010. According to one estimate, doing business the old way would require 250,000 more branches and 400,000 more customer service representatives to reach the billion-customer goal.[5] Significantly, the person responsible for increasing Citigroup's global franchise tenfold in a decade is not a sage old banker but a technology whiz from the entertainment industry. Ed Horowitz spent eight years as head of multimedia for Viacom, creators of "Beavis and Butthead"; before that, he was with the cable company HBO (Home Box Office). Like William Randle, Horowitz believes that the hardest part of his job is not technical but cultural—changing the way Citigroup thinks and uses technology. The job, he says, "is not too unlike what I had to do in the entertainment business. . . . We had traditional television, and then came cable, satellite services, videotape, DVD. All of them required us to rethink the product and how it got to its destination and what the customer would use to see it."[6] Horowitz plans to offer banking via any technology that can attract customers, even screen phones, PalmPilots, and public terminals linked to Citicorp by satellite from rural China.[7] If Citigroup has not yet penetrated the Chinese hinterlands, its partnership with Blockbuster Video is already making inroads in Latin America. So successful is the program in Peru and Colombia that the company website reports that "four months after their introduction, 44 percent of Citibank's Peruvian consumer transactions were taking place on ATMs in Blockbuster stores."[8]

Yet technology, as Eugene Ludwig has observed, can either resolve long-standing problems with access to financial services or raise new ones. Technology makes it possible to reach more people more cheaply and can reduce the cost of "connecting dangerous or isolated areas to financial services."[9] But as the Commerce Department's study of the growing digital divide implies, the cost of new technology often is beyond the reach of low- and moderate-income consumers.[10] Economist Robert E. Litan has compared the growth of electronic banking to the popularity of the automobile: "Like . . . the suburban lifestyle that the family car made possible, digital finance offers a potentially vast expansion of choice and opportunity for those who have access to it; but, also like the automobile, it may imply a widening relative gap for those who are left behind in the 'inner city' of finance."[11]

This chapter presents an overview of how technology is changing the organization and delivery of financial services, including the rise of electronic banking, in-store branching, fee-based banking, and the increasing use of customer profitability analysis to customize products and segment the market. The aim is to understand how technology is affecting the cost, availability, and accessibility of financial services in lower-income communities.

The Rise of Electronic Banking:
Cost Cutting Meets Consumer Convenience

For banks facing stiff competition from mutual funds and other nonbanks, the ability to cut costs by adopting new technology is a powerful lure. As Litan observes, "Sending messages by chip, over telephone lines, or through the air is half to two-thirds cheaper than printing or processing billions of pieces of paper and moving them around by truck and plane."[12] According to one study, the average cost per banking transaction for a full-service bank is $1.07, but 54 cents for a telephone transaction, 27 cents for ATM—and just 1.5 cents for PC banking.[13] PC home banking, which has been around since the mid-1980s, is frequently confused with Internet-based banking. With PC home banking, "banks usually send out a proprietary financial software package on disk, users fill in details offline and then send them into the bank system over its private network." On the other hand, Internet banking customers "can access their accounts from any standard browser, through a standard Internet connection, no matter which access provider they subscribe to."[14] Internet banking systems include encryption software for security.

The overhead cost of an online banking system is expected to be about a half to a third of the cost of today's branch-dominated retail banking operation. This is one reason that, globally, the financial services industry's information technology expenditures on Web-based retail delivery systems are expected to almost double by 2000, from $550 million in 1996 to about $1 billion.[15] Thus, by reducing overhead costs and enabling high-margin products to be targeted to affluent customers, technology allows banks to maintain profit margins in highly competitive product markets with narrow interest spreads and to "compete on a price basis more aggressively with such non-branched entities as money market funds."[16] This is why so many banks are repricing their services to encourage the greater use of lower-cost technologies. According to Steven Davidson of America's Community Bankers, a Washington, D.C.-based trade organization, banks in the past charged as much as $15 a month for home banking services—an amount that was far greater than most consumers were willing to pay. "Today," says Davidson, "financial institutions recognize that home banking should not be considered a profit center but instead as a relatively inexpensive delivery channel."[17] Citigroup's Ed Horowitz goes even further, arguing that banks need to see online banking "as the powerful communications medium it is, an exclusive channel for building the industry's position with its customers as broad-based financial information and transaction providers; for defining the special, trusted relationship that they share with banks; and for building that relationship into something even larger."[18]

Consumer Demand for Convenience Increases

Just as banks are rethinking the role that home-banking services should play in their distribution systems, consumers are taking a second look as well. Initially, concerns about complexity and security had dampened interest in banking by computer,[19] but recent statistics indicate that electronic banking and electronic commerce are mushrooming as consumers become more comfortable with the online environment. Worldwide, consumers went on a $30 billion shopping spree over the Internet in 1998, more than three times greater than the previous year.[20] In the United States, an estimated 8.2 million adults spent $2.4 billion on gifts bought over the Internet near the end of 1998, which is more than three times the 2.4 million customers who spent $750 million on gifts during the holiday season of 1997.[21] According to one estimate, by 2003, Internet commerce will reach $3.2 trillion.

An estimated 13 million U.S. households already shop online, and that number is expected to more than triple between 1999 and 2003, to 40 million.[22] The greatest growth in Internet shopping in a recent ten-month period was in airline ticket reservations, according to a survey of Internet users by the market research group @plan. Between July 1997 and March 1998, online airline ticketing increased 301 percent, followed by four other retail categories: stocks and mutual funds, up 291 percent; computer hardware, up 111 percent; car rentals, up 105 percent; and books, up 91 percent.[23] Consumers also are gaining confidence in the security of Web transactions. For example, the percentage of people who shopped online for stocks and mutual funds and then were actually willing to buy them online rose from 14 percent in July 1997 to 28 percent in March 1998.[24]

Online banking has increased at a similar rate, jumping 78 percent in 1997, to 4.8 million,[25] and by a similar rate in 1998, to about 7.8 million.[26] Most of the forecasts for electronic banking predict that growth will continue, although they vary in their degree of optimism. By 2000, according to the New York-based consulting group Jupiter Communications, as many as 18 million customers may be banking online,[27] while a study by Forrester Research expects more gradual growth.[28] According to Forrester, online finance will jump to 10 million households in 2001, and 14.2 million in 2002. Another study by Ernst & Young projects a 600 percent increase in home banking by the year 2000—from 1 percent of the population to 6 percent.

Other observers are more skeptical. Eugene Ludwig, for example, thinks that many forecasts of shopping by home computer are grossly optimistic. As he said in a 1996 address:

> With all due respect to those who think everybody in the world will be on the Internet by the year 2004, I think we need to take projections like these with a large grain of salt. . . .
>
> For example, one major consulting firm recently projected

that 20 percent of U.S. household spending would take place on the Internet by the year 2005. Just to put things in their proper perspective, to achieve that level of spending, Internet commerce would need to grow more than 130 percent each year for the next ten years.

Maybe that's not inconceivable, but I think it's unlikely. Consider the growth of some other recent technologies. Between 1986 and 1995, the sales of compact discs achieved a compound annual growth rate of just 30 percent. Sales of color televisions increased at an annual compound growth rate of 10 percent from 1970 to 1985.[29]

Yet despite uncertainty about the future, U.S. banks believe there is a consumer demand for online banking and are moving rapidly from "brochureware" websites—as of the fourth quarter of 1997, 60 percent of bank Web sites were static, information-only—to transaction-based.[30] Today, more than 400 banks and 225 credit unions are online: that is, they provide account balance and transaction detail to retail customers over the Web. This is twice the number that offered such services only two years ago. Then, as now, big banks were the technology leaders.[31] For example, Wells Fargo, the acknowledged industry leader in electronic banking, reported in 1998 that it had "450,000 online customers, up 50 percent from the start of [1997]."[32] By the year 2000, "the percentage of big banks offering Internet transactions is expected to reach 92 percent, and 44 percent among smaller banks," according to a forecast by the Mentis Corporation, an international research firm based in Durham, North Carolina, that studies technological issues.[33] In addition to setting up their own Web pages, some banks are forming alliances with Internet Service Providers (ISPs) to expand their reach. In May 1999, America Online signed a multiyear contract with five banks as part of the restart of its full-service banking center within its Personal Finance Channel.[34]

The Rise of the "Virtual" Bank

While hundreds of conventional banks deliver services online, banking regulators have also granted charters to several banks that operate exclusively on the Internet. Two of these, Security First Network Bank (SFNB) and Atlanta Internet Bank (doing business as NetBank), are the first and second Internet-only banks to be chartered by the Comptroller of the Currency.[35] Since then, several new virtual banks have received charters, among them Des Moines, Iowa-based Principal Bank (February 1998), Houston-based CompuBank (October 1998), Indianapolis-based First Internet Bank of Indiana, and USAccess Bank in Louisville, Kentucky (February 1999).[36]

Saying, "if your bank could start over this is what it would be," Wingspanbank.com—one of the newest virtual banks—distinguishes itself from traditional banks with some online services this way: "While traditional banks trundle online with the same old thinking, we're harnessing the power of the Internet to give you new financial power. Like loan answers in 51 seconds. Electronic bill pay. Even a credit card that saves you 5 percent at leading web merchants. Someone has to lead banking in a new direction. Why not you?"[37] Because Wingspanbank.com and other virtual banks and financial services companies do not have the overhead of a bank with branches, they can pass on their savings to customers by charging lower fees for services and offering higher rates.

The average bank spends 4.1 percent of earning assets annually on noninterest expenses, which is a big part of why a Citibank customer needs a $6,000 balance to collect 1 percent interest on a checking account.[38] Yet NetBank had this cost ratio down to 1.6 percent in the fourth quarter of 1998.[39] These kinds of cost efficiencies have also helped NetBank show its first profit—$4.5 million in net income for 1998 versus a $5.6 million loss the year before—"demonstrating that the words 'cyberbank' and 'profitable' aren't mutually exclusive."[40] Consequently, NetBank's minimum balance is $100, and the account pays 4 percent.[41] SFNB requires no minimum balance and offers checking account customers twenty electronic payments each month and unlimited check-writing privileges, both at no charge.[42]

Lower overhead is also helping Internet-only banks and nondepository financial institutions offer some of the most aggressive interest rates in the nation. In June 1999, for example, when one-year bank CDs across the country were yielding an average 4.67 percent, NetBank and Security First Network Bank were offering 5.8 percent and 5.45 percent, respectively.[43] Taking its cue from discount online brokerages, NetBank announced on March 26, 1999, that it would begin offering new and existing customers 6 percent interest on a no-fee checking account through January 1, 2000.[44] According to Bank Rate

Monitor, at the time of this announcement, the average rate on an interest-bearing checking account nationally was 1.38 percent.[45]

Because technology enables a bank to expand its market reach without opening or acquiring new branches—a substantial savings, considering that a new bricks-and-mortar branch costs about $300,000, or ten times as much as a new ATM installation[46]—the lower cost of online banking may eventually set a new industry cost standard.[47] This possibility is highlighted in a number of surveys and studies. For example, a 1996 survey by Booz-Allen & Hamilton concluded that in ten years "the Internet will be the most important delivery system," with traditional branches ranking only eighth in importance.[48]

One entrepreneur has begun to exploit the Internet's market-aggregation potential by creating what might be one of the nation's first "affinity group" virtual banks—to serve the homosexual community. Recognizing that gays and lesbians, especially couples, often face obstacles when trying to access banking services like opening a joint checking account or getting a mortgage to buy a house, Pensacola, Florida-based Steven Dunlap founded G & L Internet Bank (www.g-lbank.com).[49] Dunlap believed that, despite their strong demographics, the homosexual community was too small to support a typical branch operation— even in such big cities as New York and San Francisco—but because of its "strong sense of community" it would support a virtual bank. According to Dunlap, "of the estimated 25 million gay and lesbian Americans, 52 percent are paying for online services. If we can attract one-half of 1 percent of that population, that's 66,000 customers—and about $1 billion in assets."[50]

Competitive pressures to eliminate real estate and associated overhead from banks' balance sheets through technology are a global phenomenon. *Online Banking Report*, which monitors online banks, is currently tracking 86 non-U.S. banks around the world that provide true Internet banking services.[51] In the United Kingdom, for example, online banking is forecast to grow more than 30 percent a year until 2005.[52] By then, Britain's Stationery Office anticipates more than one in seven of its customers are expected to be using the Internet, PC banking, or interactive television to carry out their banking transactions.[53] Use of electronic banking is expected to grow to about 30 percent of the banking population in Sweden by 2005. In New Zealand, with ASB Bank showing the way, the number of bank branches dropped from 1510 in 1993 to 1278 in 1996.[54] ASB Bank "was the first to install real time online banking in 1969, the first to introduce Cashflow lobbies in 1987, the first with telephone banking service in 1988, and first off the mark with bank transactions over the web in 1996."[55] Half a world away, Banco de Brasil is spending more than $1.8 billion for a variety of network computing and technology projects to cut costs, and expects electronic transactions to account for as much as 85 percent of total transaction volume by 2000.[56] Finally, the Saudi Arabian Monetary Agency hopes to use technology to transform the kingdom from a cash-oriented country to a plastic card–oriented society, bypassing the checking stage entirely.[57] Saudi Arabia now boasts the Middle East's largest ATM system, with the majority of all cash withdrawals in the country performed at ATMs.[58]

Experts generally agree that "advanced technologies will have a more lasting effect on the way banks interact with and serve their customers than almost anything else in recent history."[59] But many smaller institutions are poorly prepared to operate in the twenty-first century world of electronic banking. For example, a recent survey of community banks found that only 19 percent have a chief information officer to oversee their use of technology and just 5 percent are planning to hire one in the near future. In addition, most are jumping onto the Internet with little time, expense, or planning. Nearly two-thirds created their Web sites in less than three months; half spent less than $5,000, and not even a third have written business plans for their Internet sites. "This lack of strategic planning where technology investments are concerned is a theme that resonates through a number of studies," the survey concluded.[60]

This is a serious problem because the effective use of technology can help smaller banks compete with the leviathans. According to Gerald H. Little, president of the New Hampshire Bankers Association, "there was the concern not too long ago that technology would be the demise of community banks, who could not keep up with the larger institutions. But this has been turned on its head. Technology is much more affordable and is the great equalizer that allows a lot of community banks to spin out new products quickly and helps them stay in the ball game."[61]

Like many of the smaller banks, low-income consumers are also ill-prepared for the transition to an online system. Although sales of personal computers outpaced sales of televisions for the first time in 1997, in low-income households "a home computer is [still] as rare as a home telephone was in the early years of this century."[62] In fact, a significant number of such households still do not have phones, let alone modems. In the mid-1990s, about 10 percent of non-Hispanic white, 25 percent of Hispanic, and 23 percent of black households with incomes below $15,000, were phoneless.[63]

However, continued innovation in Internet technology is expected to reduce significantly access problems to electronic banking. WebTV, for example, permits the viewer to go online without a computer and modem. It cost less than $500 when it was introduced in late 1996, and the price has now fallen to less than $300. The development of such inexpensive technologies has the potential to vastly increase access by low-income householders to electronic shopping, including online banking.[64]

New Delivery Systems

Other technological applications are already increasing access to basic financial services by creating new delivery systems. American Express, for example, now has ATMs that read encoded data and record travelers' checks as they are dispensed, the same as if the transaction were completed at a typical branch.[65] Diebold, in partnership with Standard Bank of South Africa, is overcoming illiteracy problems by combining voice and graphics to lead customers through ATM transactions and by building biometrics into the touch screen software, so that a fingerprint rather than a personal identification number (PIN) can be used for identification. According to Diebold officials, "The bank had signed up about 500,000 people in the last year for this account, focusing basically on the unbanked."[66] Also in South Africa, a program called Cash Paymaster Services from First National Bank brings late twentieth century technology to pensioners of the remote region of KwaZulu Natal:

"Until recently, a pension-payout vehicle would arrive every two months to give residents of retirement age (60 for women, 65 for men) their government stipend of 300 rand (about $67). Pensioners would wait for hours for the vehicles to arrive; then they'd wait some more as IDs were checked and verified. . . . The pension vehicles that arrive now are security trucks outfitted with modified automated teller machines (ATMs). And the lines move quickly: The ATMs identify pensioners by their thumbprints, so all a person has to do is place his thumb on a biometrics reader. The system also cuts down on fraud. Since it was introduced, the number of people who receive payments has dropped by 20 percent."[67]

In the United States, an eye identification system is being tested that would increase access to ATMs. The aim is to improve the security of transactions and increase access to ATMs for people with poor reading skills. This technology would eliminate the PIN in favor of a "map" of a person's eye, which is "billions of times more accurate than DNA testing and identifies customers in less than two seconds." Developed by Sensar, a biometrics technology firm in Moorestown, New Jersey, the system takes a quick video picture of a person's iris and "maps it into 250 points of information that is translated into a bar code. The bar code is then stored on file with the bank."[68] This system may be perceived as less intrusive than fingerprinting, although some privacy experts suggest it may take as much as a decade before consumers accept it. Other innovative electronic delivery systems abound. Universal Federal Credit Union in Austin, Texas, installed a computer-banking kiosk that talks back; users can see and talk to a teller, who can answer questions about their accounts on the spot. To activate various banking services, including bringing the teller into view on the video screen, a customer need only touch the kiosk computer screen. Transactions include transferring funds, applying for a loan, stopping payment on a check, opening an account, and applying for an ATM card. A fax machine also is part of the technology.[69]

Spurred on by threat of a class-action lawsuit by four blind persons who argued that in the information society, access to information technology for disabled people is as important as physical access, Wells Fargo & Co. will soon begin installing talking automated teller machines in all of its 1,500 Wells locations in California.[70] The ATMs, which are being developed with NCR and Diebold, Wells's ATM vendors, will be equipped with headphones to ensure privacy.

Several banks, including Deposit Guaranty Corporation, which serves thirty-eight Mississippi communities, have introduced in secure, heavily traveled areas kiosks with automated loan machines (ALMs) using touch-screen technology. A customer can apply for a loan and, if it is approved, the loan documents and check are then printed—all at the kiosk and all within fifteen minutes. Deposit Guaranty's ALM kiosks also include "Autolibrary," an electronic listing service for used cars, boats, motorcycles, and personal watercraft, with a financing option that calculates monthly payments that vary with loan terms. ALMs, however, may never be as ubiquitous as ATMs. Because they must attract enough customers to offset their rental cost and servicing, they may be limited to middle-class areas, where they seem to produce the highest volume and where typical loans run about $2,500.[71]

The Rise of the In-Store Branch

As banks have become more reluctant to invest in stand-alone branches, supermarkets and similar locations have become increasingly attractive as alternative outlets for providing customers with a broad array of financial services. "In-store banks [offer] everything that a traditional bank branch provides," notes Charlie Akin of International Banking Technologies in Norcross, Georgia, except that "the lobby just happens to be a 40,000-square-foot food store."[72] In the beginning of 1996, for example, NationsBank had only twenty-five in-store branches. By mid-1998, this figure had grown to 360 in-store branches spanning twelve different retailers in ten states.[73] The recent merger with Bank America created a total combined network of about 700 in-store branches in seventeen states. In some declining markets, NationsBank has replaced stand-alone branches with smaller, less expensive in-store branches. In other areas, in-store branches provide extra access for growing markets. These in-store branches are usually open fifty-one to sixty-five hours a week and staffed by two to five full-time employees. Almost half of them, mainly those in growing markets, have no tellers; the staff is totally focused on winning business.

With nearly fifty banks having at least 10 percent of their branch networks in supermarkets and with suburban retail markets awash in excess capacity—by the end of 1998, an estimated 7,000 in-store banks will be operating in grocery stores[74]—many leading U.S. grocery chains are beginning to turn their attention to seriously underserved urban markets.[75] Over time, this nascent renaissance could help mitigate the impact of branch closings in low-income neighborhoods by providing attractive retail locations for in-store bank branches in these inner-city communities.

The same logic that is attracting new retail investment in the inner city applies to the banking sector. Research shows that despite lower household incomes, inner cities' greater population densities give them far greater aggregate buying power than surrounding suburbs. Take inner-city Chicago, as an example. As Robert Weissbourd and Christopher Berry report, "Primarily as a result of concentration, neighborhoods like South Shore . . . have more buying power than even the wealthiest suburbs. For example, . . . while South Shore's median family *income* is only $22,000, compared with $124,000 in the affluent suburb of Kenilworth, South Shore packs $69,000 of retail *spending power per acre*, nearly twice Kenilworth ($38,000) . . . Thus, it is not surprising to learn that indivdiuals with reported incomes under $30,000 make almost one-third of all consumer expenditures in this country . . . This amounts to $920 billion annually, a huge business opportunity by anyone's account."[76]

According to Professor Michael Porter of Harvard Business School, the moneymaking potential of inner city retailing may be one of the industry's best kept secrets. "Sears' Boyle Heights store in East Los Angeles is one of the most profitable Sears stores in the region. Ikea's store in Elizabeth, N.J., near Newark, is the furniture store chain's No. 1 store in North America. Costco's Warehouse Club in Brooklyn, N.Y., has been an 'above average' performer within the chain since its opening a year ago. Many inner city supermarkets generate sales per square foot up to 40 percent higher than the regional average. Pathmark stores in Brooklyn's Bedford-Stuyvesant and Newark's Central Ward and the Stop & Shop store in Boston's South Bay Center are all success stories."[77]

With many new inner-city retail outlets proving to be high performers, these showcases should be attractive to mainstream banks as possible in-store branch locations. More importantly, inner cities, which banks have abandoned in droves, could provide profitable business opportunities for innovative financial institutions that best understand these emerging neighborhood markets.

Computers Magnify the Power of Telephone Technology

As competition with nonbanks heats up and the rising cost of face-to-face transactions erodes profits, computers are having yet another impact: the good old telephone is becoming a more critical component of electronic banking. At North Carolina's First Union Bank, "routine services now provided by branches are increasingly being shunted to huge telephone banks . . . where sophisticated computers display a customer's entire relationship with the bank."[78] Recognizing that "if we don't still have the human element we will lose," First Union plans to use lower cost telephone service to maintain personal contact with its customers.[79] The hope is that maybe "person-to-person" will prove an adequate substitute for "face-to-face"; for those who demand more personal service at the branch, it will continue to be available, but at a higher price.[80] Even in the world of electronic benefit transfer, where less-than-full service is the norm, telephone communication is important; EBT customers at Citicorp have twenty-four-hour access to a toll-free customer service number.[81]

Telephone technology is also being used to grow an entire franchise. Headquartered in northern Virginia, TeleBank is the successor to Metropolitan Bank for Savings, F.S.B., whose new owners found expansion in the Washington, D.C.,-area market too costly through the traditional strategy of branching. Instead, TeleBank followed the lead of many companies that provide consumer products and services nationwide from a single source; in 1989, it became one of the nation's few telephone-only banks. Similar to Internet-only banks, TeleBank emphasizes premium deposit yields, which are made possible by lower overhead costs. In 1995, the company's ratio of costs to assets was 1 percent; for similar sized banks in the Southeast the average ratio was 2.33 percent. While a typical $550 million savings institution required more than 150 employees in 1995, TeleBank operated with fewer than forty full-time employees. At the heart of the system is a sophisticated PC-based database network that enables customer service representatives to offer personalized service to every client. In addition to tracking the name and address of every caller, the database stores other vital information, such as customer account activity, size of deposits, and any specific questions a depositor might have.[82]

During the fourth quarter of 1998, TeleBank reported that it had become the first branchless bank to rank among the top fifty federally chartered savings institutions. Today, TeleBank has more than 50,000 accounts, more than $1.1 billion in deposits and $2.3 billion in assets, and has expanded its operations to include Internet, fax, and ATM banking. With the recent launch of its new product TeleBank ATM Refunder, Telebank believes it has found a way to expand its account base even more by tapping growing customer resentment of having to pay "foreign" ATM fees. Through an exclusive collaboration with world wide web–leader Yahoo!, any user of Yahoo! Finance who opens a new TeleBank account through the Internet will have their accounts automatically credited for any ATM fees charged by another bank when using that bank's ATM, up to $1.50 per transaction, up to four transactions per month.[83]

The Rise of Fee-Based Banking and the Segmented Market

According to the Federal Deposit Insurance Corporation (FDIC), banks recorded their seventh straight year of record profits in 1998, with full-year industry earnings totaling $61.9 billion, up 4.7 percent from the previous year.[84] However, according to the FDIC, fee income is growing even more rapidly than overall profits. Noninterest income, including ATM fee income, rose to $19.4 billion, an increase of 18.4 percent. Even for those banks not motivated by a desire to increase access to financial services, adding ATMs makes sense because they have become such a huge cash cow for financial institutions. Between 1995 and year-end 1997, the number of ATMs in the United States went from 123,000 to over 175,000 and the number of annual ATM transactions from 9.7 billion to over 12 billion.[85] One forecast predicts that there may be 220,000 ATMs in the United States by 2000.[86] With advancing technology, ATMs have become much more than money machines, further increasing their profit potential. By year-end 1998, 11 percent of financial institutions in the nation were providing money orders, stamps, coupons, travelers' checks, or documents through ATMs, up from 7 percent a year earlier.[87]

Both the number of ATMs and their revenues have soared since the largest ATM networks, PLUS and Cirrus, lifted their long-standing ban on ATM double charges in April 1996. Not only do most "deployers of ATMs get issuer-paid interchange of between 40 cents and 50 cents for each ATM transaction, but many also surcharge consumers 25 cents to $2 a transaction."[88] In 1998, the U.S. Public Interest Research Group (USPIRG) found that 71 percent of banks charged noncustomers to use their ATMs; one year later in 1999, 93 percent charged a fee. USPIRG also found that ATM fees are more often charged by bigger banks, which also tend to levy higher fees.[89] Nationally, 95 percent of big banks, and 91 percent of small banks, imposed surcharges. For the big banks, fees averaged $1.42, compared to $1.30 for small banks.[90]

More credit unions are also adopting surcharges. Of the thirty-one member-owned credit unions surveyed, 42 percent imposed surcharges in 1999, up from only 13 percent in 1998.[91] Surcharges alone are estimated to generate as much as $2.1 billion in bank revenues in 1999.[92] Such surcharges have their critics; legislation to ban or cap them is or has been under consideration in at least twenty-five state legislatures in 1997, 1998, or 1999,[93] as well as in Congress. However, many experts agree that such fees "were a clear incentive to both banks and retailers to introduce ATMs in many more locations."[94]

Despite the dramatic rise in the use of ATMs for accessing cash and, increasingly, other goods and services, the machines are still not very popular as depositories. While deposits accounted for 18 percent of ATM transactions in 1997, this was up only marginally from 15 percent in 1992.[95] As a result, banks have begun to use both fees and incentives to encourage customers to use ATMs rather than a human teller for routine banking transactions, including deposits. Fleet Financial Group, for example, was the first of New England's big banks to begin charging customers who sign up for a new electronic account but then conduct business with a teller. A fee of $2 a transaction is charged to Fleet's Self-Service Checking customers who use a teller for something they could have done at an ATM.[96] Among other banks with similar programs:

—First Chicago NBD Corporation charges its Self-Service Checking Account customers $3 for a teller transaction, such as cashing a check or making a deposit, that could be done at an ATM. This popular account option, which was introduced in 1995, requires no monthly fee or minimum balance. As a result of the program, customers now handle more deposits through ATMs than through human tellers.[97]

—Cleveland-based KeyCorp introduced the KeyMoney Access account in late 1996, which gives customers 25 cents per deposit, up to $1 per month, for every ATM deposit but charges them $1.50 for every teller-assisted withdrawal or deposit. This combination of incentives and penalties boosted ATM deposits to 21 percent in early 1998, from 9.5 percent in 1995.[98]

—Michigan National Bank in Farmington Hills, Mich., sent 50,000 of its 400,000 debit cardholders three $1 coupons to add to ATM deposits. The promotion was geared to cardholders that make ATM withdrawals but not deposits. A similar promotion is underway at LaSalle Banks in Chicago.[99]

—Charlotte, North Carolina-based First Union Bank's Express Checking account provides free check writing and First Union ATM access but charges $8 a statement period for an in-branch deposit, transfer, or withdrawal.[100]

If there is any good news on the ATM fee front, perhaps it is in Chase Manhattan Bank's decision not to impose a foreign ATM fee on the poor and the adoption of a no-fee ATM policy as a marketing strategy by a regional chain of convenience stores. On January 9, 1999, Chase began charging noncustomers a fee ranging from $1.00 to $1.50 per transaction, depending on market conditions, to withdraw cash from a Chase ATM, but elected not to impose any fee on noncustomers who receive public assistance payments electronically and on customers at sixty branch locations in low-income neighborhoods.[101] Citing research that shows as many as three out of four ATM customers make a purchase when they stop to use an ATM, and that they spend more on average than customers who do not use the ATM, in March 1999, Robert B. Stein, chairman, president, and CEO of Dairy Mart Convenience Stores, announced that approximately 600 stores throughout the chain's Midwest and Southeast system will begin to offer customers No-Fee ATM Service.[102] Based on the belief that customers generally make their destination decision based on convenience of the ATM and an awareness of fees, Stein is confident that its No-Fee ATM service will give Dairy Mart a competitive advantage and help build more traffic and sales.

Bounced check fees are yet another source of big profits for banks, generating an estimated $6 billion in annual profits, according to the Consumer Federation of America (CFA).[103] Large banks charge the highest average bounced check fee, $20.29, compared to $15.05 for small banks. Fees of $28.29 in Philadelphia were the highest of the twenty-five markets surveyed, while average fees of $11.71 in Los Angeles were the lowest.

Data Mining to Improve the Bottom Line

Technology is also helping banks accumulate and analyze vast amounts of customer information in a more cost-effective way, enabling them to "zip through accounts looking for better ways to make money for both you and the bank."[104] "Data mining" is about discerning customer behavior patterns—for example, with deposits, check writing, investments, and the management of retirement accounts—so that savvy bankers can hone marketing efforts, more accurately measure relationship profitability, and expand the amount of business done with each customer.[105] According to Mentis Group, "U.S. financial institutions spent more than $1 billion on data mining hardware, software, and services in 1996 alone . . . and annual outlays are projected to reach $1.75 billion by 2000."[106] These enhanced database management capabilities are essential, because as Guenther Hartfeil, vice president of BankOne, has explained, "It takes at least twice as much raw information to measure customer profitability as it does to measure product profitability." And according to Hartfeil, a growing number of banks are concluding that "products aren't profitable, customers are." While there is no industrywide profitability benchmark, for banks, a typical "bad customer makes frequent branch visits, keeps less than $1,000 in the bank and calls often to check on account balances. The most profitable customers, who keep several thousand dollars in their accounts, use a teller less than once a month and hardly ever use the call center. And while favored customers generate more than $1,000 in profits apiece each year, the worst customers often cost the bank money—a minimum of $500 a year."[107]

Using its own standards, in 1994, BankOne set out to assess the profitability of various customer segments, the results of which might raise a red flag in low-income communities. Among the hard truths of this exercise was that about 20 percent of the bank's customers accounted for more than 100 percent of its profits.[108] A market segmentation project at First Commerce Corporation showed similar results. The top 20 percent of the bank's residential customers accounted for 60 percent of revenues and 140 percent of profits, while the bottom 20 percent, with costs exceeding revenues by a factor of 2.5, generated losses equal to 55 percent of the bank's total profits.[109]

Once identified by "data mining" procedures, top-profit customers are targeted for retention and cross-sell programs. These customers are also the most vulnerable to competition from other financial institutions.[110] Centura Banks, based in Rocky Mount, North Carolina, now rates its 550,000 customers on a five-point scale, with one being the most profitable, and the most pampered.[111] At Westamerica Bancorp. in San Rafael, California, "about 5,000 'VIP' customers get a secret toll-free number allowing them to jump ahead of unprofitable callers."[112] After completely redesigning its 218 branches in Louisiana, Bank One

Corporation has plans to position a "concierge" near the front door to whisk away "Premier One" customers to a special teller window or to the desk of a specially trained bank officer.[113]

Chicago-based Northern Trust is a $28.1 billion bank using technology to target its wealthiest clients, or those whose assets top $50 million. Its Private Passport Internet Banking service brings together more than 200 Web pages and several of the bank's back-office systems that allow customers to build personal account profiles and conduct various activities with the bank in one session.[114]

But there is a fine line between using data mining as a way to retain preferred customers and technological redlining, where data mining is used to discourage business and chase away lower income customers. Recall the earlier reference to First Union Corp.'s new high-tech call center in Charlotte, North Carolina. Here is some of what goes on there:

> Fielding phone calls at First Union Corp.'s huge customer-service center here, [customer service representative] Amy Hathcock is surrounded by reminders to deliver the personal touch. Televisions hung from the ceiling so she can glance at the Weather Channel to see if her latest caller just came in from the rain; a bumper sticker in her cubicle encourages, "Practice random kindness & senseless acts of beauty."
>
> But when it comes to answering yes or no to a customer who wants a lower credit-card interest rate or to escape the bank's $28 bounced-check fee, there is nothing random about it. The service all depends on the color of a tiny square—green, yellow or red—that pops up on Ms. Hathcock's screen next to the customer's name. For customers who get a red pop-up Ms. Hatchock rarely budges; these are the ones whose accounts lose money for the bank. Green means the customers generate hefty profits for First Union and should be granted waivers. Yellow is for in-between customers: There's a chance to negotiate. The bank's computer system, called "Einstein," takes just 15 seconds to pull up the ranking on a customer, using a formula that First Union declines to detail of minimum balances, account activity, branch visits and other variables.[115]

First Union estimates that its Einstein system will boost annual revenues by at least $100 million, with about $50 million of that amount coming from extra fees and other revenues from retaining its best customers who might otherwise leave were it not for the extra pampering.

Like ATM surcharging, data mining also seems to be on the way to becoming a business necessity even in the nonprofit credit union community. BMI Federal Credit Union in Columbus, Ohio, started a relationship-pricing strategy (the more profitable the customer, the better the price) in 1997, when the $96 million credit union stopped issuing free checks to all members, reserving them instead for only those with combined balances (both savings and loans) of at least $10,000.[116] Members with combined balances of more than $35,000 also receive discounts on fixed-rate loans, plus premiums on certificates of deposit (CDs). Critics of this trend argue that segmenting credit union customers into more profitable and less profitable groups punishes low-income members who cannot afford to use more services, and is the same as saying, according to Al Menard, vice president of $525 million IAG Federal Credit Union in Rye, New York, that "rich people deserve more and poor people deserve less."[117]

Yet despite its growing use as a marketing tool, not all experts agree on the value of profitability analysis—whether it measures what it is supposed to measure and how to put it into practice. Some argue that "the underlying characteristics of customers do not fit the assumption that some customers are consistently profitable while others are not."[118] Research by First Manhattan Consulting Group, for example, shows that customer demographics are not clearly associated with profitability and that "even those who only cash checks can be profitable to banks with check cashing fees."[119] According to Giltner and Thompson, there are three reasons why profitability may not be consistently tied to specific customers:

—Revenue per household is driven partially by balances of loans and deposits, which vary substantially throughout a person's life cycle. Customers less desirable at one stage are more desirable at another.

—Profitability is most affected by how a customer uses bank services. Cost allocations, because of the fixed nature of many costs, are difficult to relate to ever-changing usage activity.

—Loyalty is clearly profitable over the long run but may seem less profitable in the short run.[120]

Finally, profitability analysis can negatively affect overall customer service, because profitable and not-so-profitable customers talk to one another. So while a complaint about poor service could be dismissed if it comes from a less profitable customer, the problem is that "unprofit-able customers share their experience with prime customers."[121]

Another problem with data mining is that it diverts attention from product development, and according to some experts product development is what banks must do to improve their competitive position relative to nonbanks. As one commentator pointed out, data mining can tell a bank manager, for example, that you have children of college age, or that you are nearing your fiftieth birthday, or that demographics make you likely to buy a second home. After finding this out, however, all the manager can offer you are the same inferior loans, CDs, or mortgages that banks have always offered.[122] The point is, many of these account-based products are still not competitive with the investment products being offered by nonbanks, which is why large bank holding companies are buying securities firms that will enable them to broaden their product lines.

Conclusions

As this discussion has indicated, new technology is speeding the re-structuring of the financial services industry that started with the rise of nonbank institutions such as mutual funds. Edward E. Crutchfield, chief executive officer of First Union Bank, has gone so far as to call the traditional part of the banking business—taking deposits, making loans, and profiting from the spread in the respective rates—a "dinosaur" in long-term decline.[123] As fee-generating activities such as money management, underwriting stocks and bonds, and selling annuities grow in importance, banks are finding that unbundling and pricing their services separately is paying off. In the third quarter of 1997, Chase Manhattan realized a 28 percent return on equity from investment banking but just 19 percent on its retail operations. Likewise, fee in-come from asset management, insurance, and stockbroking for the Cleveland-based KeyCorp grew by 36 percent, much faster than income from lending.[124] This explains why long-term plans at First Union Bank call for building a business that is half traditional bank and half "a combination of Merrill Lynch, Fidelity, and Charles Schwab."[125]

The trend for the future suggests that fees for financial services will only continue to rise, because "increasing competition from other providers of financial services [is forcing] banks to curtail cross-subsidies that enabled them to provide low-cost accounts at the expense of the implicitly better-heeled customers."[126] Moreover, an analysis of the costs and profits of banks since 1995 suggests that the recent round of bank mergers may only exacerbate this trend rather than counteract it with greater economies of scale. The analysis showed that small banks consistently operated more efficiently per customer than their much larger competitors and turned higher profits per customer than their larger rivals.[127] In 1997, the smallest banks (those with assets less than $10 billion) spent around 20 percent less on expenses, loan provisions, and restructuring charges per customer than large banks and "super-large banks" with assets over $35 billion.[128] A study undertaken for the Conference Board in New York has also found little evidence to suggest that large banks are more efficient, productive, or profitable than smaller banks.[129] Because technology levels the playing field—bank holding companies of all sizes have access to the same hardware and software—the study suggests that costs are relatively homogeneous, and that profits probably vary with other factors like management performance, regional economic activity, and product choices.[130] After analyzing income statements and balance sheets of 661 bank holding companies from 1991 to 1997, economist Kevin Stiroh found that "when nontraditional outputs (net non-interest income) are included, there are few differences in either cost or profit efficiency across size classes."[131] This research seems to suggest, as *Time Magazine* recently observed, that "if recent mergers serve as a guide to the future, the brave new world of financial services means higher costs for consumers, at least initially."[132]

The combination of new delivery systems with the increasing use of fees suggests that the poor may be able to access financial services more easily in the future—but probably at higher prices. The next chapter examines the implications of this change, paying special attention to check cashers—those very profitable pariahs of the financial services industry—and their partnerships with mainstream banks.

CHAPTER FOUR

Banks Become More Like Check Cashers— and Vice Versa

As technology and competition prompt banks to rethink their use of traditional branches, they have begun forming new partnerships to deliver financial services without heavy investments in bricks and mortar. From supermarkets and high-volume discount stores to community development organizations and check cashers, banks are relying on third parties to provide cheaper locations and greater expertise in reaching consumers that they have been unsuccessful in reaching in the past.

Many of these partnerships have proved to be win-win situations, with consumers benefiting from improved access to financial services and banks saving on overhead and labor costs. Branches in supermarkets, for example, typically operate with fewer staff than traditional bank branches but for longer hours, making it easier for consumers who work to get access to bank services. At the same time, as discussed in chapter 3, in-store branches save banks money because they do not have all the operating costs associated with stand-alone buildings, including property taxes, utilities, and maintenance. Similarly, community development organizations offer culturally sensitive outreach and education programs to help their customers access financial services successfully and develop credit histories so they can qualify for mortgages and other services, which are profitable for banks and consumers alike.

However, some of these partnerships are blurring the lines between mainstream financial institutions and so-called "fringe banks" that operate without significant consumer protections and community reinvestment obligations. As traditional financial institutions move to a fee-based services system and fringe bankers adopt increasingly sophisticated technology and broaden their market appeal to customers *with* bank accounts, banks are beginning to look more like check cashers—and check cashers more like banks. Proponents say these new alliances will provide more reasonably priced, basic financial services to the unbanked and underserved, while critics predict that the alliances will only further exploit the poor and the debt-ridden. Ultimately, the value of these initiatives to society will depend in large part on whether they help the unbanked—and those who have abused, or been abused by, the consumer credit system—establish credit ratings so they can enter the financial mainstream. This chapter focuses on banks' relationships with these third parties, starting with a discussion of new partnerships with community development organizations. It then analyzes the changing interaction between banks and check cashers, detailing not only the rise of new partnerships but also of a handful of new bank products designed to compete directly with check cashers on their own turf. The chapter concludes with a discussion of the policy issues raised by electronic banking and the restructuring of the financial services industry and of their effect on low-income consumers and communities. With reference to EFT'99, at least two important issues arise. First, should the federal government allow check cashing outlets to provide recipients access to their federal benefits and, if so, should their fees be regulated? Second, with the growing popularity of high-cost "payday loans," should federal regulations ban the practice of cash advances against federal benefits?

Partnerships with Community Development Institutions

Prodded by the Community Reinvestment Act (CRA) to do more to meet the credit needs of their local service areas, mainstream banks have found it helpful to make community-based organizations an integral element of their affordable housing and mortgage credit delivery systems. Over the years, community-based partners have played a variety of important roles, including credit counseling, developing affordable housing financed by mainstream banks, and administering publicly funded down payment and second mortgage programs for working families. Unfortunately, there are few examples of banks inviting community-based partners to help deliver more basic financial services in lower-income neighborhoods. One of the only examples of such partnerships is Operation Hope, Inc., in the Baldwin Hills section of South Central Los Angeles.

When Operation Hope was founded in the wake of the 1992 Los Angeles riots, its main goals were to return mainstream financial services to the community, to educate inner-city residents on how to manage their finances, to operate small businesses, and to lure outside investment into South Central Los Angeles. Founder John Bryant has described Operation Hope as a model for how to meet the financial needs of inner-city residents at a time when commercial banks are reducing their presence in poorer neighborhoods.[1] Subsequently, the organization got into the banking business itself, but not as a depository. Operation Hope's banking centers offer a full range of financial services through participating financial institutions, and community residents who join can open checking accounts with participating banks, cash checks, make financial investments, apply for mortgage loans and credit cards, and use computers to do banking over the Internet. They can also enroll in classes offered by participating banks on personal finance and entrepreneurship. Most customers pay an annual membership fee of $10 to $30, depending on the level of services they choose. While start-up costs were financed with a $1 million investment from Hawthorne Savings Bank, Operation Hope's banking centers are fee-for-service operations that aspire to break even in five years and, eventually, to turn a profit.

There are now two Operation Hope banking centers in Los Angeles. The first, on La Brea Boulevard just north of Baldwin Hills, boasts 3,000 community customers. The second, which opened in May 1998 in the city of Maywood in East Los Angeles, brings together under one roof the expertise and services of Home Savings of America, Union Bank of California, and more than forty lending institutions offering a full menu of financial services. Prior to the center's opening, there was not a single bank in the entire city of 27,000 residents, 93 percent of whom are Hispanic.[2] To help clients understand and make use of the center's financial products and services, Operation Hope has assembled a seven-member team that is fully bilingual. The third in what Bryant hopes will be a network of nine banking centers in Los Angeles County is now under development in the city of Watts.

The Rise of the Check Cashing Industry

As discussed in chapter 2, millions of Americans operate outside the banking system, relying upon check cashers and other fringe banking outlets to meet their financial services needs. For many years, mainstream banks and check cashing outlets (CCOs) coexisted in a two-tiered market, but times are changing. For a variety of reasons, not the least of which is the rise of electronic banking and EFT, the two industries are forming strategic alliances that are raising serious concerns in the advocacy community. As a lead-in to a discussion of these controversial partnerships, a brief overview of the check cashing industry follows.

Many consumer advocates peg the rise of fringe banking to the beginning of financial deregulation in the 1980s and a growing bifurcation in the financial services market, with traditional banks serving primarily middle- and upper-income households and CCOs serving low-income households.[3] Since then, alternative moneychangers have become a growth industry, and more pawnshops and check cashing outlets exist today, both in absolute numbers and on a per capita basis, than at any other time in U.S. history.[4] Between 1986 and 1992 the number of CCOs more than doubled.[5] With an estimated $200 billion in annual transactions, the fringe banking industry—which delivers a host of financial services from cashing checks to issuing money orders and short-term "payday loans"—is both very big and highly profitable.[6] The core of the fringe banking industry is the network of an estimated 6,000 check cashing centers across the country that cash more than 180 million checks a year, with a face value of $55 billion.[7] And check cashing is a growth industry. In just the last four years, for example, the number of check cashing stores has risen 11 percent in New York City, and the value of checks cashed by outlets in New Jersey has risen by one-fifth, to $3 billion.[8] Check cashing is also the most profitable component of the fringe banking business, with the $55 billion of transactions producing about $1 billion in profits.[9] One study found that between 1988 and 1991 the average rate of return on equity for national banks was 9 percent; for manufacturers, 12 percent; but for currency exchanges in Illinois, a whopping 104 percent.[10]

Recent immigrants who regularly send funds to their relatives abroad may value convenient wire transfers as much or more than any other financial service.[11] The undisputed leader in this business is Western Union. With almost 50,000 locations and more than 8 million customers nationwide, Western Union handles about 35 million money transfers, 58 million public utility payments, and 235 million money orders a year.[12] The two largest groups of repeat customers are unbanked individuals and immigrants sending money overseas. The company "is clearly as convenient as a bank for many people, and is far more convenient than a bank for lower-income populations that live in communities underserved by traditional banking institutions," says Tom Norton, Western Union's vice president and business manager of consumer products. In fact, Western Union executives report that many of their customers resist using banks because they perceive banks as lacking interest in their particular needs, a perception fueled by the closing of branches or the lack of capital for new businesses—or both—in their neighborhoods.[13]

In contrast to conventional banks, CCOs historically have been concentrated in inner cities rather than outlying urban areas and suburbs, although this is changing.[14] According to industry representatives, "check cashing services are no longer confined to inner-city neighborhoods, and poor people who don't have or can't get bank accounts."[15] With technology and consolidation combining to increase electronic transactions, raise bank fees, and reduce branch locations, "check cashing stores are poised to keep filling this void by diversifying their services, extending hours of operation and adding locations where banks have closed, many in suburban strip centers."[16] CCOs are able to survive in areas where banks have struggled in part because they generally have lower facilities costs.[17] Surveys also suggest that "customers are satisfied with the services they receive from check cashers, which include convenient locations, flexible hours, short lines, ancillary services such as bus passes and lottery tickets, and, perhaps most important, immediate cash without waiting for a check to clear."[18] Market research by mainstream banks, such as Chase Manhattan, confirms check cashers' competitive advantages. Chase's Kenneth Rosenblum points out, "check cashers are far superior to banks in terms of the days and hours they are open for business and their ease of access."[19]

Consumer Groups Rise Up against Check Cashers' Fees

If the growth of fringe banking has been fueled in large part by the withdrawal of conventional banks from older neighborhoods, then why should their spread raise such opposition among consumer advocates?[20] The answer has to do with their fee structure—which is particularly exorbitant for small loans. According to the National Consumer Law Center, which has led the charge against the fringe banking industry, CCOs, finance companies, pawnbrokers, and rent-to-own stores "are currently bleeding residents of poor communities by charging interest rates from 60 percent to 600 percent."[21]

Even for more basic services such as cashing checks, there is controversy over fees. A consortium of the country's six nonbank providers of money transmission services has defended their rates, demonstrating that the charges—at least in the Washington, D. C., area—are lower than those of mainstream banks. According to a letter from the consortium to the Department of Treasury, a money order cost $7 at NationsBank but 75 cents at Western Union. Similarly, a wire transfer of under $100 cost $13 at MoneyGram but can cost $30 at area banks. While Thomas Cook charges $7.50 either to obtain or cash a foreign currency check, some commercial banks in the area charge $20 to $35 to obtain a foreign currency check and $15 to cash one.[22]

Notwithstanding these examples, other surveys suggest that check cashers and money transmitters can be costly alternatives to mainstream banks for customers who do not qualify for banks' most preferred rates. Check cashing fees across the country generally range between 1 percent and 3 percent for payroll checks but can go as high as 12 percent for personal checks. Twenty-one states plus the District of Columbia regulate check cashing fees, and their caps vary widely.[23] Among the states that cap fees, Georgia has the highest *allowable* rate—at 10 percent on personal checks. Other caps on check cashing fees include 3 percent to 3.5 percent in California for government and payroll checks and 3 percent in Ohio for government checks. In Illinois the caps are 1 percent on welfare checks and 1.4 percent on other checks, plus an additional 90 cents per check.[24] While North Carolina began regulating pawnbroker charges in 1989, it was not until 1997 that the General Assembly passed a law limiting check cashing fees. Now regulated by the North Carolina Commissioner of Banks, check cashers are limited to charging 3 percent of the amount for a government check, 10 percent for a personal check, and 5 percent for all other checks, including payroll checks and money orders.[25]

Some states, like Massachusetts, regulate the check cashing industry but do not limit check cashing fees. Massachusetts check cashers,

however, must post a schedule of fees and charges "in a clear and con-
spicuous place within each location" where they conduct business.[26]
Still, half the states do not regulate the industry at all, and check cashers
have resisted efforts in Congress to impose caps on check cashing fees,
arguing that "competition is the key and the market itself assures customers of a competitive service fee."[27]

A study by the New York Office of the Public Advocate, cited by the
Organization for New Equality (ONE), found that a customer with an
annual income of $17,000 will pay almost $220 a year at a check cashing business for services that would cost $30 at a bank.[28] The Federal
Reserve Bank of Kansas City reached similar conclusions: A family with
an annual income of $24,000 will spend almost $400 in fees at a CCO
for services that would cost under $100 at a bank.[29] The Massachusetts
Division of Banks found that, depending on the customer's income,
the cost of cashing a weekly payroll check and writing money orders is
3.2 to 40.5 times more expensive at a check casher than if she used a
low-cost Basic Checking Account offered under the Commonwealth's
basic banking program.[30] These high fees add up. Over the course of a
lifetime, ONE estimates, "the cost of using a check cashing outlet . . . is
more than seven (7) times the cost of using a basic checking account."[31]
Reliance on fringe bankers also has serious wealth implications. According to ONE, if the difference in fees saved by using a basic checking account instead of a CCO were deposited in a standard savings
account, a person would be able to save more than $17,000 over an
average lifetime of work.[32]

While locational advantage is the reason most commonly offered
as to why consumers are willing to pay such high check cashing fees, it
is probably only a partial explanation at best because banks and check
cashing outlets coexist in many neighborhoods. In New York City, for
example, as of June 1990, while 70 percent of all CCOs were in low-
income neighborhoods, 71 percent of them shared a zip code with at
least one bank branch, and about 19 percent were in neighborhoods
with more than ten branches.[33] The co-location of banks and check
cashers in the same neighborhoods is even more pronounced in Charlotte, North Carolina, where there are about 2.4 banks for every CCO
in the city. Two-thirds of all CCOs in Charlotte are located in zip codes
that contain between six and 20 banks.[34] Nor are check cashers disproportionately concentrated in the poorest neighborhoods, which suggests that CCOs are meeting the financial services needs of working

people. There are more than five CCOs per 10,000 households in Charlotte neighborhoods where the median income is between $20,000–$40,000, compared with 3.4 per 10,000 households in neighborhoods where the median income is less than $20,000. This suggests that other factors are at play, such as check cashers' more convenient hours, and preferred product mix, including customer access to immediate cash.

Payday Loans: A Legal Form of Loan Sharking

Criticism of CCOs for their short-term credit prices is even more vocal; interest rates as high as 100 percent are typical for small loans of $300–$400. This was the case in South Carolina until recently, when loan rates were capped at between 50 percent and 60 percent. But the most serious attacks are reserved for CCOs' so-called "payday loans," a growing business in which a customer receives a very short-term cash advance against his or her next paycheck or benefit check. These loans frequently carry annualized interest rates of 500 percent or more. According to a 1998 survey by the American Associated of Retired Persons (AARP), "[t]he biweekly fee charged for these loans generally ranges from $15 to $25 (per $100), and requires the consumer to write a postdated check for the amount they want to borrow plus the fee."[35] In Milwaukee, for example, a customer can receive $50 for a $60 check dated 14 days later. If the customer returns within 14 days with $55, he or she gets the check back, thus paying $5, or 10 percent, for the privilege of borrowing $50 for two weeks—an effective annual interest rate of 1,092 percent. If the customer fails to return, the check is cashed, and the customer will have paid a 20 percent fee for the two-week loan— an effective interest rate of 11,348 percent.[36]

Payday lending—which the Consumer Federation of America (CFA) calls legal loan sharking—is highly lucrative. It is also a big business, having increased to nearly 8,000 companies today from 300 seven years ago.[37] Fringe banking expert John Caskey attributes the payday lending boom to three factors: check cashing companies are looking for new business as more people get paid by direct deposit and there are fewer checks to cash; friendly state legislatures continue to "cut holes" in usury laws to allow CCOs to charge fees that, while moderate in absolute terms, translate into extremely high compounded interest rates; and, despite the booming economy, the number of people with damaged credit ratings is growing, thus creating the market for payday loans.[38]

While comprehensive national data are not available, CFA's state reports indicate that payday lending is growing rapidly in several regions. In Colorado, for example, 188 lenders made almost 375,000 payday loans totaling $42.8 million in 1997, with an average true annualized interest rate of 485 percent and an average term of just under 17 days. More than 58,000 of these loans were refinanced, meaning that the borrowers failed to pay off the loans when intially due, and therefore were assessed additional fees to roll over the debt. Check cashers in Washington state originated an even higher volume of payday loans in 1997—more than 562,000, averaging $255 per loan, for a total of $145 million. At the same time they collected more than $21.5 million in payday loan fees and, despite arguing that their high fees were justified by the high risks of loss, they had to charge off only a little more than $2 million.[39] "In Ohio, payday lenders have gone from 88 outlets in 1997, the first year the state started keeping track of them, to 382 outlets as of March [1999]. Indiana lenders have had even more success, growing from 15 outlets with $12.7 million in business five years ago to 454 branches and $287 million in business last year. Kentucky now has 327 new branches since April 1998."[40]

Because of such high effective interest rates, on July 1, 1998, the Alabama State Banking Department filed cease and desist orders against 150 CCOs in that state that made payday loans. The department cited the Alabama Small Loan Act, which prohibits making loans for $749 or less without a license.[41] On January 26, 1999, the U.S. District Court for the Middle District of Tennessee clarified disclosure requirements by holding that payday loans that do not inform the borrower about certain aspects of the loan—including finance charges that amounted to an annual percentage rate of interest of 400 percent—violate the federal Truth in Lending Act.[42] Although according to the Consumer Federation of America, "19 states, including all of those in New England, as well as Pennsylvania, Virginia and Texas, prohibited payday lending, most by limiting annual, small-loan interest to less than 40 percent," some states like North Carolina prefer to regulate payday lending rather than ban it altogether.[43] Under a North Carolina law that became effective in October 1997, check cashing/payday lending companies can make payday advances of up to $300 for no more than thirty-one days with interest capped at 15 percent. Because it is the compounding effects of rollovers that can cause the interest to exceed the initial principal in relatively short order, North Carolina prohibits payday loans from being renewed.[44] However, passing a law and enforcing it are two different things. Although Ohio bans renewing payday loans, a June 1999 informal survey of 10 local payday lenders by the *Cincinnati Post* found "four of them willing to roll over loans and only one that could provide the annual percentage rate as required by state law."[45]

Perhaps because of such prohibitions, the National Check Cashers Association (NaCCA) has begun to change the way the industry refers to these high-cost, short-term cash advances. They are no longer referred to as payday loans, or any other kind of loan, but rather as "deferred deposits." This is how NaCCA defends deferred deposits and the high fees: "Many people do not have relatives to turn to or other means when the family car breaks down or an unexpected bill becomes due. Deferred deposit is sometimes the only viable option when people are strapped for cash . . . Businesses that offer deferred deposit service take a risk that traditional financial institutions are unwilling to assume. That is why service fees for deferred deposit transactions are higher than the interest rates charged by banks and credit card companies."[46]

Within the context of EFT, some consumer advocates have urged Treasury to ban payday loans, or expedited withdrawal, of government benefits. This is not a matter of theoretical concern, since the practice has already surfaced in at least one state. According to Florida Comptroller Robert Milligan, "in an expedited withdrawal service already available in Florida, a benefit customer can overdraw his/her account by $30 for an additional $19.95 fee. The overdraft protection, whether used or not, costs the customer $7 a month. In fact, the customer, when contracting with the service provider, does not have the option of *not* getting the overdraft protection."[47]

Whether CCO fees are truly excessive depends upon many variables, including assumptions one makes about the base cost of conventional banking services—which, as discussed in chapter 3, can include additional fees if a depositor's balance falls below a required minimum, bounced check fees, ATM charges, and other charges. David Davis, president of the 300-member Kentucky Deferred Deposit Association, invites his critics to do the math. "A borrower," says Davis, "has three bills due on Wednesday, and won't be paid until Friday. If he is late on his bills, there are late charges. If he bounces one check, it's $60. If he bounces three checks it's $180. It makes a lot of sense to people who need temporary financing to pay our charges, which are a lot less than fees they would face if they bounced their checks."[48]

While in many places CCOs may enjoy some monopoly power, economist John Caskey does not think this accounts for their high fees, which can be four to six times as expensive as those of banks. Fringe banking fees are high, he writes, because the cost of providing the services is high relative to the size of the transaction.[49] To say check cashers prey upon the poor, says Caskey, "is like saying Mercedes dealers prey upon the rich. It's a competitive market with free entry."[50] Other scholars have reached a similar conclusion. In their study of the check cashing business in Milwaukee, Gregory D. Squires and Sally O'Connor found that CCOs are small, for-profit businesses with higher costs per transaction than most banks, and that "their fees are affected by the relatively high-risk market they serve. Their longer hours add to their expenses. And they are often located in high crime areas, which increases their business insurance and security costs."[51]

Industry reports indicate that individuals own some 65 percent of all CCOs, but that check cashing is becoming more concentrated.[52] Ten large check cashing chains control 35 percent of all outlets, and are growing rapidly.[53] The same competitive forces affecting mainstream banks are at work in the fringe banking industry, with scale economies and technology as the principal drivers. For example, Dallas-based Ace Cash Express, the nation's largest check cashing chain, has more than 700 outlets in more than forty markets, up from just 273 stores five years ago. In fiscal 1997, Ace reported revenues of $87.4 million, up 27 percent from the previous year.[54] Not only are revenues up, but earnings are as well. For the six months ending December 31, 1997, Ace reported profits of $1.43 million, a 66 percent increase in one year.[55] And while not all of Ace's stores are permitted to make payday loans, and "lending only makes up 10 percent of its overall business, the company's revenue from payday lending has grown from $164,000 in 1994 to $10.1 million today."[56]

In-Store Branching

Like their mainstream counterparts, check cashers are cultivating new markets by introducing their own kind of in-store branches. Whereas banks are targeting the high-end retail markets for their in-store branches, CCOs are focusing more on discount groceries and other retailers whose customers generally live paycheck to paycheck. These are "retailers with stores in metropolitan areas with demographics that historically were not attractive to traditional bankers."[57] Among the leaders, Ace Cash Express opened a number of outlets in Wal-Mart Supercenters in 1998.[58]

Retailers like having check cashers in their stores for two reasons: They bring people into the stores and they put money in their hands, making it likely that the people cashing checks will use the money to make purchases where they are, rather than going somewhere else.[59] This is why Ace's Wal-Mart facilities not only cash checks but also offer payday loans, putting cash in the hands of the unbanked and credit-impaired shoppers.[60] In addition, in-store branches generate rental income for retailers as well as save them money; by handling all the store's check cashing chores, the branches thus take over their bad check risk.[61]

Technology is also making it possible for check cashing facilities to complement rather than replace mainstream bank services in super-markets and other retail locations. In August 1998, an agreement was reached between Crestar Bank, which is based in Richmond, Virginia, and is a unit of the $26.1 billion-asset Crestar Financial Corp., and Mr. Payroll Corporation to deploy the Mr. Payroll Check Cashing Machine in selected supermarket mini-branches in Virginia. "Our objective is to assist both retailers and shoppers by providing easy access to cash," said Kerry L. Brashears, vice president and alternative distribution channel manager with Crestar. "Thanks to Mr. Payroll, we can now offer an automated solution that empowers people to cash any check from any bank at any time."[62]

Technology is also making it feasible to locate check cashing facilities in smaller retail stores in older suburban strip centers, where there is not enough room for traditional full-service, staffed operations. Semi-automatic check cashing units take up as little as 150 square feet and provide a wide range of services. These powerful kiosks contain a high-level ATM, which can handle deposits, withdrawals, and all other ATM functions. It also features an automatic loan machine (ALM), which allows customers to get on the phone and initiate a loan application. The applicant gets a response to his or her request in five to ten minutes and, if the application is approved, the machine actually prints a check right there on the spot.[63]

EFT'99 Blurs the Lines Even Further

As the above discussion indicates, banks and check cashers began competing, feeding off each other, and collaborating long before EFT'99 came along. In fact, some banks, like Provident Bankshares in Baltimore, own check cashing stores outright.[64] However, the move to electronic funds transfer has increased the trend toward partnerships as check cashers try to hold on to their profits from cashing government checks and banks look to the large number of potential customers who receive government benefits. Some of the more prominent ones include:

Chase Manhattan and Check Cashers

Since June 1996, cardholders for ATMs in the NYCE teller-machine network in New York have been able to get cash at a CCO just as they would at an ATM machine. The hope is eventually to open the network to people without bank accounts, enabling them to access direct-deposit payroll accounts with swipe cards at check cashing locations on the day they are paid.[65] By virtue of this partnership, check cashers would be able to do virtually anything that Chase could do and in effect would become an extension of Chase in underserved communities and neighborhoods.

BankOne's Direct Deposit Plus

According to the Organization for a New Equality, quite possibly "the most exploitive scheme" partnerning a mainstream bank with CCOs is Direct Deposit Plus from BankOne, which allows recipients to access their federal benefits electronically at check cashing outlets.[66] The outlets pay a fee to become a provider, and benefit recipients pay a fee to open a special electronic account at BankOne. The bank electronically transmits the recipient's benefits to the check casher, which then issues a paper check to the customer, written on the customer's BankOne account. The customer then cashes the check at the CCO, for the usual fee, or somewhere else. The net result of this creative use of electronic banking is that the recipient pays a service charge for a benefit check that used to be issued for free, and moves no closer to becoming a part of the financial mainstream.

SecureCheck

In February 1997, the Community Currency Exchange Association (CCEA), the trade organization for check cashers in Illinois, launched

SecureCheck in partnership with two Chicago financial institutions, LaSalle National Bank and Corus Bank. For Corus, working with fringe bankers is nothing new. The bank, which has $2.2 billion in assets and a 1 percent deposit share of the Chicago-area market, specializes in handling deposits, providing cash for daily operations, and clearing money orders for CCOs. With SecureCheck, CCEA-member customers can have their federal benefits deposited directly to a participating bank and pick up the benefit payments at a CCO. The Comptroller of the Currency and the Social Security Administration have approved the program, and market response has been very favorable; almost 20,000 customers signed up in the first two months, and by July 1998, the program had 50,000 enrollees.[67] With about 20 percent of CCO business coming from cashing government checks, CCEA began SecureCheck to secure its members' market share. This is how SecureCheck works:

> A federal benefit recipient can enroll in the program at any of the 400 currency exchanges in Illinois participating by completing the requisite forms, which include full disclosure. The completed forms are forwarded by the currency exchange to Corus Bank, which makes the necessary arrangements with the Federal paying agency. To comply with federal consumer protection regulations (i.e. Reg. E), the recipient can choose to have a statement mailed to him/her or to pick it up at the currency exchange.
>
> The recipient's payment is deposited via EFT to the recipient's account at Corus Bank and is then swept into a commingled Currency Exchange Disbursement trust account, which is Federally insured. The currency exchange receives a bulletin board file and prints a check drawn on the trust account for each recipient registered at the exchange, and the recipient can only pick up the check at the currency exchange where he/she opened the account. The enrollee must cash the check for the full amount of the benefit payment, since no partial withdrawals are allowed.[68]

CCEA promotes SecureCheck, with a monthly fee of only one dollar, as "the most economical program for the consumer on the market today."[69] However, this fee is just for the electronic delivery of the benefit check from the bank to the currency exchange; before the payment is transferred, the bank automatically deducts an additional service charge of about $1.10 if the check casher is in Illinois and $1.60 if the store is out of state.[70] If the recipient cashes the check at the currency exchange, a check cashing fee of 1.8 percent is assessed. Thus, for a benefit payment of $700, the check cashing fee would be a relatively high $14.10.[71]

Benefits Quick Cash

Western Union's Benefits Quick Cash (BQC) program, one of the first to respond directly to EFT'99, enables federal benefit recipients to receive their government payments directly from a Western Union location of their choice. However, because Western Union is not a federally insured financial institution and thus cannot receive benefit payments directly from the Treasury Department, the company has contracted with Basin Industrial Bank of Cortez, Colo., where Western Union has a regional financial services center.[72] Basin sets up a deposit account for each BQC customer, who is issued a magnetic stripe identification card to use when withdrawing a benefits payment at a Western Union location. The BQC card is not compatible with any other credit or debit card and cannot be used at an ATM or point-of-sale (POS) terminal. Benefits Quick Cash customers, like those who use SecureCheck, must withdraw their entire benefit in one transaction.

Benefits Quick Cash has stirred up quite a fuss among advocates and federal financial regulators. Immediately upon its introduction, BQC raised serious concerns because of its high fee structure and its marketing strategy. In addition to a one-time enrollment fee of $4.00, BQC customers incur a charge of $7.50 per transaction. And because the BQC program prohibits a recipient from combining federal benefits into one account, a person who receives both social security and supplemental security income (SSI) benefits would incur a $15 charge to withdraw both benefits. Needless to say, a high fixed fee that does not vary with the size of the withdrawal does little to encourage good financial management or savings on the part of the recipient.

Western Union's original marketing strategy came under attack as well. At best, it was premature and misleading, possibly frightening benefit recipients into making banking choices that might not be in their best interest; at worst, it misstated federal policy. Among other promotional materials, Western Union had this to say about electronic benefits transfer:

"EBT stands for electronic benefits transfer. The government has ruled that federally funded benefit payments must be distributed electronically by 1999. That means that social security, disability, SSI and other federal benefits will no longer be mailed to you by check."[73] At the same time, the company made it clear to their agents that EBT could cut into their check cashing profits in a big way unless they signed on to offer the BQC program: "Federal checks are going away—don't let your customers go with them. Western Union has the simple and ready solution. You can ensure a profitable future by signing-up your customers for the Western Union Benefits Quick Cash program now!"[74] A packet for BQC advertised, "Increase your revenue opportunities with commissions and PBC bonuses as your customers return to your stores instead of competitors. . . . Build customer traffic, repeat business and increase customer loyalty by being first to deliver this new service in your area. . . . Cross-sell expanded Western Union product line to attract new customers and incremental revenues. . . ."[75]

The NaCCA Preferred Card

The National Check Cashing Association and Citibank have created a new electronic product called the NaCCA Preferred Card that will enable federal benefit recipients to open a Citibank account and thereby access their benefits at any ATM or participating check cashing outlet of their choice. Preferred Card customers will have Citibank accounts that are federally insured, provide monthly statements, comply with all consumer protection regulations, and offer toll free bilingual customer support.[76] Fees vary depending on the check casher; monthly fees range from $3 to $6, with withdrawals ranging from $1 to $4 depending on whether customers access their benefits at check cashers, ATMs, or point-of-sale terminals.[77]

Eagle National Bank's Cash 'Til Payday Loans

Blurring the line between banks and check cashers even further, in late 1995, Eagle National Bank, located in suburban Philadelphia, joined forces with Dollar Financial Group check cashers to enter the highly lucrative payday loan business.[78] Because Pennsylvania does not regulate bank loan fees, Eagle National, as the loan originator, is able to export its state's deregulated fees to other states. In practical terms, this means that by partnering with Eagle National, Dollar Financial Group can arrange Cash 'Til Payday loans for consumers at Eagle's fees, even in states that prohibit check cashers from charging typical payday loan rates or extending credit. Eagle charges up to $17.50 per $100 for fourteen-day payday loans, which translates to a 454 percent APR. The maximum loan amount is $500.

In 1997, a little more than a year after start-up, Eagle National Bank booked almost 205,000 payday loans for a total of $31 million. This accounted for 36 percent of the bank's consumer loan business. Remarkably, despite complaints about payday loans by consumer organizations, the Comptroller of the Currency gave a "Satisfactory" CRA rating to Eagle National Bank in 1998. The Community Reinvestment Act (CRA) evaluation of Eagle National did address the Cash 'Til Payday loan issue, however, and noted, among other things, that none of the loans were made within the bank's four-county assessment area, leaving one to wonder whether this was a positive consideration in Eagle National's final CRA rating.[79]

Treasury Gets Nervous

The announcement of these new partnerships to offer access to electronic benefits began several months before the federal government finalized its plans for implementing EFT'99. Concerned about the premature characterization of EFT'99 requirements as well as about hidden fees, Treasury took action. In March 1998, Treasury Undersecretary John D. Hawke Jr. notified Alan Greenspan, chairman of the Federal Reserve Board, about the problem. The Treasury recognized that partnerships like Direct Deposit Plus and BQC "could provide recipients with an expanded range of alternatives for payment services," Hawke said, but "they also raise the possibility that recipients would not clearly understand the fee structures involved, the legal nature of the relationship, or the other options available under the EFT'99 regulation." He asked Chairman Greenspan to share with "appropriate executives at the institutions you regulate" his letter calling for all banks that enter into arrangements with third-party, nondepository providers of payment services, such as check cashing outlets, to "provide appropriate disclosures to customers."[80]

Such disclosures, Hawke added, should fully and fairly convey information about the fees and costs imposed by all of the parties to the arrangement, as well as the legal relationships involved, and should explain the applicability of federal deposit insurance insofar as it is relevant to the arrangement. In addition, disclosures should be framed so as not to mislead recipients as to the requirements of EFT'99. With the further introduction of such products as the NaCCA Preferred Card, Treasury decided to take a more systematic look at the need for federal regulation of these proliferating partnerships between mainstream banks and check cashers. On January 8, 1999, Treasury requested public input on whether the federal government should regulate the arrangements between banks and check cashers and others for the delivery of electronic federal payments to recipients. In what is formally called an Advance Notice of Proposed Rulemaking, Treasury asked for comment on, among other things, whether such products as BQC, SecureCheck, or the NaCCA Preferred Card deny the recipient an account at a financial institution, or access to such an account, or access at a reasonable cost, and more generally, whether this is an area ripe for federal regulation.[81] As the next chapter discusses at length, problems like those mentioned above weighed heavily in Treasury's decisions about key provisions of the final rule.

Banks Are Also Competing Head-to-Head with Check Cashers

While some banks have joined forces with check cashers, others have blurred the lines between themselves and check cashers in other ways. First, like check cashers, many banks have begun to charge fees for cashing government and payroll checks of noncustomers. Second, several banks are creating electronic products that directly target the unbanked. Third, some banks have taken the final plunge and opened their own freestanding check cashing operations. Examples of each of these follow:

First Union National Bank Introduces Fee-Based Check Cashing

Consistent with the move to fee-based banking and over the opposition of consumer advocates, more than half of all commercial banks nationwide that cash government checks for noncustomers charged fees for the service, a 1997 industry survey found.[82] In Florida, First Union National Bank moved into this market in September 1997.

Noncustomers of First Union now have to pay 2 percent of the check's value or $3, whichever is greater, to cash government checks, including social security, welfare, unemployment compensation, and government payroll checks.[83] The average social security check in Florida is $678.50 a month, which translates into an annual fee of $162 a year. The fees have provoked bitter criticism from consumer advocates. "Charging my grandmother $14 to cash a check that cannot bounce is tantamount to purse snatching," said Mark Ferrulo, director of the Florida Public Interest Research Group.[84]

Payroll Debit Cards

The second way that mainstream banks are going head-to-head with check cashers is by developing new fee-based electronic products that target the unbanked. One of the oldest, Chase's Redi-Pay remote access program, has been up and running for more than a decade.[85] Like its newer counterparts, Redi-Pay is an ATM-based payroll service that allows companies, through direct deposit to Chase, to pay employees who do not maintain checking accounts. As originally designed, the cost of paying employees through Redi-Pay was borne by employers. More recently, however, Redi-Pay has expanded to employees of non-participating companies; unbanked workers from any company can pay to join the program. Banks such as NationsBank and Citibank offer similar electronic payroll products. CashPay, NationsBank's new payroll debit card, enables employers to save money by paying their unbanked employees electronically. Employees benefit by having access to twenty-four-hour ATMs without having to provide identification, which at some CCOs means fingerprints. Although NationsBank touts CashPay as "a win-win proposition for all concerned," cardholders have to pay $1.50 each time they withdraw cash and an additional $1.50 or more for using an ATM outside the NationsBank network.[86] This is in addition to the employers' set-up fees for opening the account and issuing the cards.

Under Citibank's PayTM program, a company's payroll is placed into a single account at Citibank, which issues online debit cards and personal identification numbers to individual employees, who can then access their earnings at ATMs or POS locations that accept the cards.[87] In addition to charging employers set-up fees, Citibank imposes on PayTM cardholders a fee of $1 per transaction both at Citibank and foreign ATMs. By contrast, other Citibank customers are not assessed a fee when using Citibank's ATM network.

Bank-Owned Check Cashing Outlets

Finally, some banks have opened separate check cashing businesses that compete head-to-head with check cashing outlets. Chase Manhattan calls its new check cashing business line Chase Check-to-Cash Clubs. For customers whose employers do business with the bank, check cashing is free; for others the bank charges a $15 annual fee, plus 1 percent of the check cashed.[88]

A recent article in *Fortune* was critical of Chase's Check-to-Cash Clubs for the same reason:

"On West 30th Street, the bank built by the Rockefellers has opened its own check cashing storefront . . . at the Club . . . there's no big visual departure from a regular Chase branch: It's got the navy awning, even a few Georgia O'Keeffe posters on the wall. The disconnect is subtler. There are no ATMs here. Tellers monotonously dispense cash from automatic chutes. And there's not a shred of literature about Chase's regular accounts."[89]

Like Chase, Union Bank of California has also gone into the check cashing business, but its Cash & Save program is focused much more on consumer development and creating a market for its mainstream services.

Union Bank's Cash & Save Program

California's third largest commercial bank has $31 billion in assets, 240 branches in California, and another 20 in Oregon, Washington, and the Pacific Rim. Its Cash & Save is a hybrid program that goes beyond check cashing by using education and consulting services to transition previous check-casher users to traditional banking services. Make no mistake about it, with profit margins ranging from 14 percent to 51 percent at its fifteen locations, Cash & Save competes with other check cashing outlets.[90] But what differentiates it from Chase's program is the way it tries to bring unbanked customers into the financial mainstream rather than simply exploiting profit from their financial alienation.

Begun at its Hawthorne location in South Central Los Angeles in 1993, Cash & Save provides a full range of services targeted to lower-income, ethnic markets with large contingents of unbanked workers. While each location provides basic check cashing services—at lower fees than those generally charged by CCOs—what really distinguishes Cash & Save from other check cashing operations is the range of banking services that it provides. Under its Money Order Plan, which carries a one-time fee of $10, customers get six free money orders per month plus a 1 percent check cashing charge. With Nest Egg Savings, a customer can open a no-fee, passbook interest rate savings account with an initial deposit of $10 and a commitment to deposit $25 monthly for at least one year. Cash & Save also offers a basic checking account for an initial deposit of as little as one dollar, a secured credit card for people who are repairing their credit rating, and a direct deposit option for the electronic delivery of government benefits. Union Bank reports that a growing number of its customers are moving on to homeownership.

Cash & Save programs are promoted through grassroots marketing strategies. Before a site opens, the manager meets with community leaders and key stakeholders to assess local needs and then tailors the product line to meet them. Each location also is required to offer quarterly seminars covering the basics of money management.

Conclusions

Despite their pariah-like status among consumer advocates and some financial regulators, check cashing outlets will find a way to serve as EBT delivery points because they meet the market test of providing a service for which people are willing to pay. Henry F. Shyne, NaCCA's executive director, explains his industry's competitive advantage over banks on the basis of volume and turnover. "Banks," he says, with some exaggeration, "prefer to have [one] million-dollar account and check cashers would prefer to have a million $1 accounts."[91] In his seminal book on fringe banking, economist John Caskey argues for an expanded role for CCOs; allowing them to function as agents for banks *and* to take deposits, he says, would give people living in communities without bank branches access to bank services and save banks the cost of establishing full-service branches. If these partnerships should materialize, however, Caskey cautions that "[s]uch an approach should not, of course, excuse banks from the obligation to ensure that credit is available in low-income and minority communities for legitimate business and housing needs."[92]

Moreover, in the extraordinarily competitive world in which they operate, it is becoming increasingly indefensible for mainstream banks to continue ignoring the fringe bankers' highly lucrative market. Wrapping up a forum on financial access in the 21st century, then Comptroller of the Currency Eugene Ludwig said that one of the lessons he drew from the day's discourse was that technology has the potential to change the economics of serving the poor. "We learned," said Ludwig, "that profitability, in itself, may not be a barrier if providers are willing to be creative in their product design, marketing, and delivery to low-income consumers. We learned that opportunities exist for expanded customer relationships among, not only those who have never had a relationship with a banking institution, but also among those who have recently left the depository fold and those who are only marginally in it. And we recognized that the congressional mandate to make all government payments electronic by 1999 will change, not only how millions of today's unbanked federal payment recipients access their funds, but also the competitive landscape of financial service provision in lower income communities."[93]

One can be virtually certain, for example, that Charlotte-based First Union Bank Corp. knows the economics of payday lending and has taken note of the fact that of the four PayDay Now! offices that opened in North Carolina in 1998, the one in the shadow of the First Union Tower in Raleigh has been the most profitable.[94] About 1,200 customers a month come through that office, many of them state employees—all of them with checking accounts at a mainstream bank, since they must write a check to get a payday loan—who willingly pay a 15 percent interest charge for a thirty-day loan to help get them to their next payday. Some banks have begun to deliberately target this market. For example, TCF Financial Corporation—a $10 billion institution with branches in 140 supermarkets and 156 other locations throughout Minnesota, Illinois, Wisconsin, and Colorado—is a mainstream bank that makes most of its money from small-balance accounts. Believing that "a little number times a big number is a big number," TCF specializes in serving the lower half of the financial services market.[95] "For a customer with $250,000 to invest," says TCF's Chairman and CEO William Cooper, "rates are the issue." From the middle-class on down, Cooper believes that customers want convenience. And convenience TCF's customers get—all branches are open from 7 a.m. to 7 p.m. weekdays, plus Saturday hours, and all of its supermarket branches are also open on Sundays and holidays.

Finally, while it is encouraging to see mainstream banks using technology to compete with check cashers in both price and convenience, too often, these products do nothing to bring poor workers into the financial mainstream. With market forces pushing banks and CCOs to collaborate, the most appropriate role for policymakers may be to create a fair playing field rather than to try vainly to bar such partnerships. This is the subject I now turn to—the rules that will govern America's transition to an electronic benefit transfer system.

CHAPTER FIVE

The Challenges and Opportunities of EFT'99

The goals of EFT'99 are easily stated but not so easily achieved: significantly increasing the participation of payment recipients in the country's financial system; making certain that they have access to their benefits at a reasonable cost; providing appropriate consumer protections; and ensuring that the system delivers payments and information accurately, conveniently, and promptly.[1] At the beginning of the EFT'99 rulemaking process, in November 1996, then-Treasury Undersecretary John D. Hawke Jr. sketched the key features of the kind of electronic transfer account (ETA) that would fulfill the Clinton administration's hopes:

> One might expect, for example, that banks would, at minimum, seek these new customers by offering them a basic account into which their monthly payments could be made by EFT, and from which withdrawals could be made by plastic card at ATMs and [point-of-sale] terminals. Additional deposits could be accepted, and other attributes of the account could be based on expected balances.
>
> Some specified number of withdrawals per month might be permitted before service charges were imposed, and the ability to make some number of free third-party payments by telephone transfer or other means might also be afforded.
>
> Additional services, such as balance inquiries, could also be provided. By making such accounts purely electronic—with no

paper checks to process or account statements to send out—
banks could hold both their costs and customer charges to a
minimum, and the risk and cost of overdrafts could be entirely
eliminated. At the same time, these new accounts could provide customers with a safe and convenient means for receiving,
holding and accessing their EFT payments.[2]

The line from vision to reality is not a straight one and not every
unbanked benefit recipient will end up with an ETA like the one Hawke
envisioned. Treasury's four-pronged game plan for moving the estimated
10 million unbanked benefit recipients into EFT'99 has been substantially modified during the rulemaking process. As originally conceived,
the EFT'99 campaign would have:

—Mounted a massive public education campaign to encourage
unbanked recipients to open bank accounts on their own to receive
their benefits through direct deposit. Though slow in getting started, a
grassroots education program finally got underway in 1998.

—Urged financial institutions to offer unbanked benefit recipients
a reasonably priced alternative to traditional checking accounts.

—Selected federally insured financial institutions competitively to
serve as Treasury's authorized agents to provide ETAs for unbanked
recipients who failed to open their own accounts in time to meet the
law's deadline. To ease concerns about cost, access, and fairness, Treasury later decided to allow all qualified financial institutions to participate and to allow all payment recipients to open ETAs regardless of
whether they already have bank accounts.[3] Because crafting the ETAs'
features took longer than expected—the accounts' attributes were not
published for public comment until November 1998, while it took seven
more months before the first financial institutions reached a preliminary agreement with Treasury to offer the ETA—Treasury also extended
the deadline for conversion to EFT by one year to January 2, 2000.

—Provided waivers for unbanked recipients for whom EFT poses
an undue hardship. For reasons discussed in this chapter, Treasury later
opened the waiver door so widely that it effectively converted EFT'99
from a mandatory program into a voluntary campaign, so that all recipients who do not have an ETA or other direct deposit account designated
by January 2, 2000, will continue to receive paper checks by default.

As of this writing, several months have past since the original implementation deadline for EFT'99, yet the process is not very near to where

Undersecretary Hawke hoped to be when he started the rulemaking process three years ago. Although the goals and concepts of EFT'99 have been universally lauded, the practicalities of implementation have proved difficult. The reality of EFT'99 is that the final rule published in November 1998 is much less ambitious than what had been hoped for. By extending broad waivers, the final rule delays the inevitable transition to an all-electronic benefit delivery system, with the result that, in the short run at least, EFT'99 will probably attract relatively few unbanked benefit recipients into the financial mainstream. Nevertheless, EFT'99 is an important piece of social policy because it is forcing a continuing national conversation, as Treasury Secretary Rubin has suggested, about how the banking system treats the poor—and how technology and a new sensitivity can change history.

This chapter presents a road map through EFT'99, from the start of the rulemaking process in November 1996 to the announcement of the first seven banks to offer the ETA thirty months later. It begins with an analysis of the most contentious issues surrounding EFT'99, including the administration's surprising decision to make EFT'99 voluntary for benefit recipients, and goes on to discuss the proposed costs and features of ETAs and Treasury's efforts to minimize the role of fringe bankers in EFT'99. The chapter concludes with a discussion of state-sponsored electronic benefits transfer (EBT) programs. While states are required by federal law to convert food stamps to electronic delivery by 2002, these EBT initiatives have taken on a new significance because forty states are adding cash assistance to their electronic transfer programs as an economy move. A handful have gone even further, helping welfare recipients open their own bank accounts so they can receive their benefits by direct deposit.

Amidst the controversy surrounding the parameters of EFT'99, some states, banks, and social services providers are quietly and effectively working together to bring unbanked benefit recipients into the financial mainstream through the use of technology. This is precisely what EFT'99 is all about, and we can learn some important lessons from these early experiences.

Markets or Mandates

At the outset, one of the most important issues the Clinton administration had to address was whether to use EFT'99 legislation as a basis for

requiring banks to provide low-cost accounts to unbanked benefit recipients. In response to concerns about high fees in the 1980s, several
states enacted so-called "lifeline" banking laws, although early efforts
for a national policy failed. There are many variations, but most lifeline
laws require banks to offer low- and moderate-income families accounts
with low minimum-balance requirements, some check writing privileges,
and modest monthly fees.[4]

The American Association of Retired Persons (AARP) and the
National Consumer Law Center, among others, urged Treasury to adopt
this approach with EFT'99. Martin Corry, director of AARP's federal
affairs department, argued that the cost of providing such accounts
would be only "modest" for financial institutions because they would
receive a windfall from the interest they would earn by investing the
idle balances on these accounts. "Banking is becoming increasingly
expensive as financial institutions charge for services previously offered
free of charge, and most have raised fees for such core banking needs
as writing a check, using an ATM machine, or making balance inquiries," Corry wrote in 1996. "Increasing costs are a significant reason why
ten million recipients of federal checks do not have bank accounts—
they cannot afford it."[5] Rising costs are a continuing problem to this day,
with the Federal Reserve reporting that banking fees increased significantly from 1997 to 1998.[6] As in the past, the Fed found that most fees
charged by big banks are higher than those charged by smaller banks.

On the other side of the issue, the New York Clearing House Association made a two-part case against a federal lifeline rule. This group
of ten large banks in New York argued that such a requirement would
greatly complicate the burden on banks to comply and would force
them to offer services below cost. The association urged the Treasury
to adopt "as a cardinal principle" the policy of the state of New York
that "no banking institution be required to offer lower cost banking
services at a cost to the account holders which is less than the actual
cost to the banking institution to provide such services."[7]

The Size of the "Float"

In assessing the economics of EFT'99, accurately calculating the size of
the interest float that banks would earn on investing benefit recipients'
idle account benefits quickly became a critical issue. The higher the
earnings on undrawn balances, the lower the fees that banks would

have to charge for various account services in order to cover their costs and, possibly, make a profit serving benefit recipients. Some consumer advocates have argued that the float on EFT would be substantial. For example, ACORN, a national organization of community-based organizations, estimated that aggregate bank earnings from undrawn balances just from the electronic delivery of welfare and food stamp payments could range between $10.5 million and $31.5 million a year.[8] There were two problems with this estimate, however. First, on a per account basis, even the high-end estimate is still quite modest. More importantly, in the case of state electronic benefit transfer programs, states—not banks—earn the float, because food stamps and welfare funds are retained by the state until they are withdrawn by recipients or disbursed to participating merchants.

The only empirical estimate of the float that might be earned from direct federal payment programs under EFT'99 was developed for Treasury by Citibank, which measured the float in a ninety-day pilot test in Texas. From the end of August to late November 1996, Citibank recorded the total deposits for all social security and supplemental security income benefit payment accounts, the withdrawals made through ATM networks, and the undrawn balances, which were used to calculate the interest earnings that could be expected from idle EFT funds. According to this calculation, a financial institution might see earnings of $0.19 per account per month.[9]

The nonprofit Organization for a New Equality has suggested that one way to improve the economics of ETAs would be for Treasury to advance the date for transferring benefits to recipients' accounts, thereby extending the float period.[10] However, this would require congressional action and would have to be scored as a budget outlay, because earnings from the float would no longer accrue to the federal government. Even if this approach is not feasible, the same result could be achieved, over time, by recipients changing their behavior and withdrawing funds as needed rather than in lump sums.

EFT'99 and Household Savings

Benefit recipients might be encouraged to save more if they were connected to the mainstream financial system and if more culturally sensitive savings vehicles were developed.[11] If they can be convinced to leave their benefits in the bank longer, the float would increase. Although there were insufficient data from the Texas pilot test to measure a learning curve, Citicorp recognized the possibility that benefit recipients might increase their savings over time or, at the least, slow the pace of withdrawals from their electronic accounts. To determine whether there is a learning effect among recipients, the authors of the study suggested, the government would have to track the history and account activities of individual recipients under the various programs and analyze the resulting data, either in a cross-sectional approach by comparing withdrawal patterns of the program population as a whole or in a longitudinal study of individual accounts over time. Citicorp also observed that because of the turnover among the population in the Texas study, "the test may not be representative of what can be expected in a more established [electronic benefit transfer] environment." In a mature electronic delivery system, account holders might take longer to spend all the funds in their accounts, and they might maintain larger balances.[12]

Food Stamp Data Suggest Changes over Time

Research indicates that food stamp recipients who receive their benefits by electronic benefits transfer make more and smaller food stamp purchases through the course of the month than those who receive their benefits by coupon.[13] This same pattern was found in Maryland's electronic cash assistance program, the only one for which empirical data on recipient behavior are known to exist. In that state, 1994 data show that those who received their benefits by check cashed or deposited the checks on average within 1.02 days of receipt. Those who received their benefits through electronic transfer, on the other hand, accessed their funds on average 3.32 days after receipt. Once recipients had cashed their checks, there was no way to track their spending patterns, but electronic funds could be followed more closely. The percentage of EBT cash benefits withdrawn, and possibly spent, rose quickly from 38.3 percent on the day of receipt to 59.7 percent the next day, to 71.6 percent on the next. Within one week of receipt, 86.2 percent of the EBT benefits had been withdrawn or spent, while 98.8 percent of paper checks had been cashed.[14]

Markets Win

Notwithstanding the disparities over potential earnings from account balances, Treasury stood firm with the banking industry in the belief that the goals of EFT'99 could best be met through the marketplace, not by mandate. From the beginning, Treasury sought to maximize competition from the private sector for the business of handling federal benefit payments, so that unbanked recipients would have a broad choice of payment services and service providers.[15] Treasury believed— incorrectly, as it turned out—that financial institutions, motivated by enlightened self-interest, would be eager to step up to the plate to vie for the business of millions of unbanked benefit recipients. As Undersecretary Hawke put it in early 1997:

"[P]rofit and business expansion opportunities are a fundamental reason for seeking this market, using the cost savings available in the electronic environment to make money, and still provide a service to the unbanked population that receives federal payments. Financial institutions should be interested in this market to protect their franchise. If they allow this population to be lured permanently to nonbank intermediaries, they may lose the opportunity to create long-term relationships. Check cashers, data processing companies, and other innovators will find ways to serve this population. They will be competing and trying to find ways to attract this population away from banks and into other forms of payment services."[16]

At that time, the administration's fondest hope was that a thousand flowers would bloom, that the industry would use EFT'99 to bring basic banking services for the poor into the technology age, which would be good for the bottom line. "In the past," said Hawke, "policymakers and social activists have thought about 'lifeline banking' in the context of a paper-based system. The objective has been to provide a low-cost means of cashing checks and maintaining checking accounts. Financial institutions, who understand only too well the costs of processing paper payments, have understandably resisted the idea that they should provide subsidized banking services. It is time to radically change our thinking about these questions. If we properly design *electronic* products—if we can capture for the benefit of the presently unbanked the advantages of electronic payments—it should be possible to provide 'lifeline banking' services not only without subsidy, but on a profitable basis."[17] However, should the banking community not respond satisfactorily in meeting the needs of unbanked recipients, he added, Treasury was ready to wield "a heavier hand of government."[18]

Heavy-handed regulation of ETAs could undermine market competition and nip innovation in the bud, Treasury believed. For EFT'99 to achieve its full potential would require creative responses from the banks. Yet without knowing how they would respond, Treasury could not intelligently address pricing and access-to-service issues without forcing banks to conform prematurely to an arbitrary standard. Litan and Rauch's assessment of the early regulation of smart card and digitized money technology seems to apply equally to EFT'99:

> In trying to set rules of the road . . . the government faces an especially delicate problem. On the one hand, the advent of these new and potentially useful monetary vehicles could be slowed if some rules of the road are not set early. Indeed, if sufficient protections to consumers are not provided against abuses, then if and when problems emerge, the danger arises that policy makers may overreact and thus thwart the technology. But, on the other hand, until the instruments themselves appear and settle into regular patterns, it is impossible to know just what is to be regulated, let alone how to regulate. And if the government lays down too many rules too early, it may distort or misdirect the development of the very instruments whose usefulness it seeks to refine. So, even in principle, it is impossible to know with any precision how many rules, or what sort of rules, the government should try to set.[19]

In accordance with its emphasis on encouraging diverse, market-based solutions, Treasury also decided to scrap its original plan to contract with a handful of financial institutions to become exclusive ETA providers in various regions of the country. Instead, the department decided to "franchise" the account so that any federally insured financial institution could participate in the ETA program as long as its version met minimum standards for product features, attributes, and fees. This decision was applauded by financial institutions that had lobbied for more flexibility in designing ETAs for a number of reasons. Crestar Bank, for example, had questioned whether it was appropriate for the Treasury "to contract with a select group of banks or non-banks for a nationally franchised banking product." Instead, banks should be allowed to "respond to the EFT'99 mandate by providing convenient products and delivery channels at good values that meet the needs of consumers and are still profitable for the banks. Banks should then be responsible for promoting their account offerings to the target 'unbanked' market to facilitate selection. Treasury could assist by using its resources on consumer education . . . At Crestar Bank we currently have a basic electronic banking product (Self-Service Checking), and we have plans to offer a 'check-less' version of this product in 1998."[20]

The American League of Financial Institutions (ALFI), the national trade association of African American, Hispanic American, and Asian American community savings banks and thrifts, also opposed Treasury's initial plan for big banks to compete to become default bankers for unbanked benefit recipients. Not anticipating the banks' subsequent lack of interest in becoming default bankers, ALFI argued that contracting with a select number of banks would allow those banks to benefit from EFT'99 even though they do not provide low-income and minority communities access to loans and other financial products and services on a day-to-day basis, as ALFI members do.[21]

The credit union industry also argued for a voluntary approach to providing ETAs, but for a different reason. Three-fifths of all credit unions—90 percent of those with assets of more than $10 million and 96 percent of those with assets of $50 million or more—already offer direct deposit of federal salaries and benefits.[22] However, many small credit unions, including community development credit unions that specifically serve low-income communities, do not, because they cannot afford ATM machines and other necessary technology. For this reason, credit unions wanted ETAs to be structured as flexibly as possible.[23]

Because of such arguments and because few financial institutions expressed interest in bidding to become default bankers before ETA features and pricing were known, Treasury decided to publish ETA standards and allow any federally insured financial institution that chooses to offer ETAs to do so. This decision, however, also had its drawbacks. Rather than dealing with a relatively small number of vendors who would be competing for a large number of accounts in a given region, the new approach meant that all financial institutions could compete for the unbanked market but that no institution could count on getting a specific number of customers. This may have made EFT'99 less attractive to some institutions that wanted a guaranteed market share before they would compete in earnest for low-income customers.

The Administration Lowers Its Expectations for EFT'99

In September 1997, recognizing the complex issues that were yet to be resolved, and stung by the industry's indifference, Treasury officially lowered its expectations for EFT'99. In an October 1997 speech, Treasury Undersecretary Hawke said "to be sure, some industry groups are planning education initiatives. But let me be quite candid: much more is needed. Industry response to EFT'99 has been disappointing so far. I have heard far more in the way of complaints about the possible costs of EFT'99 for banks than about the need to change public opinion about electronic payments. I also find, to my great surprise, that almost 18 months after the EFT'99 law was enacted, there are some bankers who have never even heard of it, and many who have only the vaguest idea of what it is about. More important, the level of awareness among the public is infinitesimal, and those who do know about it probably read some scare story, the thrust of which was 'Guess what your government is about to do to you!'"[24]

The administration's diminished hopes were reflected in two key provisions of the proposed rule that Treasury published for public comment. First, the deadline by which unbanked recipients were to begin receiving their benefits through direct deposit was pushed back by one year; recipients would be allowed to continue receiving paper checks until January 2, 2000, or until Treasury provided them with an electronic transfer account (ETA), whichever came first. The second and more problematic provision was to make it easier for recipients to obtain a waiver from EFT altogether. This represented a clear policy reversal from eight months earlier, when Treasury Undersecretary Hawke had cautioned that the "waiver authority will have to be used selectively or the benefits of the electronic program could be undermined."[25]

The EFT'99 statute gave the Secretary of the Treasury the authority to develop standards for granting hardship waivers, but the proposed rule that was released in September 1997 used that authority any way but selectively. At a news conference during which he discussed Treasury's intentions, Hawke implicitly tied the waiver decision to concerns that consumer advocates had raised about EFT. "We don't want to precipitate a broad-scale adverse reaction to [this] important program by being heavy-handed in the way it's applied," he said.[26] Understandably, the rule would grant waivers to unbanked recipients if the switch to EFT would cause them "financial hardship" and to unbanked recipients who have physical disabilities or are confronted with a geographical barrier. Less understandable was the provision to grant waivers on similar grounds to certain recipients *with* bank accounts who started receiving benefits before EFT'99 became law in 1996.[27] Furthermore, Treasury made the waivers "self-certifying," because participating agencies were unwilling to allocate the personnel necessary to run an orderly waiver system.[28] This effectively turned EFT'99 into a voluntary program.

As a story in the *Washington Post* confirmed, Treasury's liberal policy toward waivers, which converted EFT'99 to a voluntary process, was necessary because Treasury had not been able to quiet the fears of millions of unbanked recipients that EFT'99 would end up saving the federal government money at their expense. Many of the unbanked, the *Post* article said, "are poor, don't speak English and worry that they would have to pay bank fees to get their money when now they can cash their government checks for free."[29] The waiver decision also implicitly recognized that the urgently needed education and outreach campaign Treasury had planned was delayed getting off the ground. Former Undersecretary Hawke acknowledged the administration had been slow out of the block on this: "Our initial estimate vastly understated the amount of investment in public education needed merely to make people aware of what is coming, let alone how they should seek out a service to meet their needs by January 1, 1999."[30]

In June 1998, three months before the final rule was published on September 25, 1998, Treasury opened the door even wider by announcing its intention to grant automatic waivers to all federal benefit recipients who do not sign up for direct deposit on their own. The final rule, when it was adopted, would "emphasize recipient choice and the importance of ensuring that recipients are not forced into choices that are not right for them," Treasury said.[31] Not even self-certification would be required; paper checks would be the default option, until the Treasury Department provided notice that "an account meeting its specifications is available to the recipient." Even then, however, "payment recipients will be able to decide whether they wish to sign up for one of those accounts or continue receiving a paper check."[32]

True to its word, under the final rule Treasury does not require payment by electronic funds transfer in cases "where an individual determines, in his or her sole discretion, that payment by electronic funds transfer would impose a hardship due to a physical or mental disability or a geographic, language, or literacy barrier, or would impose a financial hardship. In addition, the requirement to receive payment by electronic funds transfer is automatically waived for all individuals who do not have an account with a financial institution and who are eligible to open an ETA . . . until such date as the Secretary determines that the ETA is available."[33]

Although Treasury had said it wanted the final rule governing EFT'99 "to strike the right balance between realizing the tremendous taxpayer cost savings from direct deposit while still protecting the payment recipients from possible disruption or hardship," it is hard to see just where those "tremendous savings" will come from given that paper checks will now continue by default in January 2000. Whether EFT'99 will eventually bring millions of unbanked Americans into the financial mainstream will now depend on the effectiveness of the financial education campaign that Treasury has initiated, the extent to which financial institutions will compete for benefit recipients' business, and the extent to which any companion savings or retirement incentives that Congress might enact improve the economics of low-balance accounts for both recipients and financial institutions.

Designing Electronic Transfer Accounts (ETAs)

After Treasury made the critical decision to allow all federally regulated financial institutions to offer ETAs, the debate shifted to focus on specific account features. Treasury originally intended the ETAs to be all-electronic accounts accessible at ATMs and point-of-sale terminals (POS). Taking to heart criticism from public interest groups, Treasury solicited comment on the desirability of expanding ETA services to include, among others, a provision for paying bills via an electronic debit feature rather than traditional paper checks, access to accounts at other outlets, a savings feature, and a ban or limit on ATM surcharges. Public comment was also sought on the appropriate standards by which to weigh trade-offs between increased costs and additional account features.

Most financial institutions that commented for the public record placed cost and simplicity ahead of services. Pittsburgh-based Mellon Bank, for example, was concerned that adding such features as the ability to pay bills would unnecessarily increase costs.[34] Bank of America suggested that providing payment services like check writing would increase the risk of fraud and overdrafts and result in bounced check fees for account holders.[35] Rather than larding the ETA with additional features, the banking community argued, the ETA should be very basic, providing a first step into the mainstream banking system. Benefit recipients could, at their option and at their own pace, graduate into a fuller-service account that would cost more or less than the ETA, depending upon specific account features and the financial management skills of the account holder.

Mellon Bank also argued that providing excellent customer support was more of a priority than additional account features. Since EFT'99 will probably give millions of benefit recipients their first exposure to a mainstream financial institution, Mellon Bank reasoned, every participating bank should be required to set up, as part of their ETA program, a dedicated customer service unit to answer questions relating to balances, fees, statements, and additional products. The most frequently asked questions could be answered by a voice response unit, with customer service representatives available when additional information or clarification was required.[36]

Banks also made a case, unsuccessfully, it turns out, for why they should not have to provide ETA owners written monthly account statements. This is an important issue because EFT'99 legislation requires ETAs to carry the same consumer protections that apply to regular accounts, and Regulation E of the Board of Governors of the Federal Reserve System requires that banks provide customers monthly statements. Pittsburgh-based PNC Bank, however, argued that although benefit recipients "should have the same rights under Regulation E to question unauthorized or erroneous transactions as do other depositors," they could receive sufficient account information through means other than monthly statements, including voice response units and ATM and POS transaction receipts.[37] Many ATMs now provide statements that do give transaction history although they fall short of all the information required by Regulation E.

Citicorp had a similar view about Regulation E. The bank administered the Texas Direct Payment Card pilot for the Treasury and concluded that "if there is one fee-related area . . . that requires Treasury attention, it is the matter of monthly statements." Under an exception granted to Treasury by the Federal Reserve Board, participants in the Texas program could choose whether to receive monthly statements by mail for a fee, which was deducted from their accounts. Less than 20 percent of the recipients requested statements. Citicorp found that most participants could obtain sufficient past transaction information from the bank's automated response unit, which can be accessed in English or Spanish via a toll-free call and provides the current balance as well as a recorded history of the previous ten transactions, generally at least one month's worth of transactions. Callers could also request to speak to a customer service representative, who could view one year's worth of transactions on a computer screen. In addition, Citicorp reported, since "there are no outstanding checks to reconcile, and since all transactions occur on-line, overdraws are not possible." For Direct Payment Card participants, the bank concluded, monthly statements were not necessary.[38]

Only Federally Insured Institutions Can Provide ETAs

Another point of continuing debate was whether Treasury should expand the field even wider to allow check cashers and other businesses that were not federally insured financial institutions to be involved in providing ETAs. Ultimately, Treasury decided to limit ETAs to federally insured financial institutions based on safety and soundness considerations. Fringe bankers, such as check cashers, do not provide the same consumer protections as mainstream banks and do not participate in the Automated Clearinghouse (ACH) network, which processes most electronic fund transfers. For these reasons, Treasury decided not to allow fringe bankers to offer ETAs or to enter into partnerships with financial institutions that do offer them to provide recipients access to their benefits. The prohibition against check cashers, money transmitters, and other financial services companies serving as direct ETA providers was welcomed by consumer advocates, who lobbied Treasury hard for this decision. Much to their disappointment, however, Treasury decided not to prohibit mainstream banks from partnering with third parties to provide access to federal benefits through other, non-ETA accounts voluntarily entered into by recipients, such as those discussed in chapter 4.

On November 9, 1998, the National Consumer Law Center (NCLC) renewed its plea to Treasury not to permit federally regulated financial institutions to partner with check cashers through voluntary, non-ETA accounts, because such a partnership "benefits all parties except the payment recipient." NCLC argued:

Banks operating as conduits between the federal government and fringe bankers simply add another layer of fees to the price of the fringe bankers' already costly services. We have seen a rise in the number of questionable partnerships established between fringe bankers and mainstream banks to take advantage of the opportunity and loophole that exists in the regulation of EFT payments. . . .

We believe that it is essential that Treasury require that the fees charged for these new accounts be reasonable in relation to the federal payment and the features of the account, and that consumer protections apply to the transaction from the point the federal payment is deposited in the account until the recipient withdraws the funds. Treasury should require that the banking regulators ensure the reasonableness of the fees charged for the accounts used for electronic deposit of federal funds.[39]

Embracing market competition, the National Check Cashers Association (NaCCA) extolled its members' ability "to attract customers who often choose to use our services instead of available alternatives," and urged Treasury not to ban check cashers from participating in EFT'99. "[W]e remain confident," said NaCCA, "that many recipients of federal payments will choose to utilize check cashers because of our high level of personal service, convenient locations, security and long hours. Because our primary customers are those who wish to convert financial instruments into currency, we welcome them with open arms. These customers will not be the primary customers of banks. . . ."[40]

Arguing that "fringe bankers do not need the federal government's help in grabbing market share in minority and working class communities," the National Community Reinvestment Coalition warned that if "Treasury provides non-federally insured institutions with access to a captive market of millions of unbanked recipients of federal benefits and wages, the market penetration of check cashers in underserved neighborhoods will truly dwarf that of banks and thrifts."[41] The Center for Community Change focused on costs. "Perhaps the most perverse aspect of these arrangements," said the Center, "is that they allow the cost savings, convenience and security of direct deposits to be enjoyed by the government, the insured depository institution, and the check casher, while actually increasing the cost to the benefit recipient, who no longer simply pays to have a check cashed, but also pays for an exploitative account arrangement as well."[42]

Reminding Treasury that not all opposition to strict regulation comes from fringe bankers, the Food Marketing Institute wrote about its members' vital stake in financial services issues that may affect the type of payment tendered by their customers at checkout. "Twenty-five percent of the federal benefits recipients that do not have banking relationships currently cash their checks at supermarkets," said FMI. "We value these customers . . . and we are pleased to be able to offer 'financial services' as a customer service at a very minimal charge."[43]

Treasury's decision not to ban all partnerships between fringe and traditional banks was made on pragmatic grounds, according to Undersecretary Hawke, because "[c]ustomers may prefer dealing with intermediaries that are not financial institutions." As an example, Hawke envisioned "major data processing firms developing a standardized product that could be offered to smaller depository institutions around the country." While EFT'99 is fraught with technologic challenges, he believed it also offers firms "a great opportunity to act as a kind of a franchiser to attract participants to this market."[44] However, in its rulemaking statement, Treasury did echo NCLC's concerns that some bank alliances with fringe bankers, such as those discussed in chapter 4, "may be confusing or misleading to recipients."[45]

Believing that disclosure is the best way to deal with hidden and excessive fees, Treasury advised that insured financial institutions that participate in EFTs with nonfinancial institutions should provide certain information to their customers. "This includes information about the fees and costs imposed by the financial institution and the nonfinancial institution and information about federal deposit insurance. In addition, this information should be conveyed so as not to mislead recipients."[46]

To facilitate disclosure, Treasury prepared model notification and disclosure language for federally insured financial institutions to use in conjunction with their EFT partnerships with fringe bankers and affirmed its willingness to take a stronger regulatory role if disclosure failed to curb price gouging and other abuses related to EFT accounts. Treasury also sought public comment on the need to formally regulate voluntary agreements between banks and nonbank providers of payment services, including check cashers.

Cost Shifting, Not Bridge Building

The final area of major discussion in formulating the ETAs was cost. Although ensuring access to federal benefits at a reasonable cost had been a goal of EFT'99 from the beginning, Treasury was initially reluctant to give community advocates or the financial services industry guidance on how to interpret this provision, and this reluctance was strongly criticized. Some of the friction had to do with disagreements over the anticipated size of the float. As suggested earlier, some believed the float would be sufficiently large to cover most if not all of the costs of providing basic account services. While they agreed such an outcome would be desirable, however, Treasury officials correctly asserted that there was no empirical basis for such optimism; institutions "need to determine, based on their knowledge of what their customers and potential customers want, what to offer, what is cost-justified, and what fee structure will work without it being a money-losing subsidy to recipients of federal payments."[47]

Much to the administration's frustration, bankers and consumer advocates alike continued to allege that EFT'99 is not just about building a bridge to carry the unbanked into the financial mainstream, but about cost shifting. Some financial institutions still seem to believe that the conversion from paper check to direct deposit will not save money. For example, Douglas Woodruff, a senior vice president of NationsBank Community Investment Corporation, has argued, the 41 cents per payment the Treasury will save by switching from paper checks to direct deposit will not just disappear into thin air; at some point, it will be borne by another entity. "There is a propensity on the part of people who support the concept and are not bankers to want bankers to fund the cost of the system," Woodruff says.[48] Banks are also afraid that any limits imposed on ETA charges could spill over into other areas, opening a back door for federal regulation of ATM fees. Pointing out that over 30,000 new ATM locations have been added since banks began charging ATM fees, Bank of America has argued that maintaining market-based ATM fees will encourage financial institutions to add ATMs in previously unprofitable, lower-volume locations.[49]

Consumer advocates, on the other hand, are concerned that the banks will push the costs of EFT'99 onto low-income beneficiaries by charging high transaction fees and minimizing services, such as eliminating monthly statements.[50]

Noting that bank fees had been rising at twice the rate of inflation, in July 1997 ACORN expressed concern that if ETAs did not include no- or very low-cost check writing privileges or third-party payments, consumers would have to pay for these services as well as for making withdrawals. "Given that money orders typically cost between $3 and $5 at banks, and most people pay at least rent and two utilities each month," ACORN pointed out, the cost could climb as high as $15 per month just for payments. When ATM-type transaction charges are added for accessing account balances and for using "foreign" ATMs, "depositors could pay as much as $25 in assorted fees each month—nearly $6 more than the unbanked beneficiaries pay now using check cashers for all financial transactions," ACORN argued.[51]

The Consumer Federation of America and National Consumer Law Center urged Treasury to limit fees on default accounts to a maximum of $3 per month and assure "reasonable" cash withdrawals—which they defined as at least four free ATM withdrawals per month at the institution where the account is held—plus at least two free ATM balance inquiries.[52]

Treasury Undersecretary Hawke has indicated some sympathy with this perspective. "When those rolls of paper disappear at the processing centers and the people who stack those paper checks are employed in other occupations, how do we ensure that the cost savings will inure to the benefit of recipients?" he asked at a 1997 forum.[53]

Treasury Announces the Attributes of the ETA

On November 23, 1998, Treasury published for public comment a description of the features that participating financial institutions would be required to include in their ETAs. These attributes are designed to ensure that federal payment recipients have access to ETAs at a reasonable cost and with the same consumer protections enjoyed by other account holders at the same financial institutions.[54] Several recommendations put forward by the Consumer Federation of America and other consumer advocates, including a modest fee cap and liberal withdrawal policies, were included. As proposed by Treasury, the basic ETA would be offered at federally insured financial institutions to any individuals receiving federal benefit, wage, salary, or retirement payments.[55] In addition, the ETA would:

—Accept only electronic payments;

—Be limited to a maximum monthly fee of $3;

—Allow a minimum of four cash withdrawals per month without charge through proprietary ATMs, over-the-counter transactions, or both, at the option of the financial institution;

—Provide the same consumer protections available to the financial institution's other account holders, including Regulation E protections regarding disclosure, limitations on liability, and procedures for reporting lost or stolen cards and for resolving errors;

—Allow access to the financial institution's POS network, as well as cash withdrawals and cash back with purchases;

—Require no minimum balance, except as required by federal or state law; and

—Provide a monthly statement.

Treasury also sought public input on three additional features, not included in the basic ETA account, which financial institutions could offer at their discretion at little or no cost to account holders:

—Paying interest on account balances;

—Allowing additional electronic deposits—an important feature if ETAs are to encourage household savings; and

—Providing the capability to pay bills via the automatic clearing house system.

After carefully considering public comments, Treasury will decide whether any of these features should be included in ETAs at additional costs to account holders. Not wanting to force additional costs onto consumers, Treasury put the industry on notice that if the additional features are allowed, "any financial institution that offers [them] must also make available to recipients an ETA without the additional features."[56]

There are two aspects of Treasury's ETA notice that warrant special attention: one concerns ETA attributes such as bill-paying capabilities; the other concerns the economics of ETAs.

Over-the-Counter Transactions

Notwithstanding Treasury's long-standing pronouncements to the contrary, the ETA is not an all-electronic account. Recognizing that unbanked benefit recipients "share demographic characteristics with individuals who do not prefer electronic banking solutions," Treasury agreed with consumer advocates and financial institutions that ETA accounts should offer over-the-counter as well as ATM and point-of-sale terminal access to funds.[57] This decision has three important implications. First, it could increase the supply and geographic coverage of ETAs by enabling smaller and less technologically advanced financial institutions that do not have ATM capabilities, such as many credit unions, to offer ETAs. Second, it could increase the demand for ETAs by drawing into the banking system recipients who, because of mental, language, literacy, or other barriers, are unable or unwilling to use ATMs. Treasury research indicates that about half of all prospective ETA account holders have some degree of disability, which may make it more difficult for them to access cash from ATMs, and about half do not have high school diplomas, which may make them less comfortable using ATMs for cash access and balance information.[58]

Finally, by allowing over-the-counter access to benefits, Treasury added a new competitive wrinkle to the ETA process. Because over-the-counter transactions are more costly to some financial institutions than ATM transactions, smaller financial institutions and those without ATM capabilities can differentiate their ETA products by offering recipients more "personal service" at no additional cost.

The Economics of ETAs

There is no way of knowing in advance how deep or profitable the ETA market might be because the potential profitability of ETAs depends upon many factors, not the least of which are the account attributes prescribed by the Treasury. Not only does the $3 cap on the monthly fee—and the number of withdrawals and/or account balance inquiries included with the fee—affect an institution's costs, so too does the decision to permit over-the-counter access to benefits. Other important factors include whether financial institutions have off-the-shelf products that already meet ETA specifications without requiring further investments in product development; financial institutions' cost structures, since smaller banks have higher ATM access costs than bigger banks and pay more to access the automated clearinghouse payment system; and the ability to attract sufficient account holders to realize scale economies. Research indicates that the prospective market for ETAs is highly concentrated:[59]

—50 percent of all ETA prospects live in nine states, and 80 percent of all check recipients live in twenty-three states;

—The top five cities for check recipients are Los Angeles, New York, Miami, Chicago, and San Francisco;

—40 percent of zip codes receive 91.5 percent of federal benefit checks; and within the top 10 percent of zip codes with the greatest number of check recipients, nearly one out of four recipients may not have bank accounts.

These findings suggest that financial institutions that elect to offer ETAs and heavily market them may have a good chance to achieve economies of scale.

Finally, there is the "volume impact" to consider. If ETAs shift benefit recipients who already have bank accounts away from services on which banks make more money, they will adversely affect banks' overall profitability.[60]

While the profitability of the ETA market can be determined only over time, research by Dove Associates for the Department of the Treasury concluded that creating account services for unbanked benefit recipients can be good business for financial institutions—under certain conditions. Institutions will "need to maximize float, [point-of-sale] interchange, incremental fee-based transactions and monthly account fees to generate sufficient revenues to support the ETA program."[61] With account features that are similar to those announced by Treasury, Dove estimated that "the ETA could generate a pretax profit of approximately $0.93 monthly per account for a large bank," which translates to a little more than $11 a year, or about $1.2 million in pretax profits for a portfolio of 10,000 ETA accounts.[62] Primarily because they pay higher network fees for ATM transactions, smaller financial institutions would see smaller returns—49 cents per ETA account, or about half the pretax profit generated by a large financial institution.

Because of high product development costs—which Dove estimates to range between $64,000 and $148,000 or $6 to $15 per account for 10,000 accounts[63]—a very large number of financial institutions must be able to meet minimum performance requirements with off-the-shelf products in order for ETAs to be commercially viable. Dove concluded that many banks do have such products, even though they may not heavily market them, so they could begin to offer ETAs with very modest up-front investments in systems development and set-up. With an estimated average set-up cost of $12.61 per account, assuming a 15 percent required return on investment (that is, a hurdle rate) to justify a financial institution investing in an ETA product, a large institution could expect to realize a seven-year net present value of $35.78 per ETA account, including recovering start-up costs in 13.5 months, the report found.[64] Smaller and higher-cost financial institutions could reduce these initial costs by aggregating their processing activities. "Consolidating development at third-party processors," Dove suggested, "may be an effective mechanism for gaining scale economies and thereby expanding the potential [financial institution] base that can afford to offer the ETA."[65] For this reason, according to Dove, thousands of smaller financial institutions already successfully use third parties for item and debit card processing.

Without estimating how profitable the ETA market might be, Treasury agreed that financial institutions could do well by offering an ETA product:

"Treasury research indicates that the average monthly cost of providing an account with the attributes listed in this notice, including a reasonable profit, falls within the $3.00 maximum price. Research data also indicate that, while some recipients cash their checks for free, recipients who pay to cash checks pay anywhere from one percent to six percent of the amount of the check for this service. Based on the average Federal benefit payment, recipients could pay anywhere from $6.50 to $39.30 to cash a check. Based on this information, Treasury believes that the $3.00 maximum monthly fee should provide incentives both to financial institutions to offer the account and to recipients to sign up for the account."[66]

Big Banks Disagree with the Fee

For many small financial institutions and credit unions, a $3 cap on an ETA account would seem to pose little problem. One recent survey of credit unions indicates, for example, that two-thirds of all credit unions do not charge a monthly maintenance fee on their share draft (checking) accounts, and of those that do charge a fee, nearly half charge $3 or less a month.[67] Also, many small banks routinely offer affordable checking products. For example, Citizens Savings of Summitt, Pennsylvania, offers a *free* checking account to anyone who has direct deposit of any kind, with 400 free checks, no minimum balance, and unlimited cash withdrawals at any branch.[68] And in states with lifeline banking laws or voluntary basic banking programs, large numbers of banks of all sizes offer low-cost accounts. In Massachusetts, 140 banks representing more than 80 percent of all branches and over 90 percent of all bank assets in the state have voluntarily joined the Basic Banking for Massachusetts program, under which they provide checking and savings accounts for a maximum monthly charge of no more than $3. These accounts—which allow a minimum of eight free withdrawals a month and a $10 minimum balance to open the account and keep it open—are also more generous than the proposed ETA.[69]

Despite these and other examples of affordable banking products, however, most big banks have told Treasury that $3 would not cover their costs of maintaining an ETA program.[70] The Electronic Funds Transfer Association took Treasury to task because of its "one fee fits all" mentality, when in reality operating costs vary by region and bank size. Treasury focused on average costs, says EFTA, but the association's members "do not make business decisions based on averages."[71] BB&T, The Dime Savings Bank, and other big banks echoed these concerns. BB&T, a $33.9 billion bank headquartered in Wilson, North Carolina, told Treasury that without certain added "activity fees" it cannot make money on its own Basic Checking Account which, for a $5 monthly fee, permits unlimited deposits, ten checks/debits, and ten BB&T ATM transactions per monthly cycle.[72] The Dime Savings Bank of New York, a $20 billion federal savings bank operating ninety branches in the New York City metropolitan area, reported that it offers a low-cost "Affordable Checking" account for $3 a month, and loses an average of $94 a year on every account.[73] Affordable Checking is a non-interest-bearing account that allows the holder to write up to eight checks per month, the minimum balance requirement is only a penny, and the customer gets a written statement at the end of the month. In addition, the customer gets her first fifty checks free when she opens her account.

The Dime Savings Bank continues to offer this account despite such losses, and the reason, according to bank officials, is its "dedication to serving low- and moderate-income consumers in our communities." Because a larger volume will not reduce the bank's average costs sufficiently to make up the losses, however, the bank is reluctant to extend its reach in this market by offering an ETA. "Assuming that the average per account loss on the ETA is similar to our experience with the Affordable Checking Account," bank officials commented to Treasury, "this increased demand could raise the aggregate losses beyond the point where it would be practical for any financial institution to offer, much less actively promote, the ETA."[74]

Subsidizing a Profitable Product?

Perhaps in response to such critiques, Treasury decided to subsidize ETAs with a one-time reimbursement fee per account established despite its belief that financial institutions could prosper in the ETA market. Dove Associates' studies showed that these start-up costs, which typically include the costs of enrolling and working with a customer and issuing an on-line debit card, average approximately $12.60 per account. As an added incentive—and to offset imputed costs of marketing, training, and education—Treasury is considering an additional compensation for each ETA opened above a designated threshold.[75]

Dove Associates has recommended against this decision for five reasons:

—First, EFT'99 presents an unparalleled marketing opportunity for financial institutions to sell products to millions of federal benefit recipients who need a direct deposit account.

—Second, Treasury's net saving of 28 cents a month per case for replacing a paper check with electronic delivery does not justify a significant subsidy.

—Third, research suggests that giving banks credit under the Community Reinvestment Act for offering ETAs is more important to large banks than subsidizing their set-up costs.

—Fourth, because many institutions can enter the ETA market with existing off-the-shelf products, they are likely to realize solid returns without a government subsidy.

—Finally, subsidizing set-up costs in a market that may be changing rapidly invites fraud and abuse. Dove Associates believes the ETA market may be characterized by a lot of "churning"—accounts set up and closed within a short time period—as banks move cardholders to a more mainstream product shortly after set-up, while others drop out because the account does not meet their needs.[76]

According to Treasury, however, many large financial institutions and approximately half of small financial institutions said the proposed start-up compensation of $12.60 was too low to cover the cost of opening an account.[77] Despite Dove Associates' view that many off-the-shelf products meet Treasury's proposed ETA specifications, many banks disagree, including some of the behemoths. Bank of America believes that few, if any, off-the-shelf accounts would meet all ETA requirements and that financial institutions would have to invest the resources necessary to develop a new, relatively complex account for an undetermined number of individuals.[78]

Adding Other Account Features

Recognizing that each additional feature would add cost and administrative complexity to the basic account, Treasury, nevertheless, sought public comment on whether the ETA should accept savings deposits, permit electronic bill-payment, and include other financial services.

Adding a Deposit Feature

Harking back to its larger vision for EFT'99 of bringing millions of unbanked recipients into the financial mainstream, Treasury favors permitting institutions to accept electronic deposits other than federal payments into the ETAs because this "would enable broader use of the ETA for deposits and payments from other sources, *including matching funds under individual development account programs*" (emphasis added).[79] The reason that Treasury did not incorporate the deposit option into the basic ETA account structure was because of a concern raised by consumer advocates—the fear of attachment from creditors.

Most federal benefit payments are protected from attachment and the claims of judgment creditors by federal law, even after they are deposited in a bank account. Where all the funds in an account are federal benefits, most courts have held that the account itself is wholly exempt from attachment. If exempt funds are commingled in a bank account with funds from other sources, the exempt funds continue to be protected from attachment, but the burden of proving that particular funds in an account are not subject to attachment is on the depositor.[80] Should additional electronic deposits be permitted in ETAs, Treasury has indicated that recipients must be given "appropriate disclosures regarding the possible attachment of funds." In addition, federal agencies would be encouraged "to issue clear . . . rules to help recipients and financial institutions determine which funds cannot be attached."[81]

The economics of adding a deposit/savings feature in part hinges on whether ETAs are interest-bearing accounts. Treasury research indicates that the cost of adding a savings and deposit feature to the basic ETA account is quite modest—approximately 6 cents per account. This is low enough that it is unlikely to "significantly diminish a financial institution's willingness to participate in the ETA program."[82] However, the addition of a savings option would not necessarily increase float income because banks might have to pay interest to encourage ETA holders to maintain larger balances.

In estimating float, Dove Associates assumed that banks would pay 2 percent interest and that account holders would maintain 10 percent of the average benefit amount at the end of the month. "As modeled, the increased daily balances and lower net interest income effectively cancel each other out—resulting in [a] slight reduction in float income for a [financial institution]."[83] However, Dove did conclude that incorporating additional direct deposits into the basic ETA account without paying interest on account balances would increase pretax profit by about $1.20 a year per account for large institutions and by about 72 cents a year for smaller ones.[84]

Adding a Bill Payment Feature

As convenient and economical as pre-authorized debit transactions might be for benefit recipients—because they would reduce recipients' reliance on money orders to pay recurring bills, such as rent and utilities—the implications of incorporating a bill payment feature into the basic ETA account are quite complicated. Adding such a feature might tilt the odds in favor of big banks, which have lower automated clearinghouse costs for processing direct debit bill payments than do smaller financial institutions. According to Dove, large financial institutions can "generate revenues of $0.09 per transaction from bill payments collected on behalf of their cash management customers (i.e. utilities), while smaller [financial institutions] who do not have large cash management and [automated clearinghouse] businesses face costs of up to $0.08 per transaction."[85]

For technical reasons, a payment feature would also bring to ETAs the possibility of overdrafts and their attendant high costs to financial institutions and recipients. This is because ATM systems operate with real-time balances, while the automated clearinghouse (debit) system, which uses batch processing, does not. As a result, the balance of available funds in an ETA as indicated by an ATM will not be correct on the days that clearinghouse payments are actually made. According to Dove Associates, 2.2 percent of payments could result in overdrafts, which will increase customer service costs. Dove estimates each overdraft will cost the financial institution more than $2.34, while another estimate puts the cost of uncollected payments associated with overdrafts, or charge-offs, at an additional 74 cents a month per account. "Most of these situations occur when the account holder does not know what his/her balance is at the time he/she authorizes a non-real-time payment."[86]

Critical Reaction on Both Sides of the ETA Debate

In addition to the concerns over cost and uncertainty over additional account features, other criticisms have surfaced from both sides in the wake of the ETA regulation release. In particular, banks have pointed to Treasury's requirements on opening and closing ETAs as potential deal-killers. Specifically, they object to Treasury's requirement that the ETA would be available to any individual regardless of past credit history, and that Treasury, not the financial institution, would determine the circumstances under which banks could close an ETA account.[87] This is what BankAmerica Corporation had to say about this issue:

> [A] deposit account such as the proposed ETA establishes a relationship between the bank and the account owner. In our experience sometimes these relationships simply do not work. The customer may be dissatisfied with our service or the handling of a particular matter. We may be dissatisfied with the way the customer handles the account or treats our employees. In some cases, prior experience of a financial institution with the person reflects fraudulent or other activity that suggests that there is undue risk in establishing a relationship.
>
> For these reasons, we are concerned that it may not be prudent to require a financial institution to open an account for any individual regardless of any prior unsatisfactory bank relationship. These same concerns apply to restrictions on the circumstances under which a financial institution could close an ETA. Financial institutions address these same issues every day

in deciding whether to start or continue a deposit relationship with customers who may or may not be recipients of federal benefits. The same standards that financial institutions apply to deposit customers generally should apply to opening and closing ETAs.[88]

BB&T echoed BankAmerica's concerns, underscoring the fact that Treasury's insistence that all federal benefit recipients have a right to an ETA, regardless of past performance, might do more to discourage banks from offering ETAs than any other Treasury requirement:

> Today, BB&T screens all clients opening accounts using various consumer reporting agencies, i.e. Chex-Systems. The Chex-Systems database stores the names of clients who have had accounts closed by banks due to the account being overdrawn for an excessive period of time. Other reasons clients are included in the Chex-Systems database include forgery and bankruptcy. The client's name remains on the Chex-Systems database for five years. BB&T does not open accounts for people who appear on the Chex-Systems database.
>
> If a recipient has been reported to Chex-Systems in the past, banks should not be required to open an ETA account just because the potential client is a recipient of a federal check. Also, if recipients who have an ETA abuse the account and the bank closes the account, banks should have the right to report that recipient to Chex-Systems so other banks will not be subject to the same abusive client.[89]

At the same time, consumer groups are also disgruntled with the ETA product because they argue that "Treasury's account structure is less attractive than alternatives that already exist in the marketplace, such as lifeline banking accounts and other accounts that offer free checking with direct deposit." Because it is less generous than the basic banking products being offered in lifeline banking states such as Illinois, Massachusetts, New Jersey, and New York, national advocacy organizations like Washington, D.C.-based Center for Community Change (CCC) fear that banks might be tempted to substitute the ETA for lower-cost, more attractive products, to the detriment of the consumer. "Treasury should be using its clout," says the Center for Community Change, "to nudge the market forward, not the opposite."[90] Like other consumer groups, CCC thinks that more than four withdrawal/balance inquiries should be included in the proposed $3 fee. The Center also argues that unless the ETA provides for a mechanism to pay bills, many people will end up at check cashers or other fringe bankers to buy money orders, which are prohibitively expensive at many banks. Moreover, because many people who get federal benefits also get checks from other sources, unless ETAs are able to accept other deposits, CCC argues, recipients would be "pushed back into the hands of fringe bankers."[91]

The ETA Unveiled

On June 30, 1999, at an event at the New York Customs House, Vice President Al Gore announced the names of the first financial institutions to reach a preliminary agreement with Treasury to offer the ETA: Banco Popular de Puerto Rico & N.A., Bank of America, Britton & Koontz First National Bank, Chase Manhattan Bank, Washington State Bank, and Wells Fargo & Company.[92] "These low-cost accounts will open the door for millions of Americans to receive payments in a safe, simple, and secure way," Gore stressed.[93] Of course, this can happen only if hundreds of other banks, thrifts, and credit unions in the months and years ahead follow course.

The official ETA rollout also resolved a number of unsettled issues surrounding the final specifications of the ETA. For example, Treasury acceded to consumer concerns about costs by requiring the maximum price of $3 a month to include a minimum of four cash withdrawals *and* four separate balance inquiries each month. Treasury bowed to consumer concerns in other areas as well. For example, Treasury chose to minimize service fees by allowing financial institutions to charge a higher monthly fee for an interest-bearing ETA than for a non-interest-bearing one, while maintaining the $3.00 monthly cap on interest-bearing accounts. However, this arrangement probably came at the cost of eliminating interest-bearing accounts as a viable option for financial institutions. In addition to providing a written monthly statement, Treasury also extended additional consumer protections to ETA account holders, including those pertaining to truth in savings protections and other important disclosures.[94]

The most important concessions that Treasury made to financial institutions concerns their rights regarding the opening and closing of ETA accounts. The Financial Agency Agreement requires participating financial institutions to open an ETA for any federal payment recipient who is eligible to open an account, but does not have to open an account for any individual "if it is aware that the individual previously was the owner of an ETA that was closed because of fraud at any financial institution, or, for reasons of account misuse, previously closed an ETA held by the individual at that institution."[95] Treasury limits a financial institution's right not to open an ETA for an eligible applicant to the applicant's misuse of a *prior ETA*. This means that if the financial institution had knowledge that the applicant misused a non-ETA account or committed fraud at a financial institution that had nothing to do with an ETA, it could not use this information as a reason for not opening an ETA for the applicant. The narrow construction of this provision of the Financial Agency Agreement could limit the number of financial institutions willing to take a chance on ETAs.

Treasury was more accommodating on the issue of a financial institution's right to close an ETA account for cause. A financial institution may close an ETA when it "has cause to believe that fraud has occurred in connection with the account or that the account has been misused."[96] However, Treasury requires that "any determination that fraud or misuse has occurred must be consistent with the financial institution's usual criteria for closing accounts."[97]

The Growing Importance of Financial Education

Just as Treasury was liberalizing the policy toward waivers, it was also crafting a nationwide education campaign to explain EFT'99 and help the unbanked to learn how to successfully choose and use basic financial services. This is important, because if information about the price of banking services is difficult or costly to obtain, consumers may choose to continue paying a premium to use check cashing outlets rather than switching to lifeline accounts that are no- or low-cost, but more complicated. Anecdotal evidence suggests, however, that some outlet customers are making uninformed choices. For example, a 1989 study by the Consumer Bankers Association showed that while most outlet customers realized that banks were less expensive than outlets, more than 30 percent of unbanked customers either did not know which was more expensive or thought that banks were more expensive.[98]

Treasury has used its broad outreach, which extends to civil rights, fair housing, fair lending, low-income housing, economic development, community development, and other consumer groups, to promote financial education. To bring the benefits of moving into the financial mainstream to the grassroots, Treasury wisely has engaged some of its severest critics as regional subcontractors. These include ACORN in the Northeast; the National Community Reinvestment Coalition with the National Council of La Raza and the National Coalition of the Homeless in the South and Midwest; the Texas Legal Services Center with the Texas Alliance for Human Needs and Advocacy Center and Legal Services of Eastern Missouri in the Southwest; and Consumer Action with the California/Nevada Community Action Association in the West.[99] This is the right thing to do, since these organizations represent a veritable army of community-based partners, who already routinely deal with issues of financial education and are ready to work with financial institutions and others to make EFT'99 effective for their constituents.

Financial education courses for benefit recipients need to go beyond the basics of ATM and debit card use, Swarthmore economist John Caskey suggests; they need to include money management skills, cost comparisons of fringe banking services with direct deposit, the economics of rent-to-own contracts, and credit planning.[100] Treasury officials acknowledge that local training and personalized education programs are important because, for many recipients, "the choices are complex and involve decisions about the value of entering the financial mainstream," former Undersecretary Hawke has written. "Through small-group workshops, seminars, and training programs, check recipients will receive the information they need to select the best EFT'99 option."[101] Such an expanded campaign could cost up to $20 million over two years, knowledgeable sources within the administration suggest, but these funds are not included in Treasury's budget.

Banking Unbanked Welfare Recipients: A View from the States

Although both the federal EFT initiative and state-administered EBT programs are based on electronic transfer systems, there are important technical and fundamental differences between them. Under EFT, the federal government transfers the benefits to each recipient's account at a financial institution at a certain time each month. Under most state electronic benefit transfer programs, however, the state keeps cash and food stamp benefits in its own bank accounts and merely gives recipients a plastic, magnetic-stripe debit card to allow them to access the amount of benefits they have been allocated. Specifically, clients can use an ATM or a commercial point of sale terminal for cash, but only a point-of-sale terminal installed in an eligible food store for food. The process works much the same as accessing checking and savings accounts with a standard commercial ATM/debit card, except that the clients do not actually own the accounts they are accessing.[102]

Instead, once the recipient accesses the benefits by using the EBT card, along with his or her personal identification number at an ATM or point-of-sale terminal, the EBT host system "will either authorize or decline the transaction depending on the amount of money the system records as available to the client."[103] Thus, funds remain with the state until the vendor obtains them after the fact, to settle transactions that have been completed.[104]

The critical difference between the federal EFT and state-administered EBT programs has been clearly described by Rochelle Stanfield, writing in the *National Journal:*

"The most fundamental split in approach is between direct deposit in an account in a financial institution and the use of what amounts to a debit card—in essence, the difference between having a bank account and having a credit card. The difference is important philosophically and psychologically as well as financially. A debit card—plastic money— is a convenience; a bank account is the first little step to wealth accumulation."[105]

Yet while EBT as it is currently structured has less potential to move benefit recipients directly into the financial mainstream than does EFT'99, it is still an important initiative in its own right. Twenty-nine states had already fully implemented food stamp EBT programs by January 1999[106] and all fifty states will be required to do so by 2002, which in turn will require millions of recipients to be trained to use debit card technology. Moreover, as discussed in chapter 1, forty states have decided to use electronic transfer to distribute not just food stamps but also cash benefits such as Temporary Assistance to Needy Families (TANF). Although most have focused to date on adding cash programs to their existing debit-card EBT systems, a telephone survey in June 1998 found that a majority of those states are also planning to promote direct deposit of TANF and other cash benefits. Thus, cash benefit EBT programs also have the potential to help move recipients into the financial mainstream by encouraging them to open bank accounts of their own.[107]

Direct Deposit Is a Win-Win for Distributing Benefits

Direct deposit of cash benefit programs makes sense for beneficiaries and taxpayers alike. While EBT systems may save states money over the old paper-check system, states must still pay a vendor fees for every case for every month to administer the debit card program.[108] However, states can save even more money with direct deposit because they can simply transfer benefits to recipients' accounts once a month without having to administer debit card programs of their own. The state of Connecticut, for example, paid its EBT vendor $1.30 per case month for each welfare recipient in June 1998, while direct deposit costs only 5 cents per case month. In Missouri, the costs were 58 cents and 10 cents, respectively. If all 50,000 welfare recipients in the state were to open bank accounts and go the direct deposit route, Missouri would save nearly $375,000 a year.[109]

Direct deposit also makes sense for welfare recipients because they can generally use their own banks' ATM networks for free once they have opened an account. With EBT, in contrast, they often must pay network fees and surcharges at ATMs and, in a few states, point-of-sale terminals as well. Three key factors are required to implement a successful direct deposit program: strong state leadership, a committed social services bureaucracy, and a cooperative financial services sector. The Massachusetts Community Banking Council, a consortium of 175 banks, offers low-cost checking accounts for welfare recipients. Fees on these accounts are limited to $3 a month, account holders are permitted eight free withdrawals per month, and no minimum balance is required. In 1998, approximately 31 percent of benefit recipients and 35 percent of welfare recipients in the state took advantage of direct deposit. In Connecticut, about 75 percent of the major banks offer no- or low-cost EBT accounts. Although the accounts are not promoted widely, about 10,000 of the state's welfare recipients received their benefits through direct deposit in 1998. And in Texas, more than 120 community banks and other financial institutions currently provide electronic accounts voluntarily to 22,000 federal benefit recipients under the Direct Payment Card pilot.[110]

There is more encouraging news on the welfare-banking front with the decision of a Seattle-based bank to move into the Los Angeles area. To help introduce itself to the community, Washington Mutual Bank, in conjunction with a local advocacy group, Strategic Actions for a Just Economy, is offering free savings accounts for 1,000 Los Angeles County welfare recipients, most of whom bank with check cashers.[111] They deal with check cashers, among other reasons, because in 1997, Los Angeles County contracted with the check-cashing industry to distribute welfare benefits in order to stop mail thefts of welfare checks. While the benefits gained by participating families are obvious—a free savings account that requires only a 1-cent minimum balance, five free money orders a month, and the opportunity to participate in a bank-sponsored financial education course—they are less so for Washington Mutual. According to bank spokesman Adrian Rodriguez, Washington Mutual is in the business of building long-term relationships, and sees this pilot as a way of building a loyal customer base that it hopes will remain with the bank as "they move up the financial ladder."[112]

Direct Deposit the Missouri Way

Missouri stands out among the states for its ambitious program to encourage welfare recipients to open bank accounts. The state's goal is to raise the level from less than 10 percent to at least 50 percent as a result of the switch to EBT. Caseworkers in Missouri give welfare recipients two options: having their benefits stored on a state-issued EBT card, or having their benefits deposited directly into a free or low-cost bank account.

With the EBT card, a recipient can make a purchase and get cash back at point-of-sale (POS) terminals, or use the card at an ATM to get cash. Withdrawing cash at an ATM includes an automatic network fee of 85 cents per transaction, plus a possible surcharge imposed at the discretion of the ATM owner. Caseworkers are instructed to educate recipients so they understand that with an EBT card they will pay fees and possible surcharges to retrieve cash from their accounts. However, if they use a personal bank account, there are no transaction fees unless recipients use ATMs outside their bank's system. Of the 600 bank branches participating in the state's direct deposit campaign, almost half offered accounts for free. Of those locations assessing a monthly account fee, the majority charge between $2 and $4 per month, carry no transaction fees, and offer unlimited ATM transactions at the recipient's own bank.

To encourage welfare recipients to choose this second option, the state mounted a publicity campaign to help clients learn about the benefits of direct deposit. The Missouri Department of Social Services also spent two years marketing the approach to bankers. To reduce banks' costs, the department developed an automated system banks could use to enroll its clients in direct deposit accounts. The system is accessible with a toll-free phone call, and banks use the telephone keypad to enter enrollment data.[113]

The program could never have achieved its early success, however, without the strong support of Bob Holden, the state treasurer, who personally contacted each bank in the state, asking for written information on their low-cost accounts that could be distributed to benefit recipients. The treasurer's office compiled a list of affordable bank products, organized by county, to enable caseworkers to help welfare clients make intelligent choices about how to access cash benefits. Holden also asked banks to waive opening balance requirements for benefit recipients enrolling in direct deposit, and most agreed.[114]

By April 1999, 284 banks providing more than 600 access points in all of Missouri's 115 counties—an estimated 64 percent of all banks in the state—were offering a total of 389 no- or low-cost bank accounts.[115] While it is still too early to tell whether Missouri will achieve its ambitious goal of bringing half of the state's welfare recipients into the mainstream banking system, direct deposit of welfare benefits has risen from 1 percent during the EBT pilot project to over 30 percent in a third of Missouri's counties by March 1999—with several surpassing 50 percent.[116] It should be noted that as a result of welfare reform, the number of TANF recipients has dropped by approximately 20 percent for the period October 1997 to March 1999.

Missouri's direct deposit program has received several awards for its innovative approach to bringing welfare recipients into the economic mainstream. In 1998, the program received the Mid-American Payment Exchange Marquis Award and the 1998 Governor's Award for Quality and Productivity. The program was also a semifinalist for the 1998 Innovations in American Government awards program sponsored by the

Ford Foundation, administered by Harvard University's John F. Kennedy School of Government in partnership with the Council for Excellence in Government.

Conclusions

By March 1999, the U.S. Treasury Department had made some major strides in implementing EFT'99. As Fiscal Assistant Secretary Donald Hammond reported to Congress, the volume of paper checks disbursed by the federal government has dropped by 110 million from fiscal year 1995 to 1998, resulting in significant recurring savings to the government. Today, more than 75 percent of social security and Veterans Administration benefit payments, 90 percent of federal retirement payments, and 97 percent of all federal salary payments are made by EFT, and new social security recipients are signing up for EFT at a rate of more than 90 percent. However, Hammond also acknowledged that "significant work" remained in implementing ETAs and meeting the needs of unbanked recipients.[117]

While Treasury's vision of bringing millions of unbanked recipients into the financial mainstream remains a powerful one, there is no question that EFT'99 has been severely compromised during the rulemaking process. Pushing back the deadline by a year made good sense, as did the decision to liberalize the waiver policy in order to minimize hardships. But enabling benefit recipients to certify themselves for waivers without review by any agency is a problem, and making the eventual move to an ETA purely voluntary compounds that problem. The cumulative effect of Treasury's decisions has been to significantly lengthen the transition to EFT, greatly reduce the number of unbanked who will be brought into the financial mainstream through the EFT process, and deflate the economics of ETAs by reducing their market size.

If there is any good news here it is that Treasury has begun a national grassroots education campaign to explain the benefits of direct deposit to federal benefit recipients who do not have bank accounts. This is the critical link that has been missing between EFT'99 and the community development movement. The consumer organizations spearheading Treasury's campaign are among those that have made the Community Reinvestment Act the powerful reinvestment tool it has become. They can also help make EFT'99 an effective vehicle, one that invites community participation in the technological changes now underway in financial institutions and ensures that this technology will help create affordable financial services for low-income people.

Another positive outcome of the rulemaking process was Treasury's decision not to limit the number of financial institutions selected to offer ETAs, and successfully encouraging Bank of America, with its coast-to-coast franchise, to be among the first financial institutions to agree to offer an ETA. While EFT'99's broad waiver policy may reduce the number of unbanked benefit recipients seeking ETAs, the accounts will be available to all recipients, unbanked or not, and could lead the way to more comprehensive banking services for many Americans.

Another bit of good news is the extent to which state social services departments are partnering with other state agencies and with local lenders to bring welfare recipients into the banking system. Many mainstream financial institutions appear willing to provide no- or low-cost accounts to enable recipients to receive their cash assistance by direct deposit, and many of these accounts accept nonelectronic deposits as well. However, it would help if more states followed Missouri's lead and built financial education components into their welfare reform systems, including compiling and widely disseminating guides to available low- and no-cost banking services in communities with large numbers of welfare recipients. Also, the effort would be helped significantly if banks allow welfare recipients to open ETAs, even though welfare funds are channeled through states rather than the federal government. This might encourage more states and communities to mount direct deposit campaigns, which is why the Washington Mutual bank pilot program discussed earlier is so important.

Incorporating a savings feature into ETAs is critical to the long-term success of the EFT'99 initiative because it would give recipients a concrete incentive to stop operating in a cash economy, to open bank accounts and to begin building long-term assets. By themselves, bare-bones ETAs can create the electronic infrastructure to facilitate savings by providing low-cost accounts where people can place their money, but infrastructure alone will not encourage low-wealth households to save, or help people who successfully work their way off welfare to stay off. Just like the banks that Treasury is willing to subsidize to provide ETAs, low-income customers also need a reason, or will respond in far greater numbers, if they are given a powerful incentive to change their behavior and join the financial mainstream. Offering them a financial inducement to open a bank account and begin saving on a regular basis is not only the best way to create this incentive, but would also allow the administration and Congress to fulfill their promises to share any savings made possible by EFT'99 with benefit recipients. As discussed in chapters 6 and 7, the savings program could also be structured in a way to significantly improve the float for banks and therefore their incentive to serve low-income customers.

Thus while it might not be as neat, orderly, or rapid as might have been desired, the move to electronic benefits transfer continues to have the potential to change millions of lives for the better. By itself, EFT can help large numbers of unbanked people get access to low-cost basic financial services. Partnered with a broad education initiative and savings program, it could also help them to begin to build financial assets for the long-term. Chapter 6 explains why it makes sense to link ETAs to a national savings initiative targeted to lower-income working families, and why such a program might encourage more financial institutions to participate in EFT'99.

CHAPTER SIX

Using Savings Incentives to Help the Poor Build Assets

The forces of economic change, coupled with advancements in transportation and telecommunications technologies, have accelerated the relentless decentralization of population and economic activity within metropolitan areas. Rapid suburban and exurban growth, fueled by cheaper development and operating costs, have led the private sector to abandon many urban neighborhoods, resulting in lost income and even greater lost opportunity. Many would agree with the assessment of the U.S. Department of Housing and Urban Development that "the polarization of urban communities—isolating the poor from the well-off, the unemployed from those who work, and minorities from whites—frays the fabric of our nation's civic culture."[1] There is also a growing consensus among economists that inequality harms the nation's economic growth, as well.

For instance, Joseph Stiglitz, distinguished economist and former chair of President Clinton's Council of Economic Advisors, and his colleague Jason Furman suggest that increased social inequality may reduce America's long-term economic performance. Where economists once argued that inequality was the price of economic progress, Stiglitz and Furman turn that argument on its head. Social policies to lessen inequality are not necessarily inconsistent with economic policies to maximize growth. Indeed, they believe that "governments that simultaneously pursue macroeconomic policies trying to maintain unemployment at low levels and active redistributive policies may push themselves into a better equilibrium, with sustained lower levels of unemployment, inequality, and instability. These lower levels of inequality may, in turn, help support faster economic growth. While the econometric evidence on this proposition is not decisive, it is clear that the older view, that greater inequality is associated with faster growth, is not supported by the data."[2]

University of Chicago economist Robert Townsend reached a similar conclusion—that "[p]olicymakers should realize that a policy that encourages savings could be important for long-run economic growth and increased equality"[3]—while studying formal and informal financial services in Little Village, a low- to middle-income neighborhood in Chicago. Townsend found that savings were far more important than the availability of credit in creating economic growth in the Little Village neighborhood, given that 58 percent of business start-ups there "began entirely with the owner's own savings; that is, without any loans at all."

These and a variety of other economic studies support the case that because inequality gives rise to social strife that is harmful to growth, programs that redistribute income can help the country's economic performance. There may be an even stronger case for economic development programs that attempt to increase assets rather than focusing exclusively on incomes: savings can be used to improve the long-term economic health of families, rather than simply boosting their standard of living in the short term. Sociologist Thomas M. Shapiro calls wealth a special form of money that is often "used to create opportunities, secure a desired stature and standard of living, or pass advantages and class status along to one's children. The command of resources that wealth entails," says Shapiro, "is more encompassing than income or education, and closer in meaning and theoretical significance to the traditional connotation of economic well-being and access to life chances."[4]

In keeping with this spirit, Michael Sherraden and his colleagues at Washington University in St. Louis have made a cogent case for why individual capital accumulation should be the fabric from which the nation cuts a new welfare policy.[5] They identify two phases in the transition from a policy based on increasing income and short-term consumption to one based on assets. First, it is necessary to remove the barriers to savings and investment from existing programs. This includes the asset limits that have long characterized traditional welfare policy. Second, public policies should affirmatively promote asset-accumulation by low-income households through a variety of means, including direct savings incentives. The much-maligned welfare reform bill that President Clinton signed into law in August 1996 is the beginning of phase one. Although there has been much talk about a wealth-building empowerment agenda, to date, the Clinton administration and Congress have not yet initiated phase two.

As a result, there are no savings incentives for the poor that are comparable to existing programs that target higher-income families, such as the enhanced Individual Retirement Accounts (IRAs) that were included in the 1997 balanced budget agreement. That ten-year, $17.8 billion package of tax breaks is just the most recent example of how the federal government makes it especially worthwhile for middle- and upper-income Americans to save a little extra for their retirement years. No less should be expected when it comes to encouraging and helping low-income, low-wealth Americans save and invest in *their* futures.

Government assistance to personal asset building, which a successful EFT'99 can help accelerate, is quietly becoming a core element of the grassroots community development movement. This chapter discusses the growing role that wealth-creating activities are playing in the increasingly decentralized world of welfare reform and community development, and suggests a number of ways that EFT'99 and state-run EBT programs can help move the country further along the path to an asset-based anti-poverty policy.

Helping Americans Build Assets Has a Proud Tradition

For nearly 150 years—from the Homestead Act of the nineteenth century through the home mortgage interest deduction, to the G.I. Bill, capital gains tax preferences, and tax-favored IRAs—federal policies have encouraged individual asset accumulation. However, most modern-day savings incentives such as IRAs and home mortgage deductions operate through the tax system. Thus they are not effective in encouraging the poor to save or invest because the poor have lower marginal tax rates and do not receive a large enough benefit from the incentives to make participation worthwhile.[6] However, there are examples of policies on both the local and national level that have encouraged asset building by low-income individuals. Various national policies, though modest in size and differing in their specifics, share one thing in common: built-in, special-purpose savings accounts for the benefit of participating individuals or households, who must satisfy certain program obligations before money in the accounts becomes theirs. Such programs, like the national savings initiative proposed in chapter 7, are not giveaways. They require either that recipients increase their work effort or reduce consumption in order to receive or to maximize the savings benefits.

Saving Incentives and Job Training

Since the inception of the Job Corps program in 1964, participating students have received allowances that accumulate in their personal accounts during their tours of duty and are intended to help tide them over while they look for jobs after they leave the program. Job Corps centers are required to deposit into these so-called Living Readjustment Accounts $37.50 for every $50 a student is paid in monthly living expenses. Individual students may also earn up to $850 in bonuses for obtaining a high-school equivalency diploma, a vocational training certificate, or earning college credit while in the Job Corps.[7]

Saving Incentives and Homeownership

In the last thirty years, the federal government has made at least three attempts to create special-purpose savings accounts to help low- and moderate-income households achieve homeownership. The first of these efforts came in the late 1960s. Under the Turnkey III public housing program, aspiring tenant-buyers could earn credit toward a down payment on a unit. This credit was based on the value of the labor, or "sweat equity," tenant-buyers contributed toward maintaining the units. Turnkey III managed to produce just 263 projects and a total of 6,010 dwelling units. Of these, only 18 percent of the units were ever sold because the high interest rates that characterized the 1970s made it very difficult for low-income families in public housing to get mortgages even with the equity credits.[8]

The second effort, called the Family Self-Sufficiency program (FSS), was developed in 1990 by the Department of Housing and Urban Development and has enabled more than 30,000 households to save for a down payment or other major expense.[9] The FSS program reduces the work disincentive implicit in the department's rent rules, which generally set rents at 30 percent of household income. This means that every additional dollar earned is subject to a 30 percent "rent tax." For FSS participants, however, this rent tax goes into special escrow accounts rather than into the coffers of a housing authority. Participants sign contracts agreeing to make early withdrawals only for certain activities, such as paying college tuition or buying a car to commute to and from work, and have full access to the funds in their accounts once they successfully complete the program.

The FSS program is important because it demonstrates that when properly motivated, low-income people respond positively to work and savings incentives. There is real economic value to families from the fact that would-be rent increases accrue to the household rather than to a housing authority. In 1998, the average balance in the escrow accounts was $2,267 for the 35,000 families who had been enrolled in the program for at least fourteen months.[10]

Finally, in 1996 the Federal Housing Finance Board began a program to encourage working families to save for a down payment on a home. The Board, which regulates the safety and soundness of the nation's savings and loan associations, amended the regulations for its Affordable Housing Program to permit member banks to match each dollar of a first-time home buyer's savings with up to $3 of Affordable Housing funds to help them save for a down payment and closing costs. Households must have incomes at or below 80 percent of the median income for the area in which they are located and must complete a counseling program for first-time home buyers. If a participant sells the property within the first five years of purchase, a pro-rated portion of the Affordable Housing funds must be repaid.[11]

This initiative represents a new way of helping potential home buyers overcome one of the biggest hurdles to buying a home—the lack of cash for a down payment. Where other programs offer deferred-payment second mortgages or high-risk 100 percent first mortgages to enable families to buy a home without having any cash of their own at risk, the shared savings program prepares households for the responsibilities of homeownership by encouraging them to reduce consumption in favor of saving and enabling them to build wealth right from the start. Over the past three years, several regional home loan banks have established pilot programs for their member thrifts; two of these illustrate the broad potential of savings incentives.

Under its First Home Club program, the New York Federal Home

Loan Bank allocated $1 million in Affordable Housing funds for member banks to match households' savings on a 3:1 basis, up to a maximum of $5,000. Home buyers must adhere to their personalized savings plans for at least ten months and must achieve their savings goals within twenty-four months. Under the pilot, each participating bank in the New York region can enroll up to twenty-five households in First Home Club per funding cycle. As of November 1997, twenty-eight families had achieved their savings goals and closed home loans under the program.[12]

The Home$tart Plus program of the Seattle Federal Home Loan Bank is particularly ambitious because it targets working families who live in public housing and participate in the Housing and Urban Development FSS program. Home$tart Plus matches two dollars for every dollar the family deposits in its self-sufficiency escrow account, up to a maximum of $10,000. As in New York, Home$tart Plus participants must complete a program of homeownership counseling and money management. Although the program is still in its infancy, by mid-October 1997 four families had graduated out of public housing into homes of their own. The match for these four families averaged $4,000, meaning that the individual households saved an average of $2,000 each from wages.[13]

While there has been little systematic research on the impacts of targeted savings incentives on homeownership, an evaluation of a Canadian program by Dartmouth economist Gary Engelhardt was quite positive. Engelhardt found that Canada's Registered Home Ownership Savings Plan (RHOSP) increased the rate of transition from renting to owning for young renter households by 20 percent, and that most contributions to the special savings accounts it created constituted new national savings.[14]

Savings incentives that expand homeownership opportunities for low- and moderate-income Americans should be a high national priority. For many people, homeownership *defines* the American Dream. In addition, home equity—the value of a home minus the amount owed on mortgages—represents an important source of household wealth. It has been estimated that in the United States home equity accounts for about 30 percent of total household wealth, which in 1989 was more than $7 trillion (in 1995 dollars).[15] Home equity is particularly significant for homeowners in the lowest income brackets. While half of all homeowners in 1995 held at least 50 percent of their net wealth in home equity, among those with incomes under $20,000, half held more than 71.9 percent of their wealth in home equity.[16] Perhaps even more telling is the difference in net wealth between owners and renters. In 1995, homeowners had a median net wealth of more than $102,000, compared to just $4,750 for renters.[17]

There are also community and economic development reasons why owning a home is important. Enterprising individuals frequently use home equity as a primary source of capital to start a small business or to borrow money for education and job training programs, thus further improving their economic status. Also, community redevelopment efforts are often more successful in areas with high homeownership rates because the residents are more invested in the community and less concerned that improvements will bring unaffordable rent increases. Thus, asset building through homeownership has the ability to benefit large numbers of individual working families as well as the communities in which they live.

Asset Building and Welfare Reform

With the advent of welfare reform in the 1990s, federal and state policymakers finally began to take the potential benefits of encouraging private savings into account in recrafting entitlement programs. Unfortunately, however, the widespread inclusion of measures to allow savings and asset building by the poor remains one of the best-kept secrets of welfare reform. Under the old aid to families with dependent children (AFDC) program, families would lose their benefits if they owned assets in excess of $1,000 (excluding autos), had savings accounts, or owned a car worth more than $1,500—even if it was needed to get to work. The result of these punitive provisions was that families on welfare were unable to save for school or job training, for buying a home or paying the deposit on an apartment in a better neighborhood, or for buying a reliable car.

Much to their credit, however, many states liberalized their asset rules under waivers granted them by the U.S. Department of Health and Human Services even before national welfare reform became law. California and New Hampshire, for example, increased their state asset limits to $2,000; Wyoming and other states set theirs at $2,500; Connecticut, Illinois, North Carolina, and South Carolina at $3,000; and

Maryland and Nebraska at $5,000. South Carolina also exempted the cash value of life insurance policies from the asset limit.[18]

Higher Asset Limits

By the time President Clinton signed the welfare reform bill on August 22, 1996, ending two generations under the old AFDC law, twenty-five states had already received waivers to increase their asset ceilings. Under the permissiveness of the new law, that number has risen to at least forty-five.[19] Because the new law does not contain prescriptive asset limits, states are free to set higher or lower asset limits and may keep the higher limits they established under the old waivers, as long as they are not inconsistent with the national goals of welfare reform.

Thirty-two states have also raised the limit on the value of a car that a recipient can own and still remain eligible for cash assistance—to $2,500 and $3,000 in Wisconsin and Iowa, respectively; to $4,500 in California; $5,000 in Maryland, Oklahoma, and North Carolina; and $7,500 in Virginia. Other states, including Colorado, Georgia, Maine, New York, and Pennsylvania, removed limits of any kind as long as the vehicle owned by the recipient is used for transportation to and from work or school. Recognizing that lifting value limits on vehicle ownership does not make it any easier for a poor mother to afford to buy a car, some states are even helping welfare recipients secure reliable transportation as part of their welfare-to-work strategy. Social agencies in Kentucky, for example, help recipients who land jobs get auctioned or donated cars. Pennsylvania has bought cars for recipients, who must pay the cost of taxes, tags, and registration fees to gain title; the car's value is excluded from the asset limits in determining eligibility.[20]

The Treatment of Savings

Research confirms that the old welfare law discouraged program recipients from saving, and some studies suggest that it may have also impacted saving patterns among families who were potential participants in the AFDC program. Using the National Longitudinal Survey of Women to examine state-level variations in AFDC benefits, an econometric analysis found that "a one dollar difference in the AFDC asset limit was associated with a 30-cent difference in the assets of potential AFDC recipients."[21]

In response to this empirical reality, the new Temporary Assistance to Needy Families (TANF) program permits individuals receiving time-limited cash assistance to begin saving on a regular basis. California and Virginia, for example, permit savings account balances of up to $5,000 without jeopardizing eligibility. In addition to exempting the cash value of life insurance policies, South Carolina also allows two-parent families to accumulate $2,500 in assets and to receive as much as $400 a year in interest and dividends. South Dakota and Minnesota, among others, allow children to have individual savings accounts of up to $1,000. In conjunction with the new lifetime limits on welfare benefits, the reform law also allows recipients to begin saving to prepare for the time when they are cut off from the program. In contrast to the old AFDC program, under most state TANF plans, mothers are allowed to keep a much larger portion of their earned income—up to 50 percent in some states—without losing their welfare benefits until they reach the lifetime bar against further aid.[22] Thus, notes sociologist Kathryn Eden, "mothers who combine part-time work with welfare might become better off financially than ever before, and might be in a position to save or accumulate assets if the welfare rules allow it."[23] This is why Eden believes that more states should allow welfare recipients to save money for "expenditures that ease the transition from welfare to work, particularly a car, health and medical expenditures, and a work wardrobe."[24]

The Growth of Individual Development Accounts (IDAs)

The new rules incorporated in welfare reform may help recipients *keep* assets without losing their eligibility status, but they do not necessarily help cash-strapped families *build* assets in the first place. This is why the recent rise in savings incentive programs, which were originally championed by social work professor Michael Sherraden in his 1991 seminal book, *Assets and the Poor*, is so important.[25] These Individual Development Account programs are an effort to democratize tax-driven saving policies by creating direct incentives that are more effective in helping low-income, low-tax bracket households than IRAs and similar programs. "IDAs represent a new and significant shift in anti-poverty policy—from maintenance to investment, from low expectations to respect, from consumption to production, from dependence to independence," says former Republican Senator Dan Coats of Indiana, a long-time IDA supporter. "The simple truth is," says Coats, "that investing in people makes sense, and low-income Americans deserve the same opportunity to build assets as do wealthy Americans."[26]

IDA programs have different titles in different states—Family Savings Accounts in Pennsylvania, Family Development Accounts in Missouri, and the Tenant Investment Program in Portland, Oregon—but all are administered by grassroots organizations as an integral part of their community-building missions and are carried out in partnership with participating financial institutions. In Indianapolis, for example, IDA accounts sponsored by Eastside Community Investment are managed by its own affiliated community development credit union.[27] The Philadelphia-based Women's Opportunities Resource Center is partnering with Jefferson Bank and CoreStates Bank. In Maine, financial institutions that supported IDA legislation have proposed creating a joint IDA bank in order to share the costs and benefits of serving account holders.[28]

A key feature of all IDAs is that every dollar saved by an individual is matched by a community group, foundation, church, or government.[29] Another distinguishing feature of IDAs is that participation is conditional upon the saver's completion of a financial education program. For instance, Eastside Community Investment in Indianapolis, which was one of the first community-based organizations to administer an IDA program, has collaborated with the Purdue University Cooperative Extension Service to develop a financial education curriculum entitled "Making Your Money Work." This five-session course includes lessons on money management, understanding and managing credit, financial planning, and record-keeping. In addition, each IDA participant has homework and individual meetings with a financial counselor.[30]

The final distinguishing characteristic of an IDA program is that withdrawals are limited to specific purposes. Because IDAs are designed to help low-income, low-wealth individuals build both human and financial capital, the typical program permits only three uses of savings: buying a house, getting an education, or starting a business. Permitted uses vary somewhat, however, from program to program. In Missouri IDA savings can be used to make major repairs or improvements to a home; in Maine withdrawals are permitted to buy or repair a car needed for work or for family emergencies. Central Texas Mutual Housing Association's program in Austin features youth IDAs under which a parent can open an account for a dependent child 17 years old or younger.[31] Youth IDAs earn a 2:1 match, the same as the homeownership, adult education, and small business IDAs. Other programs are more restrictive; one of North Carolina's IDA programs, for example, is targeted exclusively to homeownership.[32]

IDAs and Welfare Reform

Enabling the poor to have their first taste of the American Dream through the fruits of their own labor, which is what IDAs are all about, has strong and growing grassroots support in state houses and legislatures across the country. In addition to encouraging states to use some of their TANF funds for IDA matches as a cost-effective element of comprehensive welfare-to-work strategies, the National Governors' Association (NGA) also sees IDAs as a way to promote job retention. Since "most employed welfare recipients return to welfare because they have neither savings to weather illnesses, accidents, and setbacks, nor any means to advance beyond the sub-poverty entry-level job they first obtain," says the National Governors' Association, IDAs could provide a necessary buffer against accidents and illnesses "and the means to invest in additional training and skill upgrading."[33] NGA suggests that states might want to tie the number of IDA accounts they fund in any given year to the number of TANF recipients expected to transition off welfare in that year.

As NGA has hoped, national welfare reform has stimulated the start-up of IDA programs. The federal legislation authorizes states to create community-based IDA programs with TANF block grant funds and to disregard all IDA savings in determining eligibility for all means-tested government assistance.[34] Reinforcing the traditional values of work and individual responsibility, the legislation provides that only earned income can be saved and matched in IDAs created in conjunction with TANF programs. It also designates nonprofit, community-based organizations as custodians of IDA accounts and restricts the use of IDA balances to education, homeownership and business capitalization.[35] In the first two years after President Clinton signed the new welfare legislation, at least twenty-five states included IDAs in their welfare reform plans,[36] and several states began using TANF funds left over as welfare rolls have declined to provide matching funds for local IDA programs.

In Arkansas, the Family Savings Inititative created an IDA demonstration using $500,000 of TANF dollars and $100,000 in tax credits to businesses and individuals who provide additional matching funds for the program. The match rate is 3:1, and matches are capped at $2,000 per individual and $4,000 per household.[37] In Oklahoma, the Department of Human Services has announced a $400,000 IDA program for TANF recipients, while in Virginia the legislature has allocated $500,000 for the same purpose.[38] Iowa expects to create 10,000 IDAs and provide $1 million in matching funds by the year 2000. In Massachusetts, Michigan, and Oregon, the state workfare programs combine IDAs with wage subsidies provided to employers who hire welfare recipients. Under these "full employment plans," employers are required to pay $1 into an IDA for every hour that a welfare recipient works after the recipient has been on the job for thirty days; the employee can then use the account to pursue further education or job training.[39]

Stand-Alone IDA Programs

In addition to the TANF IDA programs, about 100 community organizations across the country are involved in local IDA activities, and several states have created stand-alone programs open to both families on welfare and the working poor.[40] Tennessee, for instance, has authorized the Tennessee Network for Community Economic Development to administer an IDA pilot in twelve communities, and in Pennsylvania, Governor Tom Ridge and the state legislature have allocated $1.25 million to an IDA initiative that will be administered by community-based organizations. Pennsylvania's Family Savings Accounts will match up to $600 over a two-year period for each account for about 2,000 families. The state will match account holders' savings at a 50 percent rate, so savers must deposit at least $1,200 over two years to get the $600 maximum match. Participants are expected to save $10 a week, and no match will be provided to savers who fail to meet the savings requirement.[41]

In 1997, the Indiana legislature created a statewide IDA program and approved $500,000 in tax credits to encourage private contributors to donate matching funds. The National Governors' Association has encouraged its members to follow this model to leverage additional money for IDA programs.[42] Indiana will combine the money provided by private contributors with $6.5 million in state general revenues over four years to support the establishment of 800 new IDA accounts per year, matching at least $3 for every $1 a participant saves, up to $900 per year. Community development corporations, including microenterprise development programs, will run the programs locally with cooperating financial institutions.[43]

Several other states have taken action in support of IDAs. The Maine legislation authorizes both TANF recipients and working poor families to participate. Missouri's program, to be administered by the Department of Economic Development, will target individuals and families at or below 200 percent of the federal poverty level and would be funded by private contributors, who will receive 50 percent tax credits from the state for their contributions. The state will cap tax credits at $4 million annually.[44]

North Carolina is also becoming a center of IDA activity, with three new initiatives now underway. In addition to a state appropriation of $600,000 to fund a pilot project of 600 IDA accounts over the next two years, the Division of Community Assistance, an arm of the North Carolina Department of Commerce, has set aside $250,000 in federal Community Development Block Grant funds for a two-year IDA pilot that is limited to homeownership. The demonstration will create 150 homeownership IDA accounts, matched 2:1 to a ceiling of $2,000, for working families in four rural and nonmetropolitan communities. The programs will be implemented by a local community development corporation or nonprofit partner that already has a low-income clientele and some past experience working with CDBG and/or homeownership programs.[45] Finally, the Durham City Council approved $50,000 in general revenues to test the effectiveness of IDAs as a way to increase homeownership among low-wealth working households. Similar to Seattle's Home$tart Plus program, Durham will match deposits for up to twenty eligible families on a 2:1 basis to cover the down payment and closing costs on the purchase of a home within the city. If the demonstration is successful, the city will consider expanding the program in the future.

Another local homeownership-based IDA program is in Denver, Colorado, where the Rocky Mountain Mutual Housing Association's First Home Savings Plan draws money from three separate sources to provide a 3:1 match for account holders' savings deposits. If participants save the maximum amount—$1,500—they will have a total of $6,000 to put toward a down payment and closing costs on their first home.[46]

The American Dream Demonstration

As is clear from the examples above, the IDA movement has strong conceptual underpinnings and widespread grassroots support. But real evidence of the impact of assets on the ability of families to get out— and stay out—of poverty so far "has been more in the realm of social philosophy than social science," as Yadama and Sherraden have said.[47] That may soon change. A national IDA demonstration project started in the fall of 1997 is the first systematic effort "designed to test the extent to which poor people can and will save if supported in appropriate ways, can use those leveraged savings to build businesses, homes and skills, and in so doing, generate jobs, profits, taxes, and economic and social development."[48]

The American Dream Demonstration (ADD), as its sponsors are calling the national pilot, is in the process of establishing at least 2,000 IDAs in thirteen low-income communities across the country.[49] The scope of the demonstration is grand not only in size but also in its intentions. "[O]ur aim," says Robert Friedman, founder of the non-profit Corporation for Enterprise Development, the "national champion" of IDAs, and one of the sponsors of the American Dream Demonstration, "is to build the case for making available to low-income people asset-building incentives equivalent to those we currently offer the non-poor."[50] In addition, the national demonstration will systematically test several propositions developed by Sherraden concerning the positive impacts of assets. These include greater household stability, increased long-term thinking and planning, increased effort in maintaining and enhancing assets, increased human capital development, increased risk-taking, greater personal efficacy and self-esteem, increased social status, increased community involvement, and increased political participation.[51]

The thirteen nonprofit community organizations, competitively selected from ninety-nine applicants, span the full range of community development missions—from traditional community action and family services, to microenterprise and self-employment for women, to affordable housing and community development finance. With the exception of Tulsa, Oklahoma, each organization will open between 50 and 150 IDA accounts. Tulsa has been selected to implement a second phase under an experimental design that will enroll 500 account holders and be subject to a rigorous impact evaluation featuring a random assignment control group.[52]

While all the pilots will target the poor—none of the participants will have household incomes greater than 200 percent of the federal poverty level—several are focusing on special target populations, such as youth, current and former welfare recipients, the working poor, single parents, low-income renters, or public-housing residents. A number of ADD programs also target African American, Asian American, and Latino communities.[53] And while the broad parameters will be similar, specific program designs, including matching rates, will vary. In dollar amounts, the matches will range from 1:1 all the way up to 7:1. At some sites, the match will vary depending upon the specific purpose for which a particular account was created. The Bay Area IDA Collaborative in Northern California, for example, intends to match education or job training IDAs on a 1:1 basis, IDAs for business development as much as 2:1, and homeownership IDAs up to 4:1. Participants in the Shorebank program in Chicago will receive a 2:1 match on the first $600 they save over three years to be used for homeownership, education, and small business development. A second program called the Shorebank Savers Club began in spring 1999 and offers a 1:1 match up to $500 a year for two years. Shorebank is also considering a teen IDA program to help families save for college expenses.[54]

As of December 31, 1998, a total of 925 individuals across the thirteen ADD sites had opened IDAs. All but twelve participants had made at least one deposit, with the median value of the participants' savings at $121 and the median value of the match at $212.[55] More than half the participants intended to use their IDA accounts to purchase a home. At this early stage, 75 percent of the participants were female, more than 80 percent had at least a high school education, and almost 80 percent were single, divorced, separated, or widowed. The median income of participants was $1,200 a month.

Special Focus on the Working Poor

The Tulsa IDA pilot, which was selected for rigorous evaluation as part of the national American Dream Demonstration pilot, is particularly important because it links IDAs to the Earned Income Tax Credit (EITC), the federal government's largest assistance program for members of the working poor.[56] The federal EITC provides around $29 billion a year to 19 million low-wage workers, and seven states have enacted additional tax credits of their own. In Wisconsin, for instance, "poor people in Milwaukee can receive combined state and federal payments that augment their yearly earnings by 30 percent, 40 percent or even 50 percent. A single mother with three children who earns $10,000, for instance, would qualify for the maximum wage supplement of $5,371."[57] This is in addition to any refund owed on taxes withheld during the year from workers' paychecks.

Tulsa's IDA coordinator is well-positioned to link the two programs because it also administers a large-scale volunteer income tax assistance program, which helped more than 7,000 low-income working families prepare their federal tax returns in 1998 alone. The Community Action Project of Tulsa County (CAPTC) hopes to encourage EITC recipients to consider investing a portion of their tax credit in a savings account rather than spending it immediately, and believes that the added incentive of the IDA match will convince some participants to begin saving for the first time in their lives. Recruitment reached high gear in early 1998 and more than 125 people had opened IDAs by August 1998, making CAPTC one of the largest of the IDA demonstration sites in the country and putting it well on the way to its goal of enrolling 500 participants over the next two years.[58]

Expanding Asset-Building Programs to a National Scale

Despite the growing support for IDA programs at the state and local level and the seemingly broad appeal of an antipoverty policy that "moves from subsistence handouts to investments, and from bureaucratically run income security systems to direct community ties," as syndicated urban affairs journalist Neil Peirce has written,[59] the IDA movement was slow to gain currency in Washington. Bipartisan IDA legislation died in committee in the 104th Congress, along with other asset-building measures including:

—KidSave, sponsored by Senator Bob Kerrey, D-Nebr., and Senator Joseph Lieberman, D-Conn., which would have provided a $500 per child tax credit to capitalize children's education or retirement accounts; and

—The Personal Economic Empowerment Act of 1996, sponsored by Representative J. C. Watts, R-Okla., and Representative James Talent, R-Mo., which would have established, among other things, Family Development Accounts to match the savings of working residents living in designated "renewal areas." Like IDAs, these FDAs could be used to purchase a home, pay for post-secondary education, or begin a small business.

It was not until the waning days of a legislative session preoccupied by presidential scandal that the 105th Congress finally approved the bipartisan Assets for Independence Act (AFIA), whose chief sponsors were Senators Dan Coats, R-Ind., and Carol Mosley-Braun, D-Ill., and Representatives John Kasich, R-Ohio, and Tony Hall, D-Ohio. AFIA authorizes the Department of Health and Human Services (HHS) to conduct a five-year, $25 million per year national IDA demonstration similar to the ongoing American Dream Demonstration discussed earlier. With one exception, HHS grants will be made to nonprofit organizations on a competitive basis. The exception applies to two states that can apply directly to HHS for funding, Indiana and Pennsylvania, which are the only ones that had committed at least $1 million in state funds to IDA programs as of October 1, 1997, when AFIA was enacted. All other states wishing to participate in the national IDA demonstration must collaborate with one or more nonprofit organizations. Congress gave HHS $10 million in first year funding to start the pilot, and the initial grants are expected to be made in summer 1999.

The Department of Health and Human Services' Office of Refugee Resettlement (ORR) decided to use some of its FY 1999 discretionary Social Services Funds for IDAs. On July 14, HHS issued a notice of funding availability for projects to establish and manage IDAs for low-income refugees.[60] Eligible refugee participants who enroll in these programs will open and contribute systematically to IDAs for specialized savings goals, with grant funds providing matches up to $2,000 per individual refugee, and $4,000 per refugee household.

Social Security Reform Boosts Savings Proposals

The Clinton administration also was slow to adopt IDAs but has subsequently moved wealth creation for working Americans to a more prominent place on its policy agenda. This not surprising, since work-centered savings incentives like IDAs complement a wide range of presidential priorities including welfare reform and the President's own community empowerment strategy. That strategy, outlined in his national urban policy report in 1995, seeks to "grow the middle class, to shrink the underclass, to expand opportunity and to shrink bureaucracy, [and] to empower people to make the most of their own lives."[61]

Moreover, as suggested in chapter 1, the likelihood that social security reform will include or be supplemented by some kind of individual savings account makes it all the more important to bring as many of America's unbanked households into the financial mainstream and to help them to invest in their futures and save for their retirements. One of the reasons why President Clinton has proposed supplementing social security with a matched retirement savings program that he calls Universal Savings Accounts (USAs) is that "[f]or many Americans, the hard work they do to provide for their families today . . . makes it difficult for them to save for tomorrow."[62]

As the social security reform debate heats up in Congress, proposals to supplement social security with a program to help families build wealth for retirement are becoming more commonplace. Senator Bob Kerrey's KidSave plan and President Clinton's USA proposals are two cases in point. For example, under the president's USA proposal, "if a couple earning $40,000 saved just $700 a year, matched by the government, a USA Account invested conservatively would be worth a quarter of a million dollars after 40 years."[63]

Because under the basic component of the President's USA plan, 98 million adults would receive an automatic government contribution to their Universal Savings Account every year, recipients would not have to sacrifice current consumption for future benefits, as they would have to do in order to participate in an IDA program. However, the President's USA proposal also includes an IDA-type option—what he calls "a powerful new incentive to save"—which takes the form of an additional $1 refundable tax credit for every dollar a low- or moderate-income worker saves, up to $350 (or $700 per couple) per year.

Getting to Scale

Momentum is also building in Congress for additional action to help working families build assets. Both houses' budget resolutions for fiscal year 2000 contained bipartisan language regarding asset building for the working poor. Showing broad support for a national IDA-type program, the Senate Budget Committee budget resolution for FY 2000, for example states that "any changes in tax law should include provisions which encourage low-income workers and their families to save for buying a first-home, starting a business, obtaining an education, or taking other measures to prepare for the future."[64] On April

29, 1999, Senator Joseph Lieberman, D-Conn., put the budget resolutions to the test by introducing the Savings for Working Families Act (SWFA), which would create a national IDA program for lower income working Americans that would be funded on the tax side of the federal budget. This legislation is discussed in detail in the final chapter.

The Time Is Right to Link IDAs to EFT'99

I believe that the growing political support for asset-based programs together with the advent of EFT'99 present a critical opportunity for the United States to adopt a full-scale IDA program that will incorporate not only families who are moving off welfare but also the working poor. As the National Governors' Association has pointed out, welfare recipients "generally comprise only about 23 percent of the poor; other people in poverty, including working families, single persons, recipients of other public benefits, and other families near poverty or vulnerable to economic changes, need and could use IDAs."[65] According to the Bureau of Labor Statistics, of the 7.5 million working poor in 1995, 3.1 million experienced at least one spell of unemployment, and nearly a quarter cited involuntary part-time work status at some time during the year. Despite a strong economy, the number of working poor is growing—by about 60,000 from 1994 to 1995 and by nearly 200,000 the next year. In both years, large numbers of working poor experienced spells of joblessness.

A national IDA program coupled with EFT'99 would help millions of families develop an emergency cushion to help weather unemployment and other short-term setbacks as well as to build their long-term financial strength by investing in homes, job training, and small businesses. While it might be possible to create a national program without linking it to EFT'99 and state EBT initiatives, coordinating the two would improve partnership-building, outreach, and education efforts.

There is a clear link between the kinds of partnerships necessary for the success of both EFT'99 and the IDA movement. To succeed in the community, both require strong grassroots support and intensive outreach, education, and training in financial education. As discussed in chapter 5, Treasury is sponsoring a two-pronged education campaign for EFT'99, one to a broad array of stakeholder groups emphasizing the benefits of the legislation, and the other to unbanked benefit recipients on basic finances, including how to maintain a bank account and how to make the best informed choices. Hundreds of local community organizations are helping with the grassroots public outreach efforts.[66] Given the shortage of funds for outreach and counseling available to grassroots organizations in the growing IDA movement and the importance of these organizations to developing support for EBT in low-income communities, it is appropriate that Treasury is funding some of these organizations as part of its EFT'99 outreach campaign.

Another similarity between EFT'99 and the IDA movement is that virtually all IDA programs are run by the kind of partnerships between community-based organizations and depository institutions that Treasury envisions for EFT'99. In this regard, two of the national IDA pilots warrant special attention because their sponsors are financial institutions. In keeping with its tradition as one of the nation's preeminent full-service community development financial institutions, Chicago's Shorebank will try to develop a prototypical IDA that is cost-effective for financial institutions.[67]

Similarly, the Alternatives Federal Credit Union (AFCU), another pioneering community development financial institution, is crafting a pilot IDA program in Ithaca, New York, that could serve as a model for other community development credit unions that want to offer IDAs in the future. AFCU will provide financial expertise, capital, information, and account management services and will partner with various other Ithaca community organizations, including the Ithaca Housing Authority, to provide training, counseling, and other essential IDA components. The housing authority's FSS program will provide financial education training and peer support to all IDA participants.[68]

Perhaps the most important link between IDAs and EFT'99 is that the electronic transfer of government benefits may actually stimulate households to start saving, a possibility discussed earlier. At a 1997 forum entitled Financial Access in the 21st Century, then-Treasury Undersecretary John Hawke cited anecdotal evidence of such behavior. "[S]ome of the early indications from the EBT programs are that if recipients do not have to turn their payments at the beginning of each month into cash which they carry around, they will keep something in their accounts and have some savings at the end of the month," Hawke said. "This suggests that there are opportunities for financial institutions to offer vehicles to encourage savings."[69]

Litan and Rauch hold similar hopes for EFT and EBT efforts. "[W]hen federal money is deposited electronically into accounts held by (or for) federal beneficiaries, many of them will prefer to withdraw cash as they need. Many will therefore maintain at least modest balances, and those balances, while perhaps too meager to support full-service checking accounts, might support low-cost, limited access accounts, whose features would depend on balances maintained."[70]

In short, a national IDA initiative could contribute to the success of EFT'99/EBT by providing benefit recipients with a substantial incentive to save. By increasing the number and size of savings deposits, a national IDA initiative would also increase the banks' float. Finally, while not directly tied to EFT, but important nonetheless, IDAs could help keep hard-pressed workers out of the clutches of exploitive payday lenders if they permitted early withdrawals to pay for family emergencies. IDA programs could allow account holders to make up the difference within a specified amount of time to avoid losing previously earned matches.

Thus the combined impact of EFT'99 and a nationwide program for IDAs could encourage more workers to join the mainstream banking system, thereby helping them accumulate savings for their own education or training or for a down payment on a first home. It could also help the working poor, who are disproportionately single parents of young children, from returning to the welfare rolls. Finally, by helping the unbanked and low-income families achieve relatively short-term goals through savings, a national IDA program could increase their ability and propensity to save for retirement as well.

Closing the Wealth Gap

As a matter of policy, a national IDA program would begin to address the widening inequalities between the rich and poor in the United States—a gap that exists not so much in terms of income as of assets. As Senator Bob Kerrey, D-Nebr., noted in introducing his KidSave legislation, there is a "stark gap . . . between those who have [wealth] and those who don't. The bottom 90 percent of Americans earn 60 percent of all income, but own less than 30 percent of net worth and less than 20 percent of financial assets."[71] The House and Senate budget resolutions for fiscal year 2000 contained similar concerns. In recommending that the federal government should utilize tax code laws or other measures to provide low-income Americans with incentives to work and build assets in order to escape poverty permanently, the Senate recognized that "33 percent of all Americans and 60 percent of all African American households have no or negative financial assets."[72] The Corporation for Enterprise Development has noted that the top 1 percent of Americans controls more net financial assets than the bottom 80 percent.[73] Perhaps even more important to America's future is the fact that nearly half of all children in the nation—including 40 percent of white children and 75 percent of African American children—live in households with no financial assets.[74]

The wealth gap is even greater for minorities than the income gap. The median income of African American workers—$387 a week—is roughly three-quarters that of white workers, but their net worth is only a tenth that of whites.[75] Moreover, middle-class blacks earn seventy cents for every dollar earned by middle-class whites but possess only fifteen cents for every dollar of wealth held by middle-class whites.[76] Findings from a recent study entitled *Minorities Face Retirement: Worklife Disparities Repeated?* estimated that "the black median household will have only 48 percent and the Hispanic median household will have only 40 percent of the wealth of the median white household at retirement."[77] Since wealth is so much more unequally distributed than income, few should argue the proposition that if the United States is ever to deal effectively with its social and economic divisions, policies that promote wealth accumulation for all Americans are needed.[78] Because such a high percentage of people of color are unbanked, a convincing case can also be made that EFT/EBT could be an important first step up the asset-building ladder for millions of minority individuals.

Another argument for why Congress and the states should undertake a major asset-building campaign for the working poor is the simple matter of fairness. A recent study found that despite growing surpluses and large income tax cuts for middle- and upper-income families, the majority of states that levy a personal income tax continue to tax families with incomes below the poverty line.[79] While eliminating the tax burden on poor and working families altogether is the most direct way for states to improve the fairness of their income tax systems, they might also consider adding a direct deposit option to their EBT cash assistance programs, increasing appropriations for existing IDA programs, and funding new IDA initiatives where they do not now exist. These options would not only improve the fairness of the system, but provide strong incentives to the affected taxpayers to save instead of spend.

Level the Playing Field

Equity should also be a paramount concern of federal programs. Analysis of the federal balanced budget legislation has shown that initiatives that primarily assist low- and moderate-income children and families, legal immigrants, and elderly people are modest in size and dissipate over time. By contrast, tax cuts for high-income individuals get much bigger over time.[80] By 2007, the tenth year of the balanced budget amendment, the capital gains tax, estate tax, corporate alternative minimum tax, and IRA provisions together will cost nearly $24 billion in a single year. This is more than six times the average annual cost—$3.8 billion—of these provisions from 1998 through 2002. Analysts in the Congressional Budget Office have found that the 5 percent of individuals with incomes of more than $100,000, who receive 75 percent of capital gains income in any year, will benefit most from the cut in capital gains taxes, and the prime beneficiaries of the higher estate tax exemption will be heirs of the top 2 percent of estates.[81] Back loading is especially egregious in the provisions for IRAs, the benefits of which will be garnered mostly by taxpayers who have incomes between $50,000 and $160,000 and who are *already covered* under an employer-sponsored retirement plan. The new Roth IRAs, which primarily benefit upper-income taxpayers, "are engineered so taxpayers can opt to pay taxes during 1999 through 2002 that they otherwise would pay in future years in return for very generous tax breaks for years to come."[82] The costs of expanding current deductible IRAs and providing Roth IRAs, according to Treasury estimates, will be $1.4 billion for fiscal years 1998 through 2002 but will balloon to $16.4 billion over the succeeding five years.[83]

One reason why President Clinton proposes to fund his Universal Savings Account initiative, which would provide an annual refundable tax credit to workers with incomes up to $80,000 a year, is to compensate for the fact that too large a slice of federal tax benefits for pension and retirement programs already goes to high-income families. Half of all American workers, according to the President, have no employer-provided pensions whatsoever. For millions of workers, "IRAs and 401Ks are something they hear and read more and more about, but don't have for themselves." Only one-third of the tax benefits for pensions and retirement savings go to families who earn less than $100,000, even though they represent the vast majority of working people in the United

States today.[84] Moreover, only 7 percent of existing tax benefits for retirement go to families with incomes of $50,000 a year or less.[85]

Another problem regarding the disproportionate allocation of tax expenditures to support IRAs and 401(k)s for higher-income families is that they may not increase retirement savings. According to William Gale of the Brookings Institution, "wide variation in effective tax rates on saving create[s] opportunities for investors to shift funds into the most tax-preferred accounts."[86] This kind of behavior has been empirically confirmed. Gale reports, for example, that "Over the last several decades, as the personal saving rate has fallen, tax-favored saving (via pensions, 401ks, IRAs, Keoghs, and life insurance) has become an ever more important component of total personal savings. Between 1986 and 1993, saving in tax-preferred accounts constituted about 100 percent of net personal saving. This does not mean there was no other saving activity, it just means that any gross saving in other accounts was fully offset by withdrawals from those accounts or by increases in borrowing."[87]

Because the poor can afford to invest only small amounts of income, IDAs may not have much of a statistical impact on the national savings *rate*, currently only about half as high as it was thirty years ago. But whatever low-income families manage to save as a result of a national IDA initiative will certainly increase *aggregate* personal savings.

In the world of the balanced budget, the only feasible way of growing an IDA program to national scale is to fund it on the tax side of the federal budget, which is not subject to spending caps and annual appropriations. This is why most higher-income savings incentives are funded through the tax system. The key to a cost-effective national IDA program is to convert the tax credits, which the poor cannot use, into IDA matching funds, which they can use. There are essentially two ways to do this. One is through a refundable IDA tax credit similar to the EITC, which is favored by Delaware University economist Laurence Seidman. "Just as the individual reitrement account (IRA) deduction encourages middle-income households to save," says Seidman, "a refundable tax credit would encourage low-income households to save."[88] According to Seidman, a refundable IDA tax credit would work this way. "If the tax credit rate is 50 percent, then for every $100 the household saves in an IDA, the federal government reimburses $50; in effect, the household contributes $50 and the government $50, to the IDA account. Private and public sources could then provide a supplemental match above the government's IDA tax credit."[89]

The second way to use the federal tax law to support IDAs is by providing businesses and high-income individuals dollar-for-dollar nonrefundable tax credits to offset their contributions to a national, regional, or local IDA match pool. For reasons discussed in the concluding chapter, I prefer limiting the tax credit to financial institutions that sponsor and adminsiter IDA programs in partnership with community-based organizations that provide required financial education services. Federal tax credits would offset the bank's costs of funding and administering their local asset-building programs, while the availability of CRA credit would be a further inducement to encourage widespread participation.

Will the Poor Take Advantage of Savings Incentives?

The national savings rate has been declining since the early 1970s. According to one recent poll, the percentage of people who have no savings at all is 44 percent among people making less than $30,000, 19 percent among those making $30,000–$49,000, and 12 percent among those earning $50,000 or more.[90] As one might imagine, there are many reasons—in addition to having too little income to meet basic family needs—why so many poor households are not in the habit of saving. Research suggests that some low-income people fear that any savings would make them ineligible for government benefits, that if they had savings family members would not help them through a financial crisis, and that family members or others in their community would insist that they share their savings.[91] A recent study of two low-income minority communities also found a sense of resignation among some residents; they might be able to save $20 to $50 a month without a noticeable hardship, they said, but they felt the money "was too little. . . to make the effort worthwhile." Others said any savings inevitably would be "wiped out in the next family economic crisis."[92] Some economists argue that another reason why the poor do not save is that they tend to "have relatively high rates of time preference and marginal propensities to consume and therefore that the poor are less 'patient' than the rich"—in short, they live for today and therefore spend rather than save.[93]

These findings and theories notwithstanding, there is evidence that many low-income households do manage to put away some money even though recurring crises such as spells of unemployment, illness, or unexpected expenses commonly and repeatedly force them to deplete these savings.[94] And while lower-income workers rarely invest in tax-advantaged IRAs, their participation in employment-based retirement savings plans is significantly higher. In 1993, for example, only 7.2 percent of eligible individuals making less than $10,000 owned an IRA, compared with 54 percent of those making $100,000 or more.[95] Yet according to the White House, 14.2 percent of workers earning between $5,000 and $9,999 participated in employment-based retirement plans that year; since only about 41 percent of workers in this income bracket had an opportunity to participate in such plans, this suggests a participation rate of about one third.[96]

Even higher participation rates among low-income workers are reported in statistics from the federal Thrift Savings Plan (TSP), which resembles an IDA program because it provides a match for federal employee contributions. More than half (51.1 percent) of covered federal employees with salaries of less than $10,000, and 73 percent earning between $10,000 and $20,000, participated in the plan in 1996. The former was up from 23 percent in 1988, the program's first full year of operation.[97] By contrast, participation rates for all eligible employees regardless of income increased to 82.9 percent during 1996, up from 80 percent in 1995 and 44.1 percent since 1988.[98] While, on average, the highest-income government workers contribute almost twice the percentage of earnings to their TSPs as do the lowest income workers, the mean contribution rate for the latter is still close to 5 percent of earnings.[99]

Three factors seem to account for higher participation rates in employment-based retirement programs. Salary reduction plans are generally more convenient since they are offered through the workplace and involve automatic contributions deducted from the worker's paycheck.[100] Employers typically market their plan to employees and educate them as to the importance for their retirement income security. Finally, employers often provide matching contributions.[101]

Other factors, including financial education and the availability of customer-friendly financial institutions that cater specifically to their needs, also affect the savings behavior of the poor.[102] This has been demonstrated time and again in developing countries. Yet though it has been stated clearly, convincingly, and with increasing evidence since the 1960s that poor "[h]ouseholds save, and they will save in a financial form if appropriate institutions and instruments are available," the message continues to fall on deaf ears among U.S. policymakers, who too often act as though they have nothing to learn from successful savings mobilization programs in the developing world.[103]

Marguerite S. Robinson, an internationally recognized expert in sustainable microfinance, believes that policymakers can learn a great deal from Third World experiences. "Extensive household savings have been reported from developing countries around the world for at least three decades," she notes, pointing out that "[t]he reasons for low institutional deposits . . . are often neither undersavings nor lack of demand for financial savings instruments, but the structure of services and institutions."[104]

A case in point is Bank Rakyat Indonesia (BRI), a state-owned commercial bank that created a saving system consisting of more than 13 million savings accounts owned by one third of all households in the country. In celebrating its great successes, J. Bryan Atwood, administrator of the U.S. Agency for International Development (USAID), praised BRI's revolutionary approach that required familiarity with the poor, willingness to design services specifically for their needs, dedication for treating them as valued customers, and an understanding that subsidized loan programs had the unintended consequence of benefiting the relatively affluent and excluding the truly needy from the formal banking system.[105] Noting BRI's "bold step a decade ago," Atwood continued:

> in deciding to expand BRI's village banking system through new services to the very poor. In doing so, you turned conventional wisdom on its head. Until then, economists, government officials in developing countries, and donors all assumed that poor people were too pre-occupied with the challenges of daily existence to save for tomorrow. They also assumed that the poor were bad credit risks and could not afford to repay loans at commercial rates.
>
> With your presence in villages throughout Indonesia, you had reason to have faith in the poor. You knew that they did indeed save, although they kept their savings hidden at home. You knew that the poor borrowed informally, often at exhorbitant rates. You also knew that the poor had enough savings collectively to finance loans.

Here at home, community development credit unions (CDCUs), which operate in some of the nation's poorest communities, have been fostering savings among low-wealth Americans for more than sixty years.

As of 1995, $250 million in savings had been deposited into community development credit unions by more than 170,000 savers with a median income of $19,000. Individual balances averaged $1,200.[106] One CDCU, the 28-year-old Bethex Federal Credit Union in New York's South Bronx, recently reported adding about 150 new members a month to its 3,500-member base, largely because of anticipation of EFT'99.[107]

Just as there is no statistically reliable estimate of how poor workers would respond to a national IDA program, it is unclear what the elasticity of demand for matched retirement savings would be as part of a USA program. However, data from the federal Thrift Savings Program cited earlier suggest that the participation rate among low-income workers could be as high as 50 percent after ten years. Surveys conducted for the White House Summit on Retirement Savings provide additional reason for optimism. According to *Public Agenda*, only 28 percent of lower-income respondents—compared to 54 percent of people with annual incomes over $75,000—said they would not likely cut back on vacation or travel expenses to save for retirement. Similarly, only 23 percent of those with lower incomes—compared to 51 percent of those with higher incomes—said they were unlikely to start shopping for groceries more carefully to save money. As President Clinton observed at the June 1998 Summit, "There may be opportunities even for relatively low-income individuals to save more than they currently are setting aside; indeed, lower-income people actually may be more willing to save than wealthier individuals."[108]

Other evidence supporting this notion has been suggested by the fact that lower income taxpayers tend to overwithhold on their taxes more frequently than higher income taxpayers. An interesting analysis of this peculiarly American phenomenon shows that for the period 1983–1992, roughly 75 percent of all U.S. taxpayers received a refund, including 49 percent of individuals with adjusted gross incomes of $100,000 and 77 percent for individuals with incomes less than $50,000. Some economists suggest that overwithholding may be used by some workers as an automatic savings mechanism, with lower income taxpayers more likely to use the system this way than higher income taxpayers. According to this theory, "high income taxpayers (because they are better able to diversify their risks, meet minimum balance requirements, and afford transaction fees) are more likely to have a broader range of financial investment instruments than are low-income taxpayers . . . which implies that the opportunity cost of overwithholding is directly related to income."[109]

Finally, although some critics might question the notion that a significant percentage of the working poor would use any portion of their earned income tax credit for investing and improving social mobility, this is exactly what economists Timothy Smeeding and Katherine Ross of Syracuse University discovered in their recent study of 830 EITC beneficiaries in Chicago. "They found that 26 percent planned to use all the money for immediate needs, like food, rent, utilities or clothes. But more than half planned to spend at least some of it on investments in the future: moving (5 percent); sending themselves or their children to school (9 percent); buying a car (14 percent); or saving (28 percent)."[110]

Conclusions

The move to asset accounts is well under way. This transition will continue because of the fiscal need for entitlement reform. Moreover, as Michael Sherraden has observed, "asset accounts are more suited to the economy and labor market of the information age." Whereas in the industrial era "mass labor markets and stable employment called for categorical programs and income protection policies," in the information age "rapidly changing labor markets will require household flexibility and control over investments in family well-being."[111] This is most evident, says Sherraden, "in the dramatic change from defined benefit retirement plans (with regular benefit payments each month) to defined contribution retirement plans such as 401(k)s, 403(b)s, regular IRAs, Roth IRAs, and the likely shift to individual accounts for some portion of social security (with payments based on lifetime contributions and investment performance). In addition to retirement, policies and proposals for other uses of asset accounts are becoming common, such as super IRAs that can be used for homeownership and education, Medical Savings Accounts, Individual Training Accounts, and Children's Savings Accounts for education and other purposes."[112]

Yet Sherraden and others are concerned that the move to decentralized, flexible government programs might once again leave behind poor and minority families unless there are special outreach efforts, education programs, and tailored incentives to participate.[113] In 1996, for example, 51 percent of whites participated in defined contribution plans such as IRAs but only 44 percent of African Americans and 29 percent of Hispanics did so.[114] Given the fact that the poor receive only trivial amounts of the nearly $140 billion per year in current federal tax benefits for retirement accounts, inclusion remains a real cause for concern.

A national IDA initiative that provides federal matching funds to encourage the working poor to invest in their own future is a direct way of democratizing asset accounts. While some might dispute Sherraden's premise that the twenty-first century knowledge-based economy calls for an asset-based policy system, two Brookings economists, Gary Burtless and Barry Bosworth, share some of Sherraden's concerns about how calls for privatizing social security will impact the working poor. They argue that privatization should not occur without a "redistribution in favor of low-wage or other kinds of workers," because "[t]he Social Security pension formula explicitly favors low-wage workers and one-earner married couples in order to minimize poverty among elderly people who have worked for a full career. To duplicate Social Security's success in keeping down poverty among the elderly, a private system must supplement the pensions from individual retirement accounts with a minimum, tax-financed pension or with public assistance payments."[115] Matching low-income workers' savings to help build their long-term economic health is an important way to address this concern.

In closing, it is important to distinguish between USAs and other proposals that focus exclusively on retirement, and IDAs that have shorter-term asset-building goals. It is also necessary to consider how both of these relate to EFT'99. While I agree with the President's sentiments on the need to help low- and moderate-income families better prepare for retirement, I would argue that before millions of lower income workers—especially the unbanked—will make effective use of USAs devoted to retirement savings, they need and deserve some help in accumulating savings for important shorter term goals, which is what EFT'99 coupled with a national IDA program for the working poor is all about.

By restricting withdrawals from a USA before age 65, the President's proposal precludes use of the matched savings program as a means of saving for a down payment or training, or starting a business. This would be the role of a national IDA program. Indeed, I would argue, a community-based IDA program that brings people into the mainstream banking system and helps them increase their financial stability and earning potential would, in the long run, improve the likelihood that low-income workers would take advantage of the federal match for retirement savings available in the USA program. This is especially true for lower-income workers and unbanked individuals. In short, USAs and IDAs are complementary, and both could improve the economics of low-balance electronic accounts that must become widely available as the nation makes the transition to electronic banking and benefit delivery in the twenty-first century.

However, at the time of this writing, the USA proposal would be centrally administered, along the lines of the federal Thrift Savings Plan model. This would mean that no bank, thrift, or credit union would hold any of the $30 billion dollars in annual deposits that would be deposited in USA accounts each year. This would also mean that none of the tens of millions of dollars a year in float income would be available to these mainstream financial institutions to help reduce the costs of desperately needed financial services—including ETA accounts—for lower income workers and unbanked benefit recipients. Because it is so important to do everything possible to ensure the widespread availability of affordable financial services to all populations and communities, it would be a mistake to prevent the very institutions that must be relied upon to provide those services from participating in the lucrative USA market. In fact, it might make sense to tie the provision of ETA accounts to a financial institution's eligibility to receive and hold USA deposits.

The final chapter discusses a proposal for a national IDA initiative in more detail, as well as suggesting other steps that the executive branch and Congress should take to increase the long-term prospects for EFT'99. Such measures could help lay the foundation for all individuals, however small their income, to begin building assets and participating fully in the nation's wealth.

CHAPTER SEVEN

An EFT'99 Action Agenda

The environment in which EFT'99 is being played out is so dynamic that within the twenty-four months it took to write this book, several chapters have had to be substantially revised—more than once. When I started this project, the federal budget was a sea of red ink; today, the surplus is more than $76 billion and growing. The pace of bank mergers and consolidations has also reached a fever pitch. The five biggest bank mergers of all time took place between August 1997 and April 1998, raising anew questions about whether scale economies within the financial services industry have become diseconomies, making it more—rather than less—costly to deliver affordable financial services to lower-income families and communities. The same forces underscore the importance of rethinking how the Community Reinvestment Act (CRA), which continues to have geography and community credit needs at its core, should be revised in light of the growth of giant regional and national bank franchises and Internet banking. While revisiting the notion of community in an Internet banking world is far from a settled issue, the Office of Thrift Supervision (OTS) is moving more aggressively than either of its counterparts at the Office of the Comptroller of the Currency (OCC) and the Federal Reserve Board.

In an April 1999 speech, OTS director Ellen Seidman argued that OTS must "guard against implicitly fostering a perverse, unintended outcome of actually lessening the CRA obligations of those who operate more and more in nontraditional ways."[1] Consequently, in the future, Seidman said that OTS will evaluate a "thrift's CRA compliance by assessing community lending, investment and service-performance throughout the markets where it does credit business, not just in its main assessment area, but well beyond."[2] Not only has this bold policy move been opposed by the powerful, conservative chairman of the Senate Finance Committee, Phil Gramm, R-Tex., who believes "her assessment area views lacked 'statutory authority,'" but it also puts OTS way ahead of its fellow regulators.[3] The OCC confirmed Seidman's worst fears when, on July 13, 1999, it approved the application of Toronto's Canadian Imperial Bank of Commerce to establish an Orlando, Florida-based Internet Bank—Columbus First National Bank—and limit its CRA assessment area to the greater Orlando region.[4] "Although CIBC will offer banking services nationally over the Internet, the OCC said, the bank's plan to designate Orlando as its initial assessment area is appropriate since it initially will operate deposit-taking automated teller machines only in the Orlando area."[5]

Moreover, the same technology that enables banks, thrifts, and credit unions to decentralize their delivery systems is now being used by check-cashing outlets, currency exchanges, and other nonbanks, with unknown consequences for the poor. Although several states have begun tightening their control over the fringe banking industry, check cashers were still unregulated in half of the country as of mid-1999. This lack of regulation was particularly striking given the amount of state and federal oversight over mainstream financial institutions, which serve customers who are far more sophisticated and able to protect themselves than many check casher patrons.[6]

Using the same technology, entrepreneurs outside of the financial services industry are also trying to catch the electronic benefit transfer (EBT) wave that could encourage more personal savings. For example, one new EFT product, the Alchemist Account Card, allows a grocery shopper to take the in-store coupon discounts against her total at the cash register, as is currently the practice, or to directly deposit the coupon savings into her bank account.[7] Other recent developments have complicated the economics of EBT. At one level, EBT is a growth industry with nothing but good prospects ahead for electronic vendors, continuing cost-savings for taxpayers, and the promise of improved access to affordable financial services for low-income benefit recipients. By spring 1999, 40 percent of all households in thirty-one states were using EBT cards at grocery stores to access their food stamp benefits, and the rest of the country will have to follow suit over the next three years by federal law.

Just in the eight months between August 1998 and June 1999, the three major EBT vendors expected to increase their collective EBT food stamp accounts by more than 1.4 million customers—and that does not count their cash assistance business. As indicated earlier, even without a federal mandate, forty states have decided to add welfare payments to their EBT systems, which means even more customers, greater economies of scale, and more fees for EBT vendors, and less fraud and lower administrative costs for government. Efforts are also underway to distribute other benefits by EBT, including women, infants, and children (WIC) benefits and child support payments. With respect to the latter, North Carolina alone collects and distributes to custodial parents more than $350 million a year in child support payments, all by paper check. So, what is wrong with this scenario?

For one thing, welfare reform is rapidly reducing the potential customer base for EBT vendors. Nationally, there were 4.5 million fewer recipients on the welfare rolls in December 1998 than there were in August 1996, when the president signed the welfare reform law.[8] Food stamp rolls are also declining—by 8 million, or 28 percent, during the past four years—rapidly enough to alarm advocates for the poor and some members of Congress.[9] Vendors are already beginning to feel the crunch. For example, in 1995, when Transactive Corp. took over the Texas delivery system and became the state's EBT vendor, the caseload for the food stamps and cash assistance programs was 1.2 million. Under Transactive's contract with Texas, the firm was to receive $2 per food stamp case a month and an additional 97 cents for cash assistance cases. Fifteen months after the contract was signed, in November 1997, however, Transactive's caseload had declined by 30 percent, with serious impacts on the contract's bottom line.[10]

Along these same lines, one of the "big three" EBT vendors (Citicorp and Transactive are the other two), Minnesota-based Deluxe Corporation, announced that it would set aside $36 million in a reserve account to cover anticipated losses in 1999.[11] After nine years of EBT contracts and subcontracts in thirty states, Deluxe is thinking about leaving the business when its current contracts expire because of the nationwide reduction in the welfare caseload. With fewer vendors and less competition, advocates fear that when the time comes for renegotiating contracts, Texas and other states may face higher costs, and allow vendors to charge recipients higher processing fees to access their benefits in exchange for contracts that cost state governments less money.[12]

As important as the changes in EBT caseloads may be, however, the biggest change of all to occur in the last two years has been the decision to grant broad, self-certifying waivers for EFT'99, changing it from a mandatory to a voluntary benefit delivery system in a matter of months. By proposing to cap account fees at just $3 per month, and then leaving to unbanked recipients the decision of whether or not to sign up for direct deposit, Treasury reduced the scale economies associated with ETAs and thereby decreased mainstream banks' incentive for entering this market. At the same time, the confusion caused by the transition to EFT'99 has given fringe bankers new opportunities to reach out to the unbanked and convince them to sign up for electronic benefit transfer programs that may not be in their own best interests.

These changes make fulfilling the promise of EBT/EFT both more difficult and more urgent. Megabanks, increasingly sophisticated fringe bankers, and an increasingly outdated Community Reinvestment Act may only make it more difficult to bring large numbers of the unbanked into the financial mainstream in the future. And the costs of being unbanked will only continue to rise. As banking experts Litan and Rauch point out, "to be without any sort of bank account is no small matter." In the modern economy, it often means "holding savings as cash, a practice that is both dangerous and insecure. It may also discourage saving in its own right, thus increasing the vulnerabilities of the poor. Furthermore, being without a checking account requires many of the poorest Americans to pay considerably more for basic financial services than other people need ever contemplate. . . . "[13]

Even if one accepts the argument that check cashers—and, increasingly, banks acting like check cashers—are meeting the demands of the unbanked for quick access to cash, for small loans, and for money orders to pay rent, utilities, and other bills, the poor have other needs that are not being met. These include "access to savings instruments, encouragement to save and not to borrow for discretionary spending, relatively inexpensive services, secure banking, and protection against theft."[14] The challenge is to use EFT'99 and the affordable banking products it spawns to meet these needs, thereby bringing millions of working people into the mainstream banking system and helping to steer them onto an asset-building course.

Fortunately, because EFT'99 is still a work in progress, it can be fortified to make it fulfill much of its original potential. However, this will require the president and Congress to embrace Treasury Secretary Rubin's vision of EFT'99 as a catalyst for changing the lives of millions of hardworking people who live at the margins of the U.S. financial system. This will also require recognizing EFT'99's potential asset-building role in the Clinton administration's agenda to empower communities. In this regard, it is notable that an interagency working group has been meeting to resolve a host of technical issues raised by EFT'99, but no comparable policy group exists to guarantee the resources needed to make electronic benefit delivery succeed.

This lack of an interagency group to focus on the larger policy issues raised by EFT'99 is not just symbolic. While the Treasury Department has the lead in implementing EFT'99, its broader goals cannot be achieved without the cooperation and, more importantly, the resources of other executive agencies. For example, the Department of Labor administers a multibillion dollar welfare-to-work initiative, and the Small Business Administration (SBA) promotes entrepreneurialism in lower-income and minority communities. Welfare reform is under the auspices of the Department of Health and Human Services (HHS); moreover, HHS oversees the new national individual development account (IDA) pilot created in the Assets for Independence Act and discussed in chapter 6. If the aim is to ensure a strong link between the EFT and EBT technologies and asset-building programs, making it possible for the poor to save and creating incentives to encourage them to save, then Treasury, not HHS, should have had the lead role in designing and implementing the national IDA demonstration.

Indeed, while virtually all domestic agencies can bring important resources to the table, two in particular can do the most to help EFT'99 succeed: the Community Development Financial Institution (CDFI) Fund, administered by the Department of the Treasury, and the Department of Housing and Urban Development (HUD). The CDFI Fund could expand its bank enterprise (BEA) initiative by providing grants to traditional financial institutions that sponsor and provide matching funds for IDA programs.[15] CDFI could also use its technical assistance funds to help federally chartered community development credit unions—which were created exclusively to meet the financial services needs of low-income persons in underserved communities—acquire the technology needed for direct deposit and ATM services; this would enable them to participate more fully in an EFT/EBT-driven financial services system.

There are also many ways HUD can promote community development policies that are asset-based and help achieve a financial services system that is more inclusive. The biggest barrier to buying a home in the United States continues to be the lack of a down payment. HUD should build upon the IDA down-payment savings pilot sponsored by the Federal Housing Finance Board (and discussed in chapter 6) and make homeownership IDAs a centerpiece of President Clinton's National Homeownership Strategy. Because homeownership rates in central cities continue to lag far behind the metropolitan suburbs, HUD could vary the rate of the match and give larger matches to families who choose to buy homes in the urban core or in designated inner-city neighborhoods.

Financial education is key to increasing savings among working families. Whether the focus is homeownership IDAs or the president's proposed USA accounts, "you can't just launch these things, throw them out and hope that people will use them."[16] Neither can succeed without an intensive grassroots educational campaign. HUD has distributed between $12 million and $15 million a year to a national network of nonprofit and community-based organizations to help prepare families for the responsibilities of homeownership. In fiscal year 1999, Congress appropriated $18 million for these homeownership counseling programs, which should be viewed as the "downstream" part of a financial education continuum. Poor English comprehension has been demonstrated as a factor in both being unbanked, and down the line, in being denied a mortgage. If HUD wants to deepen the pipeline for homeownership—especially among growing immigrant populations—it makes sense for the department to work with Treasury to ramp up the administration's financial education efforts to focus on basic financial services and personal savings.

Recognizing that "a large proportion of households do not use the savings incentives that are already available to them," Brookings economist William G. Gale identifies financial education as the best way of raising private savings. Improved education, Gale argues, "would also provide needed assistance to U.S. households as the pension system moves away from defined benefit plans and toward defined contribution plans, which place more responsibility on workers, and as social security reform is considered."[17]

In addition to greater interagency coordination and a major financial education campaign, in this final chapter I propose a four-point policy agenda to help make EFT'99 realize its potential. In ascending order of importance, I recommend that:

—States add a direct deposit option to their electronic benefit transfer (EBT) programs for recipients of emergency cash assistance.

—The Community Reinvestment Act (CRA) be strengthened to support the transition to electronic benefits transfer.

—The federal government regulate fees for cashing government checks and accessing federal benefits through voluntary (that is, non-ETA) accounts.

—Congress enact a nationwide program of Individual Development Accounts (IDAs) for working Americans, funded on the mandatory side of the federal budget. This is the same way Roth IRAs, 401(k) retirement plans, and other middle-income savings and retirement incentives are funded, and the same way that the Clinton administration proposes to fund the multibillion a year USA initiative.

Each of these proposals is discussed in detail below.

Add a Direct Deposit Option to State EBT Programs

States should take advantage of the affordable banking products that EFT'99 will generate by creating and heavily promoting a direct deposit alternative for delivering welfare benefits (Temporary Assistance for Needy Families, or TANF). This makes sense for two reasons. First, as discussed in chapter 5, it is cheaper for both the taxpayer and the benefit recipient. Direct deposit costs states less per client than does paying a third-party vendor to administer an EBT program, and for reasons mentioned earlier, the cost advantages of direct deposit are likely to grow when initial EBT vendor contracts are renegotiated in coming years. Direct deposit also makes accessing benefits cheaper for recipients, especially if they use their banks' own ATM networks for withdrawals. Second, a recipient with direct deposit is more likely to learn about other banking services and rely less heavily on expensive fringe bankers. While several states have begun promoting direct deposit as an alternative to EBT, many of them are targeting benefit recipients who already have bank accounts. Connecting significant numbers of unbanked recipients to the financial mainstream via direct deposit will require considerably more time and effort, but Missouri's experience suggests that sustained direct deposit campaigns can be successful in this endeavor.

Strengthen the Community Reinvestment Act

Financial institutions should receive Community Reinvestment Act (CRA) credit for offering and heavily marketing ETA and other low-cost/no-cost depository and payment services. In awarding CRA credit, financial regulators should carefully examine the extent to which the financial institution markets these accounts and promotes their use through the direct or indirect support of financial education services. The promotional component is critical because research on the current state of lifeline banking programs suggests that giving the unbanked inexpensive access to account services without intensive outreach will fail to draw many of them into the mainstream banking system.[18]

Existing regulations should be clarified and codified to ensure that financial institutions receive favorable CRA consideration for participating in IDA programs. This should be true regardless of the individual examiner, the location of the institution, or the nature of the federal regulator (whether the Office of the Comptroller of the Currency, the Federal Reserve, or the Office of Thrift Supervision). According to the Office of Thrift Supervision (OTS), providing retail banking services, such as free checking and ATM services, to low- and moderate-income IDA account holders results in CRA credit; deposit subsidies or matching dollars to an IDA program is currently treated as a charitable contribution for the provision of affordable housing, community services, or small business development and, therefore, counted as a qualified investment under CRA.[19] Finally, CRA credit is also awarded when bank management or staff participate in the development or implementation of financial education and training for low- or moderate-income IDA holders.

This does not mean, however, that banks should receive CRA credit when they act like fringe bankers and cash government checks for fees.[20] This is the position that a majority of the Consumer Advisory Council of the Federal Reserve Board took in April 1997, when the Council agreed that banks that cash checks in impoverished neighborhoods should receive CRA credit only if they do not charge for the service. I agree with this proposition, with one modification: I would award CRA credit to banks that operate fee-based check-cashing services as part of a larger effort to bring unbanked individuals into the mainstream banking system. For example, San Francisco-based Union Bank of California's check-cashing operation, discussed in chapter 4, is the kind of check cashing service that may warrant CRA credit, while Chase Manhattan's Check Cashing Club is not.

Increase Maximum CRA Points under the Service Test

As discussed in the beginning of this book, the CRA was enacted to encourage banks to be more sensitive to meeting local community credit needs. Since its inception, and especially since the early 1990s when CRA ratings became public, banks and community organizations have entered into community lending agreements representing more than $400 billion in reinvestment dollars for traditionally underserved populations and communities.[21] But as Litan and Rauch note, making loans represents only one side of the balance sheet. In the deregulated U.S. economy, the other side of the balance sheet—access to depository and payment services—is becoming increasingly important and has been comparatively neglected by current policies.[22] In this era of megamergers, branch closings in lower-income neighborhoods, uncertainty over whether the poor will have access to the new banking technology, and the increasing use of EBT, the federal government needs to pay more attention to just how effective a financial institution's retail delivery system is in underserved communities. It can do this by fine-tuning the CRA.

Under the Clinton administration's guidance, the Comptroller of the Currency has established three performance-based measures of CRA compliance: community development lending, investment, and service. The service test, which focuses on the availability and effectiveness of an institution's retail banking delivery system, is the compliance measure that is most relevant to EFT'99. Current CRA regulations assign twice as many points—a total of twelve—to a bank for an outstanding rating under the community development lending test, compared with a maximum of six points each for the investment and services tests; a bank must earn a total of twenty points to receive an overall rating of outstanding.[23] Because the CRA was enacted to combat credit redlining, it is understandable why the rating system was set up this way. However, to support EFT'99 and its broader vision, it is time to increase the weight assigned to the services test.

Under the services test, the substitution of technology—ATMs, banking by telephone or computer, and bank-by-mail systems—for bricks and mortar is not automatically awarded CRA points. Regulators consider delivery systems other than branches positively only to the extent that they are effective alternatives to branches in providing needed services to low- and moderate-income areas and individuals.[24] The same is true for debit cards, which do not automatically provide access to an institution's menu of products and services. However, federal regulators have ruled that if they are "a part of a larger combination of products, such as a comprehensive electronic banking service, that allows an institution to deliver needed services to low- and moderate-income areas and individuals in its community, the overall delivery system that includes the debit card feature would be considered an alternative delivery system."[25]

Giving more weight to the services component—without mandating lifeline banking—would be a strong incentive for banks to reexamine the way they provide basic financial services. At the same time, rewarding institutions for more aggressively providing affordable banking services in lower-income communities should not significantly reduce affordable lending activities. For many institutions, community development finance has proved to be profitable, as economists for the Federal Reserve Board recently found: "Lenders active in lower-income neighborhoods with lower-income borrowers appear to be as profitable as other mortgage-oriented commercial banks."[26] Thus, lenders now have a strong incentive to maintain active lending programs even without the heavy weight given such activities under the current CRA tests. Finally, a successful transition to electronic benefit delivery that brings additional millions of lower-income American families into the mainstream banking system will deepen the market for affordable banking products, help grow a new customer base, and eventually increase the demand for mortgages and other loan products, as more people invest in making themselves creditworthy. Until then, the democratization of credit cannot be complete.

Community Advocates Also Call for CRA Reform

I am not alone in proposing that the CRA should put more weight on the service test. The nationally recognized Woodstock Institute, which along with other Chicago-area nonprofits has been making community reinvestment agreements with banks since 1984, has also urged federal regulators to "look more critically at the service portion of the CRA exam, to consider such items as income of account holders, financial literacy training, account eligibility criteria, in addition to patterns of branch closings and openings."[27] Like other reinvestment advocacy organizations, Woodstock and its partner organizations use the threat of legal action under the CRA against pending bank mergers unless the affected banks agree to meet the financial services needs of their entire service areas, including the need for affordable account services. In August 1998, Woodstock and other members of the Chicago CRA Coalition reached a six-year agreement that will be implemented upon the merger of First Chicago NBD and BankOne to greatly enhance the availability of affordable financial services in lower-income and minority communities in the Chicago region.[28] The agreement includes bank allocation of $50,000 a year for financial literacy training; a commitment to increase the marketing of lifeline accounts to unbanked individuals, including EFT/EBT accounts; and a commitment to open four new full-service branches, including two supermarket branches in low- and moderate-income neighborhoods in 1998–99, and two stand-alone branches by 2002.

Under a similar threat, the Action Alliance of Senior Citizens of Greater Philadelphia and six partner organizations reached an even more sweeping reinvestment agreement that will take effect upon completion of the merger of First Union National Bank with CoreStates Financial Corporation.[29] Among the highlights of that agreement is First Union's promise to offer a choice of three low-cost accounts to low-income senior citizens and other benefit recipients, including:

Low-income personal checking account. This account would be available to low-income social security and income assistance recipients in Philadelphia. This account will have no check-writing charge or monthly maintenance fee in any month when a minimum balance of $150 is maintained. In any month where the balance falls below $150, the bank will charge 15 cents a check and a $4.50 monthly maintenance fee.

Low-income express checking account. This account would be available to low-income social security and income assistance recipients who, where possible, use First Union for direct deposit of their benefits. The account would have no monthly fee and no minimum balance requirements. There would be unlimited check writing without fee, and no fee for balance inquiry calls to First Union Direct Automated Inquiry System.

Low-income checking account for federal government benefit recipients. This account would be available after the bank's system conversion, then for at least five years from the date of the agreement to recipients of federal and state-delivered benefits whose income is at or below area median income. This account would have no monthly fee or require a minimum balance, provide up to ten checks per month without charge, up to four free over-the-counter deposits and up to four free over-the-counter withdrawals per month, and unlimited mail and drop box deposits.

While these two agreements and others like them were negotiated under threat of legal action that would delay, or possibly stop, highly profitable mergers, they demonstrate that low-income communities know what financial services their residents need and that banks have the capacity to effectively meet those needs. My proposal to increase the weight assigned to the services test under the CRA would achieve similar results in low-income and minority communities not directly affected by mergers, and without the heavy-handed threat of litigation. At the same time, it would help create and, ultimately prove, the economic viability and profitability of this new market.

Regulate Fees for Cashing Government Benefits and Voluntary Accounts

Check-cashing outlets—that part of the fringe banking system that plays such an important role in the daily lives of millions of low- and moderate-income individuals—are subject to no federal regulations protecting consumers.[30] As discussed in chapter 4, there is no national law limiting check-cashing fees, although twenty-four states and the District of Columbia impose caps of their own. However, among the states that do regulate check cashing fees, some have not been monitoring compliance effectively, according to economist John Caskey in his study of the fringe banking industry.[31]

With the check-cashing industry becoming increasingly involved in the electronic delivery of government benefits, there is a federal interest in effectively regulating check cashers' benefit access programs. These programs will compete directly with the ETAs that Treasury is hoping to offer all unbanked recipients. By capping ETA fees at $3 a month and banning their use in conjunction with check cashers, Treasury inadvertently provided mainstream banks with a strong economic incentive to reject the ETA format altogether and instead develop alternative benefit access products that can be delivered through check-cashing outlets and charge higher fees. Unless it regulates these non-ETA products as well, Treasury may have a difficult time ensuring that enough ETAs are made available to serve the millions of unbanked federal benefit recipients. This is also why Treasury called for public comment on the need to regulate so-called voluntary accounts that would provide access to benefits through nonbank entitities.

As discussed in chapter 4, the National Consumer Law Center (NCLC) has determined that financial institutions in at least twenty-five states have already entered into arrangements with fringe banking entities to deliver government benefits, with recipients gaining "only additional costs and a lack of choice each month as to where to cash the check."[32] Even where cost is not the issue, NCLC is concerned that once recipients become dependent on these providers as a conduit to their benefits, they become "excellent prospects for other high cost products such as payday loans, rent to own contracts, pawn transactions, sales of lottery tickets, and liquor."[33] Despite these problems, however, neither NCLC nor I propose prohibiting fringe bankers from participating in *any* arrangement with mainstream financial institutions that provides access to federal benefits. NCLC proposes, however, that Treasury should not permit them to "be the primary or sole access for any federal benefit recipient,"[34] which is often the case. I agree with NCLC that nonbanks should never be the sole access for any benefit recipient, but I do not think that Treasury should ban partnerships in which they may be the primary access point. If Treasury were to follow NCLC's advice, it would not only ban such voluntary arrangements as Corus Bank's SecureCheck program, for which check cashers and currency exchanges are the only conduits for government benefits, but it might also ban the NaCCA Preferred Card, which is a cobranded debit card that allows customers to access their benefits at participating check cashers, point-of-sale locations across the country, and at any Citibank ATM.[35]

Regulations should also address the growing practice of offering high-interest "payday loans" in anticipation of federal recipients' benefit payments. NCLC reports that this exploitive practice is also on the rise. They cite a program in Philadelphia that a mainstream bank offers to both check cashers and pawnbrokers that "provides a cornucopia of high priced financial services," including payday loans tied to federal benefits:

> Opening this electronic account is free. After the fixed monthly charge of $2.50, the additional monthly charges vary based on the type of access desired:
>
> 1. If the client only uses the payment service provider through whom the account was established, the money can be withdrawn in increments at a cost of $1.00 for each withdrawal.
>
> 2. If the client wants an ATM card, the "silver" card costs $10.95 a month—in addition to the $2.50 fixed monthly fee. In addition to the $1 to $3 surcharge imposed by the banks' ATM machine (there is no home bank ATM for these customers), the check casher receives a fee of $2.00 per transaction. Each ATM transaction will cost recipients between $3.00 and $5.00.
>
> 3. For the client who desires to borrow against the federal benefit, there is a "gold" card at a cost of $20.95 a month, in addition to the $2.50 a month. The transaction fees are the same as for the silver card. But we do not know the fees for the credit extension on the federal payment.[36]

Under this program, the client is required to sign a form stating that the monthly statements required by Regulation E to be provided by the bank are sent to the check casher. No phone number is available to recipients who have questions about their benefits or their accounts or the fees charged them. As indicated in chapter 4, the comptroller for the state of Florida identified another exploitive program in his state that provides cash advances against future federal benefits, which will multiply in the absence of the federal government's strict regulation of such practices.

Treasury must ensure that such loans are strictly controlled. The risk that the benefits will not arrive—particularly when access to those benefits is handled through the check casher itself—is so low that there is no justification for charging exorbitant interest rates on loans in anticipation of payroll checks as discussed in chapter 4. Treasury should ensure that fees are capped at a reasonable level and should strictly prohibit rolling over the loans for additional terms to protect recipients from digging themselves deeper into debt.

Treasury already has taken two steps down the road toward regulating such fees. First, as discussed in chapter 5, it requested federal bank regulatory agencies to require insured financial institutions that distribute federal benefits in partnership with check cashers and other nonbanks to fully disclose all customer fees associated with those delivery systems.[37] More importantly, the final rule implementing EFT'99 prohibits nonbanks from offering ETAs either independently or in partnership with insured financial institutions.

I would like to see a federal ceiling on fees that both banks and nonbanks can charge for cashing government benefit checks or providing access to federal benefits, but I believe that Treasury's ban on ETA partnerships between banks and check cashers goes too far. Early experiences with bank–check casher joint products such as SecureCheck and the NaCCA Preferred Card confirm both the check-cashing industry's resilience and resourcefulness, and that the voluntary alliances make good business sense for mainstream banks.

I propose that Treasury now adopt a "substantial equivalence" approach to regulating account fees on voluntary accounts and for cashing government checks, with the federal regulation kicking in where there are no state-imposed limits or where the state cap exceeds some specified federal standard. This is basically how Congressman Bruce F. Vento, D-Minn., would deal with fees under EFT'99. On July 22, 1998, Vento introduced the Electronic Funds Transfer Account Improvement and Recipient Protection Act, H.R.4311, which would limit fees on ATM and POS transactions to access federal benefits to the national average, and guarantee recipients five free transactions per month.[38] A "substantial equivalence" approach, like Vento's, leaves the regulatory responsibilities to those states with equally stringent or more stringent laws and encourages states with no such laws or regulations to adopt them. Caskey suggests that effective regulation need not be costly, either to fringe banks or to taxpayers, and that in highly competitive markets, ceilings on fees are scarcely necessary.

However, where there are fewer market participants and less competition, the regulations could offer much-needed consumer protection.[39] In addition to capping fees and regulating payday loans based on federal benefit deposits, Treasury should also look at requiring check cashers to post fees clearly, to give receipts with each transaction, and to disclose fully the costs and restrictions on non-ETA benefit delivery programs. However, imposing a federal ceiling on fees for non-ETA benefit accounts offered by banks and check cashers should not be confused with banning all ATM surcharges, which I think is a bad idea.[40] In 1996 nearly one-third of bank-owned ATMs—in excess of 30,000 machines—were located off the banks' premises. Between 1996 and 1997 alone, the number of new ATMs exploded. The 18 percent increase was the fastest rate of growth in ATMs in fifteen years, and the number of new off-premises ATMs as a percentage of total ATMs also increased significantly.[41] With almost 90 percent of big banks projecting further growth of their off-premises networks, these numbers are bound to rise considerably. Fee-generation—more than market penetration—is driving this expansion, and a Congressional ban on ATM surcharges would probably severely curtail the growth in off-premises ATMs, especially in impoverished neighborhoods and other areas with lower volume potential.

Enact a National IDA Program and Fund It on the Tax Side of the Budget

EFT'99 would have substantially more grassroots support and national impact if it were linked to a major effort to stimulate savings and wealth for working people. A national IDA initiative would attract tens of thousands more unbanked individuals into the financial mainstream than would EFT'99 on its own, thus advancing Treasury Secretary Rubin's vision. Community-based organizations, which are the primary points of contact for low-income consumers in EFT'99's consumer education campaign, would also benefit from having additional resources funneled to them for consumer education under local IDA programs.

IDAs would also improve the economics of ETAs for financial institutions, as previously noted, by providing a source of low-cost deposits to help offset the higher overhead associated with low-balance accounts. By helping banks enlarge their markets and reduce their costs, an IDA program could convince more banks to offer ETA programs in the first place. For these and other reasons mentioned throughout this book, enacting a national IDA program and funding it on the tax side of the budget is a critical step for Congress to take to complement welfare reform, reward work and thrift, and help EFT'99 achieve its full vision.

As implied in the discussion of the Assets for Independence Act (AFIA) in chapter 6, even with bipartisan support for fully funding this five-year, 50,000 account IDA pilot, the spending caps associated with the balanced budget agreement make it impossible to grow AFIA to national scale as long as it is funded on the discretionary side of the budget. A window of opportunity to move AFIA to the tax side of the budget opened late in the 105th Congress when the House approved the Taxpayers Relief Act of 1998, H.R.4579. Introduced by Ways and Means Chairman William Archer, R-Tex., Section 14001 of H.R.4579 authorized yet another IDA pilot, this one called Family Development Accounts (FDAs). Archer's bill included some intriguing innovations—including allowing participants to direct the Internal Revenue Service to deposit some or all of their Earned Income Tax Credit directly into their savings account—but most importantly it placed an IDA program on the tax side of the budget for the first time.

While H.R.4579 was never taken up by the Senate and died with the close of the 105th Congress, the House Ways and Means Committee validated the principle that, like Roth IRAs and 401(k)s, IDAs should be funded on the mandatory side of the budget. As indicated in chapter 6, bipartisan support for modifying federal tax laws to encourage low-income workers and their families to save carried over into the 106th Congress, in the House and Senate budget resolutions for fiscal year 2000. President Clinton's Universal Savings Account initiative gives additional political muscle to the argument that it is appropriate to use the federal tax code to encourage lower- and middle-income people to save, and raises hopes for a larger national IDA program than might have been thought possible. After all, if the President can propose spending more than $33 billion a year to help working families save for retirement, then spending $2 or $3 billion to help lower income people save for their first home, or to pay tuition, is a modest investment in the nation's future. In short, as the 106th Congress settled in, the climate was becoming increasingly hospitable to a national IDA proposal.

Having become aware of my work to use EFT'99 as a vehicle for helping the poor to build assets, in the spring of 1998, Senator Joseph Lieberman, D-Conn., a longtime champion of asset-based community development policies, invited me to work with him to create a national IDA program that would be funded on the tax side of the budget. Senator Lieberman believes, as I do, that there are not enough community-based organizations that are strong enough, stable enough, and large enough to grow a national IDA program. Instead of pursuing Seidman's idea of creating a refundable savings tax credit—which would require the poor to self-finance the matching funds for their own IDA and wait for their refund until the end of the year—we decided to target insured depository institutions because they have the capacity and motivation to create and efficiently administer large numbers of IDA accounts. In addition to receiving CRA credit, they should be attracted to the program because IDA accounts are a source of cheap deposits with lower average turnover rates that will help make profitable the transition to EFT/EBT.

Senator Lieberman introduced S.895, The Savings for Working Families Act (SWFA), on April 28, 1999, with bipartisan co-sponsors, including Senators Rick Santorum, R-Pa., Spencer Abraham, R-Mich., Richard J. Durbin, D-Ill., Chuck Robb, D-Va., and Robert Kerrey, D-Nebr. The Act provides tax incentives for federally regulated financial institutions to provide matching funds for IDA programs, which they would sponsor throughout their franchise or in selected branches or segments of their service area. Changing sponsorship from community-based organizations, as provided for in the Assets for Independence Act, to banks would still maintain the key role of community partners because every IDA program would remain a partnership between a financial institution and one or more community based organizations. The difference, however, is that the community partners would be able to concentrate on what they do best—marketing the programs and conducting financial education and credit counseling activities. Bank sponsorship would also enable financial institutions to realize scale economies by aggregating IDA programs across many neighborhoods and community-based partners.

SWFA would match dollar-for-dollar, up to a maximum of $300 per year, the deposits of working people whose household income is up to 60 percent of the local area median income—which is approximately 200 percent of the poverty level. Unlike the Assets for Independence Act, in which nonprofits would have to apply to the Department of Health and Human Services for a limited amount of matching funds in annual grant competitions, there would be no competition for funds under SWFA. Any federally regulated financial institution that chose to create and fund an IDA program and support financial education activities would receive offsetting federal tax credits to reimburse them for those costs. Lieberman's legislative proposal would provide an investment tax credit of up to $300 per IDA account per year to financial institutions to reimburse them for providing matching funds, and an additional one-time tax credit of up to $100 per account holder, to provide financial education to IDA participants.

Lieberman expects the cost of his national IDA initiative to be between $200 million and $500 million a year. While actual costs would vary, of course, with the number of IDA account holders and their savings habits, SWFA would control program costs by limiting the number of IDA accounts that any financial institution would be permitted to open. Qualified financial institutions would be limited to having an average of no more than 100 active IDA accounts per banking office during calendar year 2000, 200 per banking office in 2001, and increasing by increments of 100 accounts per year, up to an average of 500 active accounts per banking office in 2004 and thereafter.[42]

Some Final Thoughts

Long ago, Reverend Martin Luther King Jr. admonished that "we should not let our technology outdistance our need to understand and be of service to the least among us."[43] However, modern banking technology has not, up to now, been a servant of the poor.

To help the poor and underserved, existing community development partnerships with local lenders can and must be extended. Since most successful community development lending initiatives involve some level of cooperation between banks and local community organizations, it makes good business sense "for banks to incorporate low-income groups into their new technology programs," as Gail K. Hillebrand of Consumers Union has noted.[44] Yet this is not happening to any great degree.

There are a few examples, both in the United States and abroad, where the savings in overhead from electronic banking are being used to create new products for underserved populations rather than to pay higher dividends to depositors. Riverside Health System Employees Credit Union, in New York, "is evidence that you don't have to be big to join the electronic banking revolution."[45] When an employee of Riverside Health System joints the Credit Union, she can get direct deposit, arrange for electronic payment for recurring bills, access her account twenty-four hours a day by telephone, and make ATM transfers. For direct deposit account holders, there are no charges for these services.

Another innovation comes from South Africa. In the early 1990s, Standard Bank of South Africa created an electronic bank called E-Bank to serve a growing market of low-income, largely illiterate wage-earners who could no longer receive their pay in cash because of growing crime problems.[46] When employers switched to paying employees by check or direct deposits, Standard Bank was flooded by waves of unbanked customers. Operating exclusively through a "fingerprint-secured" debit card system and ATM network that is programmed to give operating instructions in each of South Africa's eleven official languages, E-Bank grew to 200,000 basic savings accounts by 1996 and at that time was opening 20,000 new accounts a month. Through incentives like free life insurance, monthly drawings with cash prizes for savers, and shopping discounts for the stores with E-Bank ATMs, Standard Bank is encouraging low-income customers using higher-cost services to switch to the cheaper E-Bank account.

These low-cost, stripped-down services are specifically designed to attract a new customer segment—the unbanked—and with it, possibly, a new profit center. Community development advocates would do well to study innovations like these, possibly adapting them to help bring low-income communities in the United States into the financial mainstream.

In conclusion, it should be emphasized that EFT'99 is not simply about technology transfer and saving the federal government money. It is about financial inclusion and the recognition that "economic opportunity cannot thrive where access is denied."[47] It is critical that the United States not enter the new millennium on the cusp of a digital divide, that there be no isolation of low-income and inner-city communities from access to and full use of banking technology. If the steps that I have recommended are taken, I believe that in ten years low-income people will have the ability to secure banking and financial services using the technology of the day and that technology will be available and abundant in communities across the country. Basic financial literacy will be made a larger part of elementary and high school curricula so that young people everywhere will learn more about the importance of credit, budgeting, and financial management, and recognize the power of compound interest at a young age. Community development programs will place greater emphasis on asset building and wealth accumulation than is currently the case, encouraging savings for down payment IDAs and promoting community development credit unions in public housing and empowerment zones. Using technology, financial institutions will partner with community-based organizations to provide access to affordable financial services at the neighborhood level.

I hope that ten years from now the financial industry will have discovered a new customer base. I further hope that the technology, delivery systems, and partnerships that the industry will have forged in low-income communities will demonstrate that they can earn good returns by serving this population. EFT and EBT have given us the opportunity to think more about ways that new markets can be created. We need to seize this opportunity creatively. If there is one thing that this study demonstrates, it is that the most effective means of dealing with the payday lender problem is "assuring that low-income households have a place to accumulate $100 of savings to pay for a car repair, rather than having to borrow $100" at exorbitant rates.[48] This is why it is important to incorporate a savings feature into the ETA and encourage mainstream banks to create more convenient and affordable account services to low-income working Americans. This is also why adding a wealth-building component to EFT'99 and state EBT initiatives is *not* about subsidizing the poor. It is about complementing welfare reform. It is about fairness. It is about making compound interest work *for* the poor and giving them a place in the American capitalist system.

Notes

Chapter One

1. John D. Hawke Jr., undersecretary of the Treasury for domestic finance. Hearings before the Senate Committee on Banking, Housing and Urban Affairs, May 22, 1997, text as prepared for delivery.

2. Jeanne M. Hogarth and Kevin H. O'Donnell, "Being Accountable: A Descriptive Study of Unbanked Households in the U.S.," *Proceedings of Association for Financial Counseling and Planning Education* (1997), p. 58.

3. More recent estimates in Missouri, where the conversion to electronic delivery of benefits is well under way, and in California, where EBT is still in the planning stages, also both place the figure at around 75 percent. State of Missouri, Nomination Form, 1998 Governor's Award for Quality and Productivity, 1998, and Brian Patrick Lawlor, Laura Fry, Michele Melden, Cheryl Nolan, and Gail K. Hildebrand, *Electronic Benefit Transfer in California: Issues, Perspectives and Recommendations* (June 1998), p. 1. Report available from Legal Services of Northern California, 515 12th Street, Sacramento, CA 95814.

4. The White House, *Saving Social Security Now and Meeting America's Challenges for the 21st Century* (1999). In his State of the Union address on January 19, 1999, President Clinton proposed to reserve 11 percent of the projected surpluses over the next fifteen years to create new Universal Savings Accounts (USAs) so that all working Americans can build wealth to meet their retirement needs. See chapter 6 for more information on USAs.

5. Robert B. Avery, Raphael W. Bostic, Paul S. Calem, and Glenn B. Canner, "Changes in the Distribution of Banking Offices," *Federal Reserve Bulletin*, vol. 83, no. 9 (September 1997), p. 2. Litan and Rauch report a further decline in the number of financial institutions to less than 10,000 in 1997. See Robert E. Litan with Jonathan Rauch, *American Finance for the 21st Century* (U.S. Department of the Treasury, November 17, 1997), p. 68.

6. Cited by Kevin J. Stiroh, "Are Bigger Banks Better?" report prepared for the Conference Board, Research Report 1238-99-RR (1999), p. 3.

7. Jeffrey Marshall, "New Banks Are Sprouting All Over," *U.S. Banker* (October 1998), p. 44.

8. Richard Korman, "Today's Bank of Yesterday," *New York Times*, June 20, 1999, Section 3, p. 1.

9. Avery and others, "Changes in the Distribution of Banking Offices," pp. 2, 18.

10. Louis Jacobson, "Bank Failure: The Financial Marginalization of the Poor," *The American Prospect*, no. 20 (Winter 1995), p. 8 (www.epn.org/prospect/20/20jaco.html (accessed August 12, 1999)).

11. Cited in Susan Headden, "The New Money Machines," *U.S. News and World Report*, August 5, 1996, p. 52.

12. "Merger Mania, Sobering Statistics," *Economist*, June 20, 1998, p. 89.

13. Litan and Rauch, *American Finance for the 21st Century*, p. 54.

14. Stacy Perman, "Is Bigger Really Better?" *Time*, April 27, 1998, p. 56.

15. Michelle Samaad, "The Final Fee: Some Banks Make You Pay to Close an Account," bankrate.com (July 6, 1999), p. 2 (www.bankrate.com/brm/news/bank/19990629.asp).

16. Ibid.

17. "American Banks: The Good Times Keep on Rollin'," *Economist*, October 25, 1997, p. 83.

18. Michelle Samaad, "Customers Feel Like Tumbleweeds in the Wake of Bank Mergers," *Bankrate Monitor*, posted on www.bankratemonitor.com, September 4, 1998.

19. P.L. 95-128, 95 Cong., 1 sess., 1997.

20. Litan and Rauch, *American Finance for the 21st Century*, p. 140.

21. Ibid., p. 141.

22. National Association of Community Loan Funds, *Business Plan 1998–2002* (Philadelphia, May 1997), p. 44.

23. "CRA: Revisiting Some Fundamentals," remarks by Ellen Seidman, director, Office of Thrift Supervision, at the Consumer Bankers' Association Annual Conference, Arlington, Va., April 26, 1999, p. 2.

24. Ibid., p. 3.

25. The amendment to the Federal Financial Management Act of 1994 is contained in P.L. 104-134, known as the *Debt Improvement and Collection Act of 1996*. 104 Cong. 2 sess. 1994.

26. Financial Management Service, *Governmentwide Treasury-Disbursed Payment Volume, October 1, 1998, through March 31, 1999*. (U.S. Department of the Treasury, 1999). The 390 million payments total does not include tax refunds, which are not included in the electronic delivery mandate.

27. "Treasury Proposal Would Implement 1996 Law Requiring Electronic Payment for Federal Salaries, Social Security Veterans, and Other Benefits," U.S. Treasury Department, Treasury News, RR-1991 (September 11, 1997), p. 1.

28. Ibid., and John D. Hawke Jr., undersecretary of the Treasury for domestic finance. Hearings before the House Government Reform and Oversight Sub-

committee on Government Management, Information and Technology, June 18, 1997, p. 2. Text as prepared for delivery, available as press release RR-1768 from the U.S. Treasury Department.

29. Financial Management Service, EFT '99, Fact Sheet on 31 CFR 208: Management of Federal Agency Disbursements; Notice of Proposed Rulemaking. September 16, 1997.

30. J. Kenneth Blackwell, "One Degree of Separation: Advances in Technology and Their Impact on Money, Banks and the Urban Poor," *Executive Speeches*, (February/March 1997), p. 33.

31. Brett F. Woods, "Comment: Food Stamps and EBT: What Price Progress?" *American Banker* (September 16, 1997), p. 16. "Each month 210,000 food retailers receive the coupons in exchange for food items. The retailers carry stacks of food stamps to 10,000 participating financial institutions, which credit the store accounts for their value. The banks send the food stamps to a Federal Reserve Bank, which credits the banks' accounts, bills the Treasury, and destroys the coupons."

32. *Personal Responsibility and Work Opportunity Reconciliation Act of 1996*. P.L. 104-193, 104 Cong. 1 sess., 1996.

33. Joseph Radigan, "EBT Rule Causes a Stir," *U.S. Banker* (July 1997), p. 76. In May 1994, the U.S. Department of Agriculture entered into an agreement with eight states—Alabama, Arkansas, Florida, Georgia, Kentucky, Missouri, North Carolina, and Tennessee—to establish a prototype for a common system to deliver federal and state-delivered benefits. The eight states called themselves the Southern Alliance of States (SAS).

34. Christopher D. Cook, "To Combat Welfare Fraud, States Reach for Debit Cards," *Christian Science Monitor*, May 25, 1999, p. 5.

35. David Barstow, "Welfare Debit Cards Offer Benefits and Some Snags," *New York Times*, June 18, 1999, p. 3.

36. Kim Girard, "Texas Ropes in Chaotic Call Center," *Computer World* (March 31, 1997), pp. 71–72.

37. Litan and Rauch, *American Finance for the 21st Century*, p. 148.

38. Joseph A. Slobodzian, "The High Cost of Food Stamp Fraud," *Philadelphia Inquirer*, January 4, 1999, p. B-10.

39. For one progress report of state EBT activity, see Joseph Radigan, "EBT Rule Causes a Stir," *U.S. Banker* (July 1997), pp. 75–76.

40. Telephone survey of current state activities by the Center for Community Capitalism, Kenan Institute of Private Enterprise, University of North Carolina at Chapel Hill, June 1998.

41. "Nation's Largest Smart Card Project for Health and Food Benefits in Western States Unveiled Today by Siemens," *Excite Business Wire*, June 10, 1999, p. 1.

42. Telephone survey of current state activities by the Center for Community Capitalism, June 1998.

43. John D. Hawke Jr., "Comment: New Law Means Millions of New Customers," *American Banker*, Nov. 6, 1996, p. 4.

44. Cited in Hawke, "Comment: New Law Means Millions of New Customers," p. 4.

45. Financial Management Service, *Governmentwide Treasury-Disbursed Payment Volumes: FY 1995-Cumulative FY 1999, through April, 1999.*

46. Booz-Allen & Hamilton and Shugoll Research, *Mandatory EFT Demographic Study, Executive Summary*, report prepared for the U.S. Treasury Department (April 22, 1997), p. 2.

47. The lifeline banking states are Illinois, Massachusetts, Minnesota, New Jersey, New York, Rhode Island, and Vermont. Joseph J. Doyle, Jose A. Lopez, and Marc R. Seidenberg, "How Effective is Lifeline Banking in Assisting the Unbanked?" *Current Issues in Economics and Finance*, Federal Reserve Bank of New York, vol. 4, no. 6 (June 1998), p. 1.

48. Cited by Richard A. Oppel Jr., "The Stepchildren of Banking," *New York Times*, March 26, 1999, p. C1.

49. Eugene A. Ludwig, in *Financial Access in the 21st Century,* proceedings of a forum held on Feb. 11, 1997 (Office of the Comptroller of the Currency), p. 1.

50. State of Missouri, Nomination Form, 1998 Governor's Award for Quality and Productivity, 1988, and Lawlor and others, *Electronic Benefit Transfer in California: Issues, Perspectives and Recommendations,* p. 1.

51. U.S. Treasury Secretary Robert Rubin, "Making 'Welfare-to-Work' Work," Remarks to a forum held Dec. 12, 1996 at the John F. Kennedy School of Government (Harvard University).

52. Thanks to Carolyn Betts of Hamilton Securities, Washington, D.C., for pointing this out.

53. Peter P. Swire, "Equality of Opportunity and Investment in Creditworthiness," *University of Pennsylvania Law Review*, vol. 143, no. 5 (May 1995), p. 1538.

54. Fannie Mae Foundation, *African American and Hispanic Attitudes on Homeownership: A Guide for Mortgage Industry Lenders* (Washington, 1998), pp. 6, 10. The question of whether late bill-payment would have a consequence on their ability to qualify for a mortgage was asked of all respondents, not just those who perceive the mortgage system to be discriminatory.

55. George C. Galster, *An Econometric Model of the Urban Opportunity Structure: Cumulative Causation among City Markets, Social Problems, and Underserved Areas,* (Fannie Mae Foundation Research Report, September 1998), pp. xi–xii.

56. Letter from ACORN to Director, Card Technology, Financial Management Service, U.S. Department of the Treasury, in reference to 31 C.F.R. Part 207, July 8, 1997.

57. Robert J. Samuelson, "Hell No, We Won't Save," *Newsweek,* February 22, 1999, p. 42.

58. Richard W. Stevenson, "Uncle Sam Learns Thrift While America Spends," *New York Times,* July 4, 1999, p. wk5.

59. Senator Bob Kerrey, "Who Owns America? A New Economic Agenda," *Assets* (Corporation for Enterprise Development, Winter 1997), p. 7.

60. See, for example, Melvin L. Oliver and Thomas M. Shapiro, *Black Wealth/White Wealth: A New Perspective on Racial Inequality* (Routledge, 1995).

61. Thomas M. Shapiro, "The Importance of Assets," paper prepared for a conference on The Benefits and Mechanisms for Spreading Asset Ownership, New York University, December 10–12, 1998, p. 18.

62. Ibid.

63. National Telecommunications and Information Administration, *Falling through the Net: Defining the Digital Divide, A Report on the Telecommunications and Information Technology Gap in America* (U.S. Department of Commerce, July 1999), pp. xii–xiii.

64. "New Commerce Report Shows Dramatic Growth in Number of Americans Connected to the Internet," U.S. Department of Commerce press release (July 8, 1999), p. 1.

65. *Falling through the Net,* p. xiv.

66. Keynote Address by Scott McNealy, in O'Reilly & Associates, eds., *The Harvard Conference on the Internet and Society* (Harvard University Press, 1996), p. 50.

67. Jane Bryant Quinn, "Direct Deposit Push: Cashing Government Checks Could Become Bigger Burden," *The Pantagraph* (Bloomington, Illinois), June 2, 1999, p. C3.

Chapter Two

1. Arthur B. Kennickell and Myron L. Kwast, "Who Uses Electronic Banking: Results from the 1995 Survey of Consumer Finances," in *Annual Meeting of the Western Economics Association Proceedings* (July 1997), p. 10.

2. "Banks Struggle to Define EC Business: Strategy, Pricing Still Lacking," *Retail Delivery News,* vol. 3, no. 19 (September 30, 1998), p. 2.

3. Phil Britt, "Profiling the Online Banking Customer," *America's Community Banker,* vol. 6, no. 9 (September 1997), pp. 6–7.

4. Steve Klinkerman, "Online Banking: Profits or Peril?" *Banking Strategies,* (March/April 1997), p. 36.

5. Carol Power, "On-Line Banking: Net.Bank Wants Clients On-Line, Not in Line," *The American Banker* (April 23, 1998), p. 14.

6. Rebecca Rairley Raney, "More Banks Leaning toward Web Transactions," *New York Times on the Web,* August 16, 1997, p. 2. The research cited is from Mentis Corporation, Durham, N. C. See also Klinkerman, "Online Banking," p. 36; Power, "On-Line Banking," p. 14.

7. "PC Banking's Next Wave," *American Demographics,* vol. 1, no. 2 (February 1999), p. 2.

8. The 6 percent estimate comes from the Yankelovitch Monitor database, the 13 percent number from the Federal Reserve Board's Survey of Consumer Finances, and the 22 percent statistic from the Population Survey of Income Dynamics. They are cited by economist John Caskey in *Financial Access in the 21st Century,* proceedings of a forum held February 11, 1997 (Office of the Comptroller of the Currency), p. 3.

9. Booz-Allen & Hamilton and Shugoll Research, *Mandatory EFT Demographic Study Executive Summary,* report prepared for the U.S. Department of Treasury, Financial Management Service (September 15, 1997), www.fms.treas.gov/eft/demogra.html#overview; Dove Associates, *ETA Initiative: Final Report,* report prepared for the U.S. Department of Treasury, Financial Management Service (June

15, 1998); Dove Associates, *ETA Initiative: Optional Account Features,* report prepared for the U.S. Department of Treasury, Financial Management Service (June 26, 1998); Dove Associates, *Focus Group Summary Report,* report prepared for the U.S. Department of Treasury, Financial Management Service (June 15, 1998); Dove Associates, *ETA Conjoint Analysis Proposed Statistical Methodology,* report prepared for the U.S. Department of Treasury, Financial Management Service (October 13, 1998). See also *Stakeholder Meetings Summary,* prepared by the Financial Management Service (U.S. Department of Treasury, July 31, 1997), www.fms. treas.gov/eft/stakehol.html.

10. Constance R. Dunham, Fritz J. Scheuren, and Douglas H. Willson, "Methodoligcal Issues in Surveying the Nonbanked Population in Urban Areas," in *American Statistical Association Proceedings,* 1998 (forthcoming). See also Office of the Comptroller of Currency, *Project on Nonbanked Households: Expanding the Financial Frontier* (May 7, 1997).

11. Dove Associates, *ETA Initiative: Final Report,* p. 21. The other four cities are Chicago, Miami, New York, and San Francisco.

12. James H. Johnson Jr. and Walter C. Farrell Jr., "Growing Income Inequality in American Society: A Political Economy Perspective," in James A. Auerbach and Richard S. Belous, eds., *The Inequality Paradox: Growth of Income Disparity* (Washington, D.C.: National Policy Association, 1998), pp. 147–48.

13. The various surveys' results are cited in Jeanne M. Hogarth and Kevin H. O'Donnell, "Bank Account Ownership and Use of Financial Institutions: Helping the 'Unbanked' Become Banked," in *Eastern Regional Family Economics Resource Management Association Proceedings* (February 1998), p. 16.

14. Jeanne M. Hogarth and Kevin H. O'Donnell, "Being Accountable: A Descriptive Study of Unbanked Households in the U.S.," in *Proceedings of the Association for Financial Counseling and Planning Education* (1997), p. 58.

15. Robert E. Litan with Jonathan Rauch, *American Finance for the 21st Century* (U.S. Department of Treasury, November 17, 1997), pp. 24–26, 145–50; John P. Caskey, *Fringe Banking: Check-Cashing Outlets, Pawnshops and the Poor* (New York: Russell Sage Foundation, 1994), pp. 100–01.

16. "Consumer Credit and Usury Edition," *National Consumer Law Center Reports,* vol. 16 (January/February 1998), p. 13; Caskey, *Fringe Banking,* p. 88–89.

17. Caskey, *Fringe Banking,* p. 8.

18. John P. Caskey, *Lower Income Americans, Higher Cost Financial Services* (Madison, Wisc.: Filene Research Institute, 1997), p. 15. Caskey interviewed a total of 900 households with incomes of less than $25,000: 300 each in Atlanta, Georgia; Oklahoma City, Oklahoma; and 300 spread over five smaller cities in eastern Pennsylvania.

19. Yolanda S. Brown, vice president and manager of community banking administration for Union Bank of California, quoted in Michael J. Major, "Check Cashing Services Offer New Profits," *Bank Marketing,* vol. 26, no. 2. (1994), p. 55.

20. Hogarth and O'Donnell, "Being Accountable," p. 61. The national data reported by Hogarth and O'Donnell are from the Survey of Consumer Finance (SCF), released every three years since 1983. The SCF contains information on

household characteristics, consumer credit, loans, financial assets, wealth, income and employment. While the SCF is based on a national probability sample that oversamples high-income households, Hogarth and O'Donnell weight the data so that "the picture of low-to-moderate income households that emerges is valid," p. 60.

21. Hogarth and O'Donnell, "Being Accountable," p. 61. The SCF question asking why people did not have checking accounts is asked of both the unbanked and people who had some other account format, such as a savings account. In 1995, 15 percent of the SCF respondents had no checking account but only 13.1 percent had no account of any kind. However, in conducting their analysis of the SCF data, Hogarth and O'Donnell reported results only for those respondents who had no accounts of any kind.

22. Booz-Allen & Hamilton and Shugoll Research, *Mandatory EFT Demographic Study Executive Summary*, p. 3.

23. In the telephone EFT'99 survey, 73 percent of respondents were age 65 or older and 84 percent were white. In the mail survey, 61 percent of respondents were age 65 or older and 70 percent were white. Booz-Allen & Hamilton and Shugoll Research, *Mandatory EFT Demographic Study Executive Summary*, p. 2. This breakdown does not correspond to the national profile of unbanked recipients from the SCF, where the average age was 43 and only 7 percent were white. Hogarth and O'Donnell, "Bank Account Ownership and Use of Financial Institutions," p. 6.

24. Booz-Allen & Hamilton and Shugoll Research, *Mandatory EFT Demographic Study Executive Summary*, p. 3.

25. The Amigo Card!, Amigo Card Systems, 2200 Clarendon Boulevard, Suite 1204, Arlington, VA 22201.

26. Elvin K. Wyly, Norman J. Glickman, and Michael L. Lahr, "A Top 10 List of Things to Know about American Cities," *Cityscape*, vol. 3, no. 3 (1998), p. 10; Caskey, *Fringe Banking*, pp. 100–01.

27. Johnson and Farrell, "Growing Income Inequality in American Society," pp. 145–47.

28. Wyly, Glickman, and Lahr, "A Top 10 List of Things to Know about American Cities," p. 10.

29. Ibid., p. 10.

30. Caskey, *Fringe Banking*, pp. 100–01.

31. Ibid., p. 101.

32. Johnson and Farrell, "Growing Income Inequality in American Society," p. 147.

33. "California Leads States and Los Angeles County, Calif., Tops Counties in Hispanic Population Increase," *Census Bureau Reports*, press release, September 4, 1998.

34. Benjamin Forgey, "A Slice of American Pie in Latino L.A.," *Washington Post*, December 12, 1998, p. B5.

35. Ibid.

36. Johnson and Farrell, "Growing Income Inequality in American Society," pp. 147–48.

37. Ibid., pp. 148–49.

38. Brian Patrick Lawlor, Laura Fry, Michele Melden, Cheryl Nolan, and Gail K. Hillebrand, *Electronic Benefit Transfer in California: Issues, Perspectives and Recommendations* (San Francisco, June 1998), p. 1.

39. Johnson and Farrell, "Growing Income Inequality in American Society," pp. 151–53.

40. The base case model sets continuous variables (such as education and income) at their sample means.

41. Cited in Louis Jacobson, "Bank Failure: the Financial Marginalization of the Poor," *The American Prospect*, no. 20 (Winter 1995), p. 9.

42. See, for example, Caskey, *Fringe Banking*, pp. 90–97 (finding no consistent pattern as to bank branch closings in low-income urban areas).

43. Marian Miller King, "The Unbanked: Who They Are and Why It Might Be Hard to Stay That Way," at http://www.bankrate.com/brm/news/bank/19980102.asp., last accessed July 8, 1999, p. 6.

44. Ibid.

45. Mitchell Ratner, "Ethnographic Studies of Homeownership and Home Mortgage Financing: An Introduction," *Cityscape*, vol. 3, no. 1 (March 1997), p. 10.

46. Susan Hamilton and Stephen J. H. Cogswell, "Barriers to Home Purchase for African-Americans and Hispanics in Syracuse," *Cityscape*, vol. 3, no. 1 (March 1997), p. 119.

47. Michael D'Ieste, ethnic segment marketing manager for Texas Commerce Bank, quoted in King, "The Unbanked," p. 2. The $23 billion-asset Texas Commerce Bank is owned by Chase Manhattan Bank.

48. "Poor Area, Profitable Venture," *U.S. Banker*, July 1995, p. 39.

49. Ibid.

50. Lisa Fickenscher, "Banco Popular Targets U.S. Mainland Card Market," *American Banker*, October 19, 1998, p. 13.

51. Ibid.

52. Ibid.

53. Letter to the author from Susan Winstead, senior vice president, NationsBank, October 27, 1998.

54. Cited in Thomas A. Shapiro, "The Importance of Assets," p. 16. See also Chenoa Flippen and Marta Tienda, "Racial and Ethnic Differences in Wealth among the Elderly," paper presented at the 1997 annual meeting of the Population Association of America, Washington, D.C.

55. Hogarth and O'Donnell, "Being Accountable," p. 59.

56. J. Kenneth Blackwell, "One Degree of Separation—Advances in Technology and Their Impacts on Money, Banks and the Urban Poor," *Executive Speeches*, (February/March 1997), p. 34.

Chapter Three

1. Eugene A. Ludwig, remarks before the Conference on Digital Commerce '96: Law, Policy, Profit & Pitfalls on the Global Information Network, held May 6,

1996, Washington, D.C. Text available at http://www.occ.treas.gov/ftf/release/96-53.txt.

2. Quoted in Saul Hansell, "Era May Be Ending for Big Local Banks," *New York Times*, September 2, 1997, p. A10.

3. Joshua Cooper Ramo, "The Big Bank Theory and What It Says about the Future of Money," *Time*, April 27, 1998, p. 49.

4. Quoted in David Bollier, *Rapporteur, The Future of Electronic Commerce* (Aspen Institute, 1996), p. 28.

5. Kevin Maney, "Citicorp's Billion-Customer Plan Relies on High Tech," *USA Today*, April 16, 1998, p. 4B.

6. Ibid.

7. Ibid.

8. "When Is a Branch Not a Branch?" *Citibank World*, June 1998, http://www.citibank.com/corporate_affairs/cbworld/0698/popcom.htm.

9. Robert E. Litan with Jonathan Rauch, *American Finance for the 21st Century*, report prepared for the U.S. Department of the Treasury (November 17, 1997), p. 139.

10. Department of Commerce, *Falling through the Net: Defining the Digital Divide* (July 1999), pp. xii, xiii.

11. Litan and Rauch, *American Finance for the 21st Century*, p. 139.

12. Ibid., p. 54.

13. Cited by Eugene Ludwig in remarks to the Women in Housing and Financing Technology Symposium, proceedings of a forum held on December 4, 1996, Washington, D.C., p. 3.

14. Bruno Giussani, "Swiss Bank to Offer Retail Services on the Web," *New York Times Online*, April 11, 1997.

15. The forecast is by Needham, Mass.-based Meridien Research, and cited in "Study: More Banks to Offer Web Transactions," *Bank Systems and Technology*, vol. 35, no. 3, March 1998, p. 41 (no author).

16. Steven C. Davidson, *The Community Banker's Guide to the Internet and Home Banking* (Washington, D.C.: America's Community Bankers, 1997), p. 41.

17. Ibid., p. 8.

18. Ed Horowitz, "In the Arena of On-line Banking, The Message Is the Medium," *Banking Systems and Technology*, February 1998, p. 48 (available at http://www.banktech.com).

19. Edward Furash, in *Financial Access in the 21st Century*, proceedings of a forum held February 11, 1997 (Office of the Comptroller of the Currency), p. 52.

20. Neil Munro, "Who Will Rule the Net?" *National Journal*, February 13, 1999, p. 406.

21. George Avalos, "Internet Shopping Soared during Holidays, But the Nation's 'E-tailers' May Have to Scramble to Keep Consumers Happy in 1999," *Contra Costa Times*, January 26, 1999, p. 1.

22. Munro, "Who Will Rule the Net?" p. 406.

23. Lisa Napoli, "For Popular Categories, Online Sales Rise Sharply," *New York Times Online*, March 3, 1998, p. 1.

24. Ibid.

25. Reported in Robert Goldfield, "Banking on the Web," *The Business Journal*, online edition, July 13, 1998, p. 1.

26. Estimate by Kenneth Clemmer of Forester Research. Cited in Christine Dugas, "Net Bank Piques Interest with Rate Offer," *USA Today*, April 27, 1999, p. 1B.

27. Ibid.

28. "On-line Financial Services Market Readying to Heat Up, Poll Says," *Bank Systems + Technology*, November 1998, p. 14.

29. Eugene A. Ludwig, The Conference on Digital Commerce '96, p. 3.

30. "Study: More Banks to Offer Web Transactions," *Bank Systems and Technology*, vol. 35, no. 3, March 1998, p. 41.

31. The 1998 data are from *Online Banking Report*, www.onlinebankingreport.com.

32. Bill Orr, "Community Bank Guide to Internet Banking," *ABA Banking Journal*, June 1998, p. 47.

33. Reported in "Bellsouth Making Web Available to Banks," *Greensboro News Record*, December 1, 1998, p. B5.

34. "America Online Banking," *New York Times*, May 11, 1999, p. 10.

35. Davidson, *The Community Banker's Guide to the Internet and Home Banking*, p. 40. See www.netbank.com, www.SFNb.com.

36. Kenneth Kiesnoski, "Cyberbanks: Carving a Market Niche?" *Bank Systems + Technology*, vol. 36, no. 5 (May 1999), p. 30.

37. Advertisement for Wingspanbank.com, *USA Today*, June 25, 1999, p. 3E. See the bank's website at www.wingspanbank.com.

38. Scott Woolley, "Virtual Banker," *Forbes*, June 15, 1998, p. 127.

39. Kenneth Kiesnoski, "Cyberbanks: Carving a Market Niche?" *Bank System + Technology*, vol. 36, no. 5 (May 1999), p. 30.

40. Ibid.

41. Scott Woolley, "Virtual Banker," p. 127.

42. James Mahan III, "Banking on the Internet at Security First Network Bank," *Journal of Retail Banking Services*, vol. 17, no. 3 (Autumn 1996), p. 24.

43. National rate from bankrate.com/brm/rate/dep.home.asp; Netbank rate from www.netbank.com; and Security First Network Bank from www.SFNB.com.

44. Christine Dugas, "NetBank Piques Interest with Rate Offer," *USA Today*, April 27, 1999, p. B1.

45. Ibid.

46. Matt Andrejczak, "Carrollton Bank on Target with New ATMs in Area," *Washington Business Journal*, December 8, 1997, p. 1.

47. Davidson, *The Community Banker's Guide to the Internet and Home Banking*, p. 40.

48. Ibid., p. 26.

49. "Internet Bank to Serve Homosexual Community," *Bank Systems Technology*, October 1998, p. 60.

50. Ibid.

51. See True World Internet Banks at http://www.onlinebankingreport.com.

52. "Electronic Banking to Grow More than 30% a Year until 2005," *Management Accounting*, vol. 76, no. 9 (London: October 1998), p. 11.

53. Ibid.

54. Sherrill Tapsell, "Brickless Banks," *Management-Auckland*, vol. 45, no. 4 (May 1998), p. 38.

55. Ibid.

56. Thomas Hoffman, "Brazilian Bank Java Bound," *Computerworld*, September 22, 1997, p. 4.

57. Henry T. Azzam, "Electronic Banking in the Kingdom," *Middle East Executive Reports*, vol. 20, no. 9 (September 1997), p. 8.

58. Ibid.

59. Grant Thornton LLP, "Community Banks' Attitudes towards Alternative Payment Systems," in *Forum on Technology-Based Services and the Internet*, proceedings of a forum held September 12, 1996, Washington, D.C.

60. Ibid.

61. Michael J. Major, "The Conundrum of Technology," *America's Community Banker*, vol. 8, no. 3, p. 25.

62. Litan and Rauch, p. 140.

63. Constance R. Dunham, Fritz J. Scheuren, and Douglas H. Willson, "Methodological Issues in Surveying the Nonbanked Population in Urban Areas," in *American Statistical Association Proceedings*, 1998 (forthcoming), p. xx, n. 11. The statistics were derived from special runs of Current Population Survey data three-year average, 1994–96, carried out for the Office of the Comptroller of the Currency by the U.S. Bureau of the Census.

64. Davidson, *The Community Banker's Guide to the Internet and Home Banking*, pp. 1, 15.

65. Thomas Swidarski, director of financial industry worldwide marketing for Diebold, Inc., in *Financial Access in the 21st Century*, p. 45.

66. Ibid.

67. Simon Cashmore, "Networking a Nation," *Computerworld*, September 9, 1996, p. 44 (available at http://www.computerworld.com/home/print9497.nsf/all/SL96net201SF56).

68. Lynn Waldsmith, "Companies Join Fraud Fight," *The Detroit News Online*, May 28, 1998, http://detnews.com/1998/cyberia/9806/01/05280052.htm, p. 2.

69. Earl Golz, "Video Banking in Austin," *North Communications Press Release Archives*, July 12, 1995, p. 1.

70. Arthur M. Louis, "Wells to Use ATMs That Talk," *San Francisco Chronicle*, June 24, 1999, p. B1.

71. D. Blair Bingham Jr., "Deposit Guaranty Pioneers Automated Loan Machines," *Journal of Retail Banking Services*, vol. 17, no. 1 (Spring 1996), p. 35; Susan Headden, "The New Money Machines," *USA Today Online*, August 5, 1996.

72. "Public Voice for Food and Health Policy, Tracking Electronic Benefits Transfer Policies and Issues," *EBT Watch* (Washington, D.C., July 29, 1998), p. 1.

73. "Changing Customer Behavior," *Distribution Management Briefing*, May 1998, p. 8.

74. "Public Voice for Food and Health Policy," p. 1.

75. Christopher Rhoads, "The Future of the Branch," *American Banker*, December 4, 1996, p. 15A.

76. Robert Weissbourd and Christopher Berry, *The Market Potential of Inner-City Neighborhoods: Filling the Information Gap* (Brookings Institution Discussion Paper, March 1999), pp. 2–4 (emphasis in original).

77. Michael E. Porter and Mark Blaxill, "Inner Cities Are the Next Retailing Frontier," *Wall Street Journal*, November 24, 1997, p. A22.

78. Robert D. Hershey Jr., "2 Banks, One Goal: Cast Long Shadows," *New York Times*, November 15, 1997, p. D1.

79. Steven G. Boehm, First Union senior vice president for customer direct access division, quoted in Hershey, "2 Banks, One Goal: Cast Long Shadows," p. D1.

80. Hershey, "2 Banks, One Goal: Cast Long Shadows," p. D1.

81. Furash, *Financial Access in the 21st Century*, p. 51.

82. Laurence P. Greenberg and Arthur M. Domingo, "A Bank No One Visits," *Journal of Retail Banking Services*, vol. 17, no. 3 (Autumn 1996), p. 19.

83. "Net Bank Introduces ATM Refunder," *Financial NetNews*, vol. 4, no. 8 (February 22, 1999), p. 5.

84. Federal Deposit Insurance Corporation (FDIC), Commercial Banking Performance, Fourth Quarter 1998, as quoted by Marcy Gordon, "Bank Profits Up 4.7%," Associated Press, March 15, 1999.

85. Joe Asher, "The Second ATM Revolution," *ABA Banking Journal*, May 1998, p. 51.

86. Ibid.

87. "Enhanced ATMs Begin to Push the Cardholder Activity Pace," *Debit Card News* online edition, May 16, 1997, p. 1.

88. Asher, "The Second ATM Revolution," p. 52.

89. U.S. Public Interest Research Group, *ATMs: Always Taking Money: A Fourth PIRG Survey of ATM Surcharging Rates April 1, 1999—The Third Anniversary of ATM Surcharging* (Washington, D.C., 1999), pp. 1–2.

90. Ibid., p. 3.

91. Ibid., p. 3.

92. Ibid., p. 5.

93. Ibid., p. 1.

94. Asher, "The Second ATM Revolution," p. 52.

95. "The Risks and Rewards of Encouraging ATM Deposits," *Debit Card News*, March 30, 1998, p. 1.

96. Associated Press, "Fleet to Electronic Users: You'll Pay," *Boston Globe*, October 5, 1998, p. D2.

97. "The Risks and Rewards of Encouraging ATM Deposits," *Debit Card News*, p. 1.

98. Ibid.

99. Ibid.

100. "Will Banks Be the Big Losers in EFT 99?" *Bank Technology News*, August 1997, p. 3.

101. "Chase to Charge Noncustomers at Its ATMs," *American Banker*, January 7, 1999, p. 28.

102. "Dairy Mart Stores in Seven States Will Offer Customers No-Fee ATM Service; Unique Service Will Make Dairy Mart a Destination Stop for Customers," *Excite Business Wire*, March 31, 1999, p. 1.

103. "CFA Creates Storm over Bounced Check Fees," *The Regulatory Compliance Watch*, vol. 9, no. 27 (July 6, 1998), p. 1. The CFA report said that banks generated over $5.2 billion in annual profits on fees for bounced checks, and $918 million in profits on bad check deposits.

104. Ramo, "The Big Bank Theory and What It Says about the Future of Money," p. 49.

105. Paul Decker, "Data Mining's Hidden Dangers," *Banking Strategies* (March/April 1998), p. 6.

106. Ibid.

107. Rick Brooks, "Alienating Customers Isn't Always a Bad Idea, Many Firms Discover," *Wall Street Journal*, January 7, 1999, p. A1.

108. Guenther Hartfeil, "Bank One Measures Profitability of Customers, Not Just Products," *Journal of Retail Banking Services*, vol. 18, no. 2 (Summer 1996), p. 24.

109. Debora Connelly and Barbara Read, "First Commerce Segments Customers by Behavior, Enhancing Profitability," *Journal of Retail Banking Services*, vol. 19, no. 1 (Spring 1997), p. 24.

110. Hartfeil, "Bank One Measures Profitability of Customers, Not Just Products," pp. 23–24.

111. Brooks, "Alienating Customers Isn't Always a Bad Idea, Many Firms Discover," p. A1.

112. Ibid.

113. Ibid.

114. Jennifer Baljko, "Northern Trust Zeroes in on Valued Clients," *Bank Systems + Technology*, vol. 36, issue 6 (June 1999), p. 44.

115. Brooks, "Alienating Customers Isn't Always a Bad Idea, Many Firms Discover," p. A1.

116. Melanie McManus, "The Price is Right," *Credit Union Magazine*, April 1998, p. 25.

117. Ibid.

118. Robert C. Giltner and Michael Thompson, "Putting Profitabil gity Information Systems to Work," *Bank Accounting and Finance* (Winter 1998), p. 4.

119. Ibid.

120. Ibid.

121. Ibid.

122. Kevin Zaney and Ken Rees, "Bankers Putting Faith in Myths—and Industry's Future at Risk," *American Banker*, February 3, 1997, p. 8A.

123. Hershey, "2 Banks, One Goal," p. D1.

124. "American Banks: The Good Times Keep on Rollin'," *Economist*, October 25, 1997, p. 83.

125. Hershey, "2 Banks, One Goal," p. D1.

126. Litan and Rauch, *American Finance for the 21st Century*, p. 146.

127. "Merger Mania: Sobering Statistics," *Economist*, June 20, 1998, p. 89.

128. "New Wave of ATM Use," *Direct Delivery International*, April 1998, p. 10.

129. Kevin J. Stiroh, *Are Bigger Banks Better?* Research Report 1238-99-RR (The Conference Board, 1999), p. 3.

130. Ibid., p. 5.

131. Ibid., p. 12.

132. Stacy Perman, "Is Bigger Really Better?" *Time*, April 27, 1998, p. 56.

Chapter Four

1. Jason Booth, "Operation Hope Opens Inner-City Banking Centers," *Los Angeles Business Journal,* June 22–28, 1998, p. 22.

2. Lee Romney, "Financial Center Brings 'HOPE' to Maywood," *Los Angeles Times,* May 16, 1998, p. D2.

3. Jean Ann Fox, Matt Gordon, and Leslie Borja, *The High Cost of "Banking" at the Corner Check Casher: Check Cashing Outlet Fees and Payday Loans* (Washington, D.C.: Consumer Federation of America, August 1997), p. 2.

4. John P. Caskey, *Fringe Banking: Check-Cashing Outlets, Pawnshops and the Poor* (New York: Russell Sage Foundation, 1994), pp. 1–2.

5. Gregory D. Squires and Sally O'Connor, "Fringe Banking in Milwaukee: The Rise of Check Cashing Businesses and the Emergence of a Two-Tiered Banking System," *Urban Affairs Review,* vol. 34, no. 1 (September 1998), p. 127.

6. Scott Shepard and Elliot Jaspin, "An 'Unholy Alliance'? Check-Cashers & Banks Seen Profiting in Paperless Era," *Times-Picayune,* September 27, 1998, p. A19.

7. National Check Cashers Association, "Q&A–NaCCA Facts," http://www.nacca.org/q&a.htm.

8. Richard A. Oppel Jr., "The Stepchildren of Banking," *New York Times,* March 26, 1999, p. C17.

9. Shepard and Jaspin, "An 'Unholy Alliance'?" p. 3.

10. Cited by Squires and O'Connor, "Fringe Banking in Milwaukee," p. 128.

11. Louis Jacobson, "Bank Failure: The Financial Marginalization of the Poor," *The American Prospect,* no. 20 (Winter 1995), pp. 63–70.

12. Western Union, written comments on proposed rule for Management of Federal Agency Disbursements, 62 Federal Register 48,713, December 11, 1997 (letter from Adam P. Coyle, counsel, to Cynthia L. Johnson, Financial Management Service).

13. Western Union, written comments on interim rule for Management of Federal Agency Disbursements, 61 Federal Register 39,253, November 15, 1996 (Tom Norton, vice president/business manager of consumer products, to Cynthia L. Johnson, Financial Mangement Service).

14. Caskey, *Fringe Banking,* p. 63.

15. Carol Frey, "Borrowing against Paycheck on Rise," *News and Observer,* December 24, 1998, p. D1.

16. Joanne Gordon, "The Service Side of Strips," *Chain Store Age,* February 1998, p. 136.

17. National Check Cashers Association, written comments on interim rule

for Management of Federal Agency Disbursements, 61 Federal Register 39,253, November 25, 1996 (letter from Stephen Wolf, board chairman, to Cynthia L. Johnson, Financial Management Services).

18. Jacobson, "Bank Failure: The Financial Marginalization of the Poor," pp. 63–70.

19. *Financial Access in the 21st Century*, proceedings of a forum held on February 11, 1997 (Office of the Comptroller of the Currency), p. 49.

20. Consumer Union, written comments on interim rule for Management of Federal Agency Disbursements, 61 Federal Register 39,253, November 25, 1996 (letter from Michelle Meier, counsel for government affairs, to Cynthia L. Johnson, Financial Management Services).

21. National Consumer Law Center, Comments on Department of the Treasury Notice of Proposed Rulemaking on Electronic Benefits Transfer: Selection and Designation of Financial Institutions as Financial Agents, 31 CFR Part 207, 62 *Fed. Reg.* 25572-25576 (May 9, 1997), July 8, 1997.

22. Thomas Cook, American Express Travel Related Services Company, Western Union Financial Services, Travelers Express Company, Comdata Network, and MoneyGram Payments System, written comments to proposed rule on Electronic Benefits Transfer, 62 Federal Register, 25,572, July 8, 1997 (letter from Howrey & Simon, attorneys, to John P. Galligan, Financial Management Service). The data were included in attachment entitled "The Non-Bank Money Transmitter Industry Serves Vital National Financial Interests," p. 6.

23. Kelly Thompson Cochran, *Making Check Cashing Services Work for Local Communities* (University of North Carolina Center for Community Capitalism, forthcoming 1999), p. 26; American Association of Retired Persons, *Check-Cashing: 1998 Survey of State Laws* (Washington, D.C., 1998).

24. Organization for a New Equality, *Cash, Credit & EFT'99: Reducing the Cost of Credit and Capital for the Urban Poor* (Washington, D.C., no date), pp. 3–4, n.1.

25. Carlene Hemphell, "The Lure of Easy Money," *News and Observer*, June 27, 1999, p. 4E.

26. Massachusetts Division of Banks, *Study on the Costs of Utilizing Massachusetts Licensed Check Cashers vs. The Basic Banking for Massachusetts' Basic Banking Account* (Commonwealth of Massachusetts, April 1997), p. 2.

27. National Check Cashers Association, "Deferred Deposit," http://www.nacca.org/defdep.htm. Last accessed on October 13, 1998.

28. Organization for a New Equality, *Cash, Credit & EFT'99*, p. 5.

29. Cited by P. Lunt, "Banks Make Check Cashing Work," *ABA Banking Journal*, December 1993, pp. 51–52.

30. Massachusetts Division of Banks, *Study on the Costs of Utilizing Massachusetts Licensed Check Cashers*, p. 5. The Massachusetts Community and Banking Council established its voluntary Basic Banking for Massachusetts program in May 1994. By 1997, 151 banks and 82 percent of bank branches participated in the program. The Basic Checking Account features a maximum monthly charge of $3, a minimum of eight free withdrawals a month and a $10 minimum balance. The Basic Savings Account features a minimum deposit requirement of no more than $10, a minimum balance of no more than $10 to open and maintain the account,

and a maximum monthly charge of $1. Massachusetts Division of Banks, *Study on the Costs of Utilizing Massachusetts Licensed Check Cashers,* p. 3.

31. Organization for a New Equality, *Cash, Credit & EFT'99,* p. 5.

32. Ibid.

33. Joseph J. Doyle, Jose A. Lopez, and Marc R. Saidenberg, "How Effective Is Lifeline Banking in Assisting the 'Unbanked'?" *Current Issues in Economics and Finance,* Federal Reserve Bank of New York, vol. 4, no. 6 (June 1998), p. 4.

34. Preliminary results from a survey of check-cashing outlets in Charlotte being conducted at the Center for Community Capitalism, University of North Carolina at Chapel Hill.

35. American Association of Retired Persons, "Check-Cashing: 1998 Survey of State Laws," chart.

36. Squires and O'Connor, "Fringe Banking in Milwaukee," p. 136.

37. Peter Kilborn, "New Lenders with Huge Fees Thrive on Workers with Debts," *New York Times,* June 18, 1999, p. A1.

38. Cited in Andrew Conte, "Growth of Payday Loan Industry Explodes," *Cincinnati Post,* June 21, 1999, p. 4.

39. Jean Ann Fox, *The Growth of Legal Loan Sharking: A Report on the Payday Loan Industry* (Washington, D.C.: Consumer Federation of America, November 1998), p. 3.

40. Conte, "Growth of Payday Loan Industry Explodes," p. 1.

41. Fox, *The Growth of Legal Loan Sharking,* p. 22, Appendix B.

42. Ali Sartipzadeh, "Failure to Disclose Finance Charges in Check Cashing Violates TILA, Court Says," *BNA Legal News,* vol. 72, no. 1 (March 15, 1999). The Truth in Lending Act (15U.S.C.1638) was enacted in 1968 (90 Cong. 1 sess.).

43. Cited in Peter T. Kilborn, "New Lenders with Huge Fees Thrive on Workers with Debts," *New York Times,* June 18, 1999, p. A28.

44. Frey, "Borrowing against Paycheck on Rise," p. D1.

45. Conte, "Growth of Payday Loan Industry Explodes," p. 3.

46. National Check Cashers Association, "Deferred Deposit," http://www.nacca.org/defdep.htm.

47. Letter to Donald V. Hammond, fiscal assistant secretary of the Treasury, from Robert Milligan, comptroller, State of Florida, concerning Advanced Notice of Proposed Rulemaking on the Possible Regulation Regarding Access to Accounts at Financial Institutions through Payment Service Providers, April 7, 1999.

48. Stephen Rothman, "Officials Call Payday Financing 'Loan Sharking,'" http://www.bankrate.com/brm/news/chk/19980217.asp).

49. Caskey, *Fringe Banking,* p. 7.

50. Quoted in Lynn Waldsmith, "Check Cashers: Saints or Sinners? Critics Say They Gouge Patrons with Big Fees: Others Say It's Service," *Detroit News,* April 6, 1997, p. C1.

51. Squires and O'Connor, "Fringe Banking in Milwaukee," p. 141. See also Caskey, *Fringe Banking,* pp. 112–14.

52. Joanne Gordon, "The Service Side of Strips," *Chain Store Age,* February 1998, p. 136.

53. Ibid., p. 137.

54. Ibid., p. 137.

55. Tyrone Beason, "Banking on the Edge," *Seattle Times*, January 26, 1998, p. C1.

56. Conte, "Growth of Payday Loan Industry Explodes," p. 3.

57. "Banking on New Markets," *Progressive Grocer*, April 1996, p. 69; Amy Baldwin, "Wal-Mart Introduces Check-Cashing Outlets at Supercenters," *Lexington Herald-Leader*, June 27, 1998, p. 1.

58. Baldwin, "Wal-Mart Introduces Check-Cashing Outlets," p. 1.

59. "Banking on New Markets," p. 73.

60. Baldwin, "Wal-Mart Introduces Check-Cashing Outlets," p. 3.

61. "Banking on New Markets," p. 69.

62. "Mr. Payroll Corporation in Alliance with Crestar Bank," *Excite Industry News, PR Newswire* online, August 18, 1998.

63. "Banking on New Markets," p. 73.

64. Provident's check-cashing chain is called Fast 'n Friendly. Laura Pavlenko Lutton, "Trying Different Strategies to Cash in on Check Cashing," *The American Banker*, October 23, 1997, p. 5.

65. David Brindley and Fred Vogelstein, "The Check Is Not in the Mail," *U.S. News and World Report*, April 14, 1997, p. 66.

66. Organization for a New Equality, *Cash, Credit & EFT'99*, p. 14.

67. Roger H. Bezdek, "Summary of Four New Electronic Accounts Being Developed by the Private Sector for the Unbanked," (Treasury Department memo, July 1998), p. 2.

68. Ibid., pp. 2–3.

69. Community Currency Exchange Association of Illinois, written comments on proposed rule for Management of Federal Agency Disbursements, 62 Federal Register 48,713, November 14, 1997 (letter from Abby L. Hans, president, to Cynthia L. Johnson, Financial Management Service).

70. Bezdek, "Summary of Four New Electronic Accounts," p. 3.

71. Ibid.

72. Telephone interview with Pete Ziverts, vice president, corporate communications, Western Union, June 1998.

73. Western Union, "Introducing the Western Union Benefits Quick Cash Program," no date.

74. Letter to Western Union agents by Jay Giesen, Western Union senior vice president, August 4, 1997.

75. "Western Union Introduces the Solution to Keep Your Customers Coming Back," Western Union, undated.

76. National Check Cashers Association, written comments on proposed features for Electronic Transfer Accounts, 63 Federal Register 64,819, January 7, 1999 (letter from Stephen H. Wolf, chairman of federal payments committee, to Cynthia L. Johnson, Financial Management Service).

77. "NaCCA Preferred Card ... Pilot Program Announced," *NaCCA Currents*, July 1998, p. 2.

78. Fox, *The Growth of Legal Loan Sharking*, p. 5.

79. Comptroller of the Currency, "Public Disclosure Community Reinvestment Act Performance Evaluation, Eagle National Bank, Upper Darby, Pennsylvania," April 6, 1998, p. 6.

80. Letter from John D. Hawke Jr., undersecretary of the Treasury for domestic finance, to Alan Greenspan, chairman of Federal Reserve Board, March 26, 1998.

81. "Advanced Notice of Rulemaking: Possible Regulation Regarding Access to Accounts at Financial Institutions through Payment Service Providers," 64 Federal Register 1149, January 8, 1999, pp. 1149–1152.

82. The survey by the Consumer Bankers Association reported that 64 percent of respondents cash government checks for noncustomers. About one third of those did not charge for the service; among the rest, the average fee was $3.93. Consumer Bankers Association, *Basic Banking Survey* (Washington, D.C., December 1997), p. 3. http://www.cbanet.org/Products/basic_banking_survey.htm.

83. Florida Public Interest Research Group, "First Union Imposes New Check Cashing Fee that Gouges Consumers," September 16, 1997, press release, at http://www.pirg.org/floridapirg/consumer/first_un.htm, p. 1.

84. Ibid.

85. Patricia A. Murphy, "Will Banks Be the Big Losers in EFT '99?" *Bank Technology News,* August 1997, p. 2.

86. Rob Chambers, "NationsBank Rolls Out Payroll Debit Card," *Atlanta Journal,* July 2, 1998, p. 14.

87. "Citibank Uses Manpower to Boost Debit Card Use by Unbanked Workers," *Debit Card News* online, September 16, 1997, p. 1.

88. Shelly Branch, "Where Cash Is King," *Fortune,* June 8, 1998, p. 210.

89. Ibid.

90. Telephone interview with Yolanda Brown, vice president and division manager for Union Bank of California, Los Angeles, October 7, 1998.

91. Anita Womack, "EFT'99 Spawns Methods for Reaching the 'Unbanked,'" *Bank Marketing,* vol. 30, no. 6 (June 1998), p. 8.

92. Caskey, *Fringe Banking,* p. 136.

93. From a foreword by Eugene A. Ludwig in *Financial Access in the 21st Century,* p. iii.

94. Frey, "Borrowing against Paycheck on Rise," p. 6D.

95. William Cooper, TCF chairman and CEO, quoted in Beverly Foster, "For TCF, It's PPI," *The Journal of Lending & Credit Risk Management,* vol. 80, no. 8 (April 1998), p. 8.

Chapter Five

1. *Proposed Rule: Management of Federal Agency Disbursements,* 62 Federal Register 48,713 (September 16, 1997) (to be codified at 61 C.F.R. 208): 48,714.

2. John D. Hawke Jr., "Comment: New Law Means Millions of New Customers," *American Banker,* November 6, 1996, p. 4.

3. Financial Management Service, "Final Rule for Electronic Government Payments Will Balance Recipient Needs with Benefits of Electronic Payment," U.S. Department of the Treasury, http://www.fms.treas.gov/eft/regs/6-25-98.html, updated June 25, 1998.

4. John P. Caskey, *Fringe Banking: Check-Cashing Outlets, Pawnshops, and the Poor* (New York: Russell Sage Foundation, 1994), p. 129.

5. American Association of Retired Persons, written comments on interim rule for Management of Federal Agency Disbursements, 61 Federal Register 39,253, November 25, 1996 (Letter from Martin Corry, director, Federal Affairs Department, to Cynthia L. Johnson, Financial Management Service).

6. "Banking Fees," *USA Today*, July 16, 1999, p. B1.

7. New York Clearinghouse, written comments on interim rule for Management of Federal Agency Disbursements, 61 Federal Register 39,253, November 26, 1996 (letter from Jill M. Considine, president, to Cynthia L. Johnson, Financial Management Service).

8. ACORN, written comments on proposed rule for Electronic Benefits Transfer, 62 Federal Register 25,572, July 8, 1997 (unsigned letter to director of card technology, Financial Management Services).

9. Financial Management Services, *Direct Payment Card Pilot: Statistical Evaluation of Float Earnings* (U.S. Department of Treasury, June 26, 1997), pp. 1–2.

10. Organization for a New Equality, *Cash, Credit & EFT'99: Reducing the Cost of Credit and Capital for the Urban Poor* (New York, no date), p. 17.

11. See, for example, discussions of this issue by Elizabeth Rhyne of the U.S. Agency for International Development and Pamela Flaherty of Citicorp, in *Financial Access in the 21st Century*, proceedings of a forum held February 11, 1997 (Office of Comptroller of the Currency), pp. 12, 14.

12. Financial Management Services, *Statistical Evaluation of Float Earnings*, p. 4.

13. Abt Associates, *The Evaluation for the Expanded EBT Demonstration in Maryland, Vol. 3: System Impacts on Demonstration Participants* (U.S. Department of Agriculture, May 1994), pp. 26–29 (reporting that the number of food purchases per month rose and that participants reported a significant drop in the number of days without food in their households).

14. Abt Associates, *The Evaluation for the Expanded EBT Demonstration in Maryland, Vol. 2: System Impacts on Program Costs and Integrity* (U.S. Department of Agriculture, May 1994), pp. D-3 to D-6. This analysis was performed not as a way to study recipients' behavior, but rather to calculate the effect of EBT on government float.

15. John D. Hawke Jr., undersecretary of the Treasury for domestic finance, "EFT '99: An Expanded Role for the Government and a Challenge for the Private Sector," remarks to the Bank Administration Institute's Symposium of Payment System Strategy, held in Washington, D.C. on October 21, 1997, p. 5.

16. Hawke, quoted in *Financial Access in the 21st Century*, p. 39.

17. Hawke, "EFT '99," p. 6.

18. Hawke, quoted in *Financial Access in the 21st Century*, p. 40.

19. Robert E. Litan with Jonathan Rauch, *American Finance for the 21st Century* (U.S. Department of the Treasury, November 17, 1997), p. 82.

20. Crestar Bank, written comments on proposed rule for Management of Federal Agency Disbursements, 62 Federal Register 48,713, December 12, 1997 (Letter from Patricia R. Tudor, vice president, strategic marketing, to Cynthia L. Johnson, Financial Management Service, and to Marcia Z. Sullivan, Consumer Bankers Association).

21. American League of Financial Institutions, written comments on proposed rule for Management of Federal Agency Disbursements, 62 Federal Register 48,713, December 16, 1997 (letter from Dina Nichelson on behalf of membership to Cynthia L. Johnson, Financial Management Service).

22. "Electronic Benefits Transfer—It's Here!" *Missouri Courier* (Missouri Credit Union System), vol. 39, no. 6 (Summer 1997), p. 13. Data cited are from CUNA Economics and Statistics.

23. Rochelle L. Stanfield, "Capitalism for the Poor," *National Journal*, July 11, 1998, p. 1620.

24. Hawke, "EFT '99," p. 6.

25. Hawke, *Financial Access in the 21st Century*, p. 38.

26. Beth Berselli, "Treasury to Exempt Some Recipients of Payments from Electronic Delivery Rules," *Washington Post*, September 12, 1997, p. A14.

27. Ibid.

28. *Proposed Rule: Management of Federal Agency Disbursements*, 62 Federal Register 48,713, p. 48,718.

29. Berselli, "Treasury to Exempt Some Recipients," p. A14.

30. Hawke, *Financial Access in the 21st Century*, p. 40.

31. John D. Hawke, quoted in Financial Management Service, "Final Rule for Electronic Government Payments," June 25, 1998, p. 1.

32. Financial Management Service, "Final Rule for Electronic Government Payments," p. 2.

33. *Final Rule: Management of Federal Agency Disbursements*, 63 Federal Register 51,490 (September 25, 1998) (to be codified at 61 C.F.R. 208.4a), p. 51,504.

34. Mellon Bank, N.A., written comments on proposed rule for Management of Federal Agency Disbursements, 62 Federal Register 48,713, December. 11, 1997 (letter from Kenneth W. Potter, vice president, to Cynthia L. Johnson, Financial Management Service).

35. Bank of America, written comments on proposed rule for Management of Federal Agency Disbursements, 62 Federal Register 48,713, December 15, 1997 (letter from John H. Huffstutler, senior vice president and chief regulatory counsel, to Cynthia L. Johnson, Financial Management Service).

36. Mellon Bank, N.A., written comments on proposed rule for Management of Federal Agency Disbursements, 62 Federal Register 48,713.

37. PNC Bank, N.A., written comments on proposed rule for Management of Federal Agency Disbursements, 62 Federal Register 48,713, December 15, 1997 (letter from Alfred F. Cordasco, supervising counsel, to Cynthia L. Johnson, Financial Management Service).

38. Citicorp, written comments on proposed rule for Management of Federal Agency Disbursements, 62 Federal Register 48,713, December 15, 1997 (letter from Mark E. MacKenzie, executive director, to Cynthia L. Johnson, Financial Management Service).

39. Letter from Margot Saunders, managing attorney, National Consumer Law Center, to Treasury Secretary Robert E. Rubin, November 9, 1998 (cosigned by fourteen other advocacy organizations).

40. National Check Cashers Association, written comments on proposed features for Electronic Transfer Accounts, 63 Federal Register 64,820, January 7, 1999 (letter from Stephen H. Wolf, chairman of federal payments committee, to Cynthia L. Johnson, Financial Management Service).

41. Letter to Donald V. Hammond, fiscal assistant secretary of the Treasury, from John Taylor, president and CEO, the National Community Reinvestment Coalition, concerning the Advance Notice of Proposed Rulemaking regarding the possible Regulation Regarding Access to Accounts at Financial Institutions, April 6, 1999, p. 2.

42. Letter to Donald V. Hammond, fiscal assistant secretary of the Treasury, from Deborah Goldberg, Neighborhood Revitalization Project, Center for Community Change, concerning the Advance Notice of Proposed Rulemaking regarding the possible Regulation Regarding Access to Acounts at Financial Institutions, April 8, 1999, p. 2.

43. Letter to Mr. Roger Bezdek, Office of the Fiscal Assistant Secretary of the Treasury, from Timothy Hammonds, president and CEO of the Food Marketing Institute, concerning the Advance Notice of Proposed Rulemaking regarding the possible Regulation Regarding Access to Accounts at Financial Institutions, April 8, 1999, p. 1.

44. Hawke, *Financial Access in the 21st Century*, p. 40.

45. "Proposed Features: Electronic Transfer Accounts," 63 Federal Register 64,819, November 23, 1998, p. 64,823.

46. Financial Management Service, "Commonly Asked Questions," http://www.fms.treas.gov/eft/question.html, updated October 27, 1998.

47. Hawke, *Financial Access in the 21st Century*, p. 39.

48. Stanfield, "Capitalism for the Poor," p. 1619.

49. Bank of America, written comments on proposed rule for Management of Federal Agency Disbursements, 62 Federal Register 48,713, December 15, 1997.

50. Stanfield, "Capitalism for the Poor," p. 1619.

51. ACORN, written comments on proposed rule for Electronic Benefits Transfer, 62 Federal Register 25,572, July 8, 1997. The $25 estimate included fees for use of recipient's bank ATMs, foreign ATM surcharges, and the cost of money orders to pay rent and utilities because the EBT pilot did not include payment services.

52. National Consumer Law Center, written comments on 61 Federal Regulation 39253. (Letter from Margot Saunders, managing attorney, and Barbara Leyser, EBT consultant, to Cynthia Johnson, Financial Management Service, November 25, 1996.)

53. Hawke, *Financial Access in the 21st Century*, p. 38.

54. Financial Management Service, "Fact Sheet: Notice of Proposed Electronic Transfer Account Features; Request for Comment," http://www.fms.treas.gov/eft/eta/etafact.html, updated November 23, 1998.

55. "Proposed Features: Electronic Transfer Accounts," 63 Federal Register 64,819, p. 64,821.

56. Ibid., p. 64,824.

57. Dove Associates, *ETA Initiative Final Report* (U.S. Department of Treasury, June 15, 1998), p. 25.

58. Ibid., p. 27.

59. Ibid., pp. 17–18, 21–22, 31.

60. Ibid., p. 49.

61. Ibid., p. 54.

62. The study assumed ETA accounts would include a $3 monthly fee, two cash withdrawals and two balance inquiries at the financial institution's ATM network, one teller transaction and four transactions at point-of-sale terminals, no minimum balance requirement, a monthly mailed statement, no interest paid on account balance, direct deposit of federal funds only, no savings or bill payment options, a "7x24" call center for customer service to notify of a lost or stolen card, and full compliance with Regulation E. Dove Associates, *ETA Initiative Final Report*, pp. 60–61.

63. Dove Associates, *ETA Initiative Final Report*, p. 68.

64. Ibid., p. 61.

65. Ibid., p. 69.

66. *Proposed Features: Electronic Transfer Account*, 63 Federal Register 64,819, p. 64,823.

67. National Association of Federal Credit Unions, written comments on proposed features for Electronic Transfer Accounts, 63 Federal Register 64,819, January 6, 1999 (letter from Kenneth L. Robinson, to Cynthia L. Johnson, Financial Management Service).

68. Citizen Savings Association, written comments on proposed features for Electronic Transfer Accounts, 63 Federal Register 64,819, December 21, 1998 (Letter from Leonard J. Lavelle, vice president, savings, to Cynthia L. Johnson, Financial Management Service).

69. Massachusetts Community & Banking Council, written comments on proposed features for Electronic Transfer Accounts, 63 Federal Register 64,819, no date (letter from Kathleen Tullberg, manager, to Cynthia L. Johnson, Financial Management Service).

70. Financial Management Service, "ETA Comment Summary: Notice of Proposed ETA Features, http://www.fms.treas.gov/eta/summary.html, updated February 11, 1999.

71. See, for example, Electronic Funds Transfer Association, written comments on proposed features for Electronic Transfer Accounts, 63 Federal Register 64,819, January 7, 1999 (letter from H. Kurt Helwig, executive director, to Cynthia L. Johnson, Financial Management Service).

72. Branch Banking & Trust Company, written comments on proposed features for Electronic Transfer Accounts, 63 Federal Register 64,819, January 5, 1999 (letter from Sonia L. Beach, vice president, marketing, to Cynthia L. Johnson, Financial Management Service).

73. Dime Savings Bank of New York, FSB, written comments on proposed features for Electronic Transfer Accounts, 63 Federal Register 64,819, January 7, 1999 (letter from Robert S. Monheit, regulatory counsel, to Cynthia L. Johnson, Financial Management Service).

74. Ibid.

75. "Proposed Features: Electronic Transfer Accounts," 63 Federal Register 64,819, p. 64,821.

76. Dove Associates, *ETA Initiative Final Report*, p. 73.

77. Financial Management Service, "ETA Comment Summary: Notice of Proposed ETA Features," p. 4.

78. Bank of America, written comments on proposed features for Electronic Transfer Accounts, 63 Federal Register 64,819, January 7, 1999 (letter from Patrick M. Frawley, regulator relations director, to Cynthia L. Johnson, Financial Management Service).

79. "Proposed Features: Electronic Transfer Accounts," 63 Federal Register 64,819, pp. 64,824–64,825.

80. Ibid., p. 64,822.

81. Ibid., p. 64,825.

82. Dove Associates, *ETA Initiative Optional Account Features: Economic Waterfall Analyses* (U.S. Department of the Treasury, June 26, 1998), p. 5.

83. Ibid., p. 5.

84. Ibid., p. 21.

85. Ibid., p. 2.

86. Ibid., p. 14.

87. Financial Management Service, "ETA Comment Summary: Notice of Proposed ETA Features," p. 2.

88. Bank of America, written comments on proposed features for Electronic Transfer Accounts, 63 Federal Register 64,819.

89. Branch Banking & Trust Company, written comments on proposed features for Electronic Transfer Accounts, 63 Federal Register 64,819.

90. Debby Goldberg, "NCLC EBT: CCC Alert on ETA Proposal," December 29, 1998.

91. Ibid.

92. The ETA Financial Agency Agreement is an agreement between Treasury and a financial institution designating the financial institution to act as Treasury's financial agent in providing ETAs. Any financial institution that offers the ETA must do so subject to the terms and conditions of the agreement. The agreement incorporates the final features of the account and other account criteria, such as standards for closing accounts. See Treasury Office of Public Affairs, Press Release RR-3229 attachment from the Financial Management Service, "Commonly Asked Questions," June 30 1999.

93. "Vice President Gore, Treasury Secretary Rubin Announce Low-Cost Electronic Account," The White House, Office of the Vice President (June 30, 1999).

94. These consumer protections are incorporated into regulations issued by the Federal Reserve Board. Regulation DD is the Federal Reserve's regulation implementing the Truth in Savings Act of 1991. Regulation DD is designed to enable consumers to make informed decisions about accounts at depository institutions by requiring depository institutions to provide disclosures regarding the rates of interest payable on deposit accounts, minimum balance requirements, and the fees that are assessable against deposit accounts. Regulation E establishes the basic rights, liabilities, and responsibilities of consumers who use EFT

services and of financial institutions that offer these services. See "ETA Electronic Transfer Account Commonly Asked Questions and Answers."

95. Ibid.

96. Ibid.

97. Ibid.

98. The Roper Organization, *Check Cashing Services Study* (Consumer Bankers Association, December 1989), p. 5. However, the size of the sample was small and not representative. Only 33 percent of the 505 participants were unbanked. For a detailed analysis of the study, see Caskey, *Fringe Banking*, pp. 74–76.

99. John D. Hawke Jr., "Sending the Right Message to Federal Payment Recipients," EFT Exchange, vol. 1, no. 2 (June 1998), p. 2 (http://www.fms.treas.gov/eft/educ/exch6-98.html).

100. Caskey, *Fringe Banking*, pp. 148–49.

101. Hawke, "Sending the Right Message," p. 2.

102. "EBT Questions & Answers," Financial Management Service web site, http://www.fms.treas.gov/ebt/question.html., updated May 8, 1998.

103. Ibid.

104. Brian Kibble-Smith, "Citibank Profitably Pioneers Electronic Benefits Transfer Programs, " *Journal of Retail Banking Services*, vol. 19, no. 4 (Winter 1997), p. 4.

105. Stanfield, "Capitalism for the Poor," p. 1620.

106. Food and Nutrition Service, "Food Stamp Program Electronic Benefit Transfer (EBT) Highlights," http://www.fns.usda.gov/fsp/MENU/ADMIN/EBT/status/EBT-CONG-Jan99.doc, updated January 1999.

107. Telephone survey by Center for Community Capitalism, Kenan Institute of Private Enterprise, University of North Carolina at Chapel Hill, June 1998.

108. States save money by converting paper systems to EBT because federal regulations effectively prevent states from spending more for an EBT system than they would spend on a paper system. Although EBT vendors charge client governments a fee for each benefit case they carry on their system each month, this "case-month" fee must meet certain "cost neutrality" criteria because federal contributions to a state's EBT costs are limited. Kibble-Smith, "Citibank Profitably Pioneers Electronic Benefits Transfer Programs, " pp. 5–6.

109. Nomination form, 1998 Missouri Governor's Award for Quality and Productivity (no date), p. 2.

110. Viveca Ware, "Governments and EFT," *Independent Banker*, March 1998, p. 20.

111. Carla Rivera, "Bank to Open Accounts for Welfare Recipients," *Los Angeles Times*, May 27, 1999, p. B5.

112. Ibid.

113. Missouri Department of Social Services, "Direct Deposit Initiative," fact sheet, no date.

114. Ibid.

115. Letter from Melba Price, April 9, 1999.

116. Ibid.

117. "Treasury Fiscal Assistant Secretary Donald V. Hammond Testimony

before the House Subcommittee on General Oversight and Investigations," Office of Public Affairs, Department of the Treasury, March 2, 1999, pp. 2, 4.

Chapter Six

1. *Empowerment: A New Covenant with America's Communities*, President Clinton's National Urban Policy Report (U.S. Department of Housing and Urban Development, July 1995), p. 2.

2. Joseph E. Stiglitz and Jason Furman, "Economic Consequences of Income Inequality," *FOMC Alert*, vol. 2, no. 6 (September 29, 1998), p. 7. The Stiglitz and Furman paper cited here was presented at the Federal Reserve Bank of Kansas City's Jackson Hole symposium on August 29, 1998.

3. Robert Townsend, "Formal and Informal Financial Services," in *Financial Access in the 21st Century*, proceedings of a February 11, 1997, forum (Office of the Comptroller of the Currency), p. 19.

4. Thomas M. Shapiro, *The Importance of Assets*, unpublished paper prepared for Ford Foundation, December 10–12, 1998, Conference on the Benefits and Mechanisms for Spreading Asset Ownership (New York University), p. 3.

5. See generally Michael Sherraden, *Assets and the Poor: A New American Welfare Policy* (M. E. Sharpe, 1991); Karen Edwards, *Individual Development Accounts: Creative Savings for Families and Communities*, Policy Report (St. Louis: Washington University Center for Social Development, 1997).

6. Edwards, *Individual Development Accounts*, p. 3.

7. Ibid., pp. 18–19.

8. Michael A. Stegman, *More Housing, More Fairly*, report of the Twentieth Century Fund Task Force on Affordable Housing (Twentieth Century Fund Press, 1991), p. 46.

9. Letter from Robert W. Gray, Office of Policy Development and Research, U.S. Department of Housing and Urban Development, August 25, 1998.

10. Ibid.

11. Edwards, *Individual Development Accounts*, p. 16.

12. Federal Home Loan Bank of New York, "First Home Club Program Guidelines" (New York: May 1996).

13. Telephone interview with Judy Dailey, vice president and community investment officer for the Federal Home Loan Bank of Seattle, November 1997.

14. Gary V. Engelhardt, "Do Targeted Savings Incentives for Homeownership Work? The Canadian Experience," *Journal of Housing Research*, vol. 8, no. 2 (1997), pp. 225, 244.

15. Total wealth was about $20.6 trillion in 1989 (in 1995 dollars). John C. Weicher, "Increasing Inequality of Wealth?" *The Public Interest* (Winter 1997), pp. 17–18.

16. Joint Center for Housing Studies, *The State of the Nation's Housing 1997* (Harvard University, 1997), pp. 18–19.

17. Ibid.

18. Department of Health and Human Services, "State Welfare Demonstrations," Fact Sheet (October 10, 1996).

19. Michael Sherraden and Robert E. Friedman, "A Saving Feature in Welfare Reform" (St. Louis: Washington University Center for Social Development, no date).

20. Department of Health and Human Services, "State Welfare Demonstrations," Fact Sheet (October 10, 1996).

21. Cited by Michael Sherraden and Sondra Beverly in "Institutional Determinants of Saving: Implications for Low-Income Households," *Journal of Socio-Economics* (forthcoming), p. 13.

22. Kathryn Edin, "The Role of Assets in the Lives of Low-Income Single Mothers and Non-Custodial Fathers," paper presented at the December 10-12, 1998 Ford Foundation Conference on the Benefits and Mechanisms for Spreading Asset Ownership (New York University), p. 8.

23. Ibid.

24. Ibid., p. 26.

25. Sherraden, *Assets and the Poor*, pp. 220-33.

26. Corporation for Enterprise Development, *Assets: A Quarterly Update for Innovators* (Summer 1998), p. 3.

27. Corporation for Enterprise Development, "How IDAs Work," http://cfed.cfed.org/idas/documents/howworks.htm, last updated January 12, 1998.

28. Corporation for Enterprise Development, "PA Funds IDA Pilot Program for Spring Kickoff" and "Bi-Partisan Maine IDA Bill Picking Up Steam," *Assets: A Quarterly Update for Innovators* (Spring 1997).

29. Neal R. Peirce, "Savings Incentives—For the Poor?" *Washington Post*, syndicated column, October 5, 1997.

30. Corporation for Enterprise Development, "How IDAs Work."

31. E-mail from Caroline Dugan to members of the IDA network, June 9, 1999.

32. Corporation for Enterprise Development, "Innovative Missouri IDA Bill Utilizes Tax Credits for Funding," "Bi-Partisan Maine IDA Bill Picking Up Steam," and "North Carolina IDA Working Group Secures Funding from State," *Assets: A Quarterly Update for Innovators*, Spring 1997.

33. National Governors' Association, *Building Assets and Economic Independence through Individual Development Accounts*, Issue Brief (January 31, 1997), p.4.

34. Personal Responsibility and Work Opportunity Reconciliation Act of 1996, section 404(h), P.L. 104-193, 104 Cong. 1 sess.

35. National Governors' Association, *Building Assets and Economic Independence*, p. 1.

36. Karen Edwards, "Individual Development Accounts (IDAs): Creative Savings Opportunities for Individuals and Families," *Bridges* (Federal Reserve Bank of St. Louis: Summer 1998), p. 6.

37. http://www.arkleg.state.ar.us.

38. Corporation for Enterprise Development, *Assets: A Quarterly Update for Innovators*, (Summer 1998), p. 13.

39. National Governors' Association, *Building Assets and Economic Independence*, p. 3.

40. Edwards, "Individual Development Accounts," pp. 1, 6.

41. Pennsylvania Department of Community and Economic Development, "Empowering Individuals: Family Savings Accounts," http://www.dced.state. pa.us/PA_Exec/DCED/project/emp-fsa.htm, last updated October 1998.

42. National Governors' Association, *Building Assets and Economic Independence*, p. 4.

43. Angela Duran, "Individual Development Accounts," *Policy Points*, vol. 2 (Pine Bluff, Arkansas: Good Faith Fund, October 19, 1998), p. 5.

44. Corporation for Economic Development, "Bi-Partisan Maine IDA Bill Picking Up Steam."

45. Corporation for Economic Development, "Innovative Missouri IDA Bill Utilizes Tax Credits for Funding."

46. Rocky Mountain Mutual Housing Association, *First Home Savings Plan*, Fact Sheet (no date).

47. Gautam N. Yadama and Michael Sherraden, *Effects of Assets on Attitudes and Behaviors: Advance Test of a Social Policy Proposal*, Working Paper (St. Louis: Washington University Center for Social Development, 1995).

48. See, for example, Peirce, "Savings Incentives—For the Poor?"

49. Corporation for Economic Development, "National IDA Demonstration Launched," *Assets: A Quarterly Update for Innovators* (Fall 1997). http:// www.cfed.org/idas/documents/AssetsFal97/afal97.htm.

50. Bob Friedman, Corporation for Enterprise Development, "What's in a Name?" *Assets: A Quarterly Update for Innovators* (Fall 1997) http://www.cfed.org/ idas/documents/AssetsFal97/afal97.htm.

51. Yadama and Sherraden, *Effects of Assets on Attitudes and Behaviors*. See also Corporation for Economic Development, "National IDA Demonstration Launched," and Michael Sherraden, Deborah Page-Adams, and Lissa Johnson, *Start-Up Evaluation Report: Downpayment on the American Dream Policy Demonstration* (St. Louis: Washington University Center for Social Development, January 1999).

52. Telephone interview with Jennifer Robey, CAPTC IDA program coordinator, August 27, 1998; Corporation for Economic Development, "National IDA Demonstration Launched."

53. Sherraden and others, *Start-Up Evaluation Report: Downpayment on the American Dream Policy Demonstration*, p. 19.

54. Letter and supplemental materials to the author by Jennifer Tescher, IDA business manager, February 12, 1999.

55. Center for Social Development, *Preliminary Report: American Dream Demonstration as of December 31, 1998* (St. Louis: Washington University, February 1999), pp. 1–7.

56. Under the Earned Income Tax Credit, which provides a refundable tax credit for poor workers, a married worker raising one child with a family income less than $25,760 can receive up to $2,210, while a worker raising more than one child with a family income less than $29,290 can receive an EITC of up to $3,656. In Fiscal Year 1999, tax expenditures for the EITC are expected to exceed $28 billion. David Stoesz and David Saunders, *Welfare Capitalism: New Opportunities in Poverty Policy* (Virginia Commonwealth University, 1998) pp. 4–5.

57. Jason DeParle, "On a Once Forlorn Avenue, Tax Preparers Now Flourish," *New York Times on the Web*, March 21, 1999, p. 2.

58. Telephone interview with Jennifer Robey, CAPTC IDA program coordinator, August 27, 1998.

59. Peirce, "Savings Incentives—For the Poor?"

60. Program announcement and application materials are available on the ORR website at www.acf.dhhs.gov/programs/orr/ida.htm.

61. President Bill Clinton, quoted in *Empowerment: A New Covenant with America's Communities*, p. 27.

62. President Bill Clinton, remarks on Universal Savings Accounts (White House Office of the Press Secretary, April 14, 1999).

63. Ibid.

64. Offered by Senator Frank Lautenberg, D-NJ, for Senators Lieberman, himself, Santorum, Binaman, and Abraham, as an amendment to the concurrent resolution, S. Con. Res. 20, 106 Cong. 1 sess., March 25, 1999.

65. National Governors' Association, *Building Assets and Economic Independence*, p. 4.

66. John D. Hawke Jr., undersecretary of the Treasury for domestic finance. Hearings before the Subcommittee on Government Management, Information and Technology of the House Government Reform and Oversight Committee. Text as prepared for delivery available from the U.S. Department of Treasury website http://www.ustreas.gov/treasury/press/pr061897.html. June 18, 1997.

67. Letter and supplemental materials to the author by Jennifer Tescher, February 12, 1999; Corporation for Economic Development, "Shorebank Corporation."

68. Corporation for Economic Development, "Alternatives Federal Credit Union," *Assets: A Quarterly Update for Innovators* (Fall 1997). http://www.cfed.org/idas/documents/AssetsFal97/afal97.htm.

69. John D. Hawke Jr., *Financial Access in the 21st Century*, p. 40.

70. Robert E. Litan with Jonathan Rauch, *American Finance for the 21st Century* (U.S. Department of the Treasury, November 17, 1997), p. 149.

71. Senator J. Robert Kerrey, "Introductory Floor Statement on KidSave," (Office of J. Robert Kerrey, June 17, 1998), p. 2.

72. Offered by Senator Frank Lautenberg, D-N.J., as an amendment to S. Con. Res. 20, March 25, 1999.

73. Corporation for Enterprise Development, *USAs, Universal Savings Accounts—A Route to National Economic Growth and Family Economic Security* (Washington, D.C., 1996), p. 9.

74. Corporation for Enterprise Development, "Sense of the Congress Resolution on the Assets for Independence Act," *Assets: A Quarterly Update for Innovators* (Summer 1998), p. 3.

75. Michael A. Fletcher, "Race Board's Focus Turns to Economic Gap," *Washington Post*, January 15, 1998, p. A8.

76. Melvin L. Oliver and Thomas M. Shapiro, *Black Wealth/White Wealth: A New Perspective on Racial Inequality* (Routledge, 1997), p. 7.

77. "Study Finds Social Security Narrows Gap in White and Minority Retire-

ment Wealth but Disparities are Still Great," PR Newswire, February 9, 1999 (online). The International Longevity Center-USA Ltd. released the study.

78. For a forceful statement of this argument, see Oliver and Shapiro, *Black Wealth/White Wealth.*

79. Elizabeth C. McNichol and Edward B. Lazere, *Most States Still Tax the Working Poor after Five Years of Economic Recovery* (Center for Budget Policy and Priorities, April 11, 1997). http://www.cbpp.org/sttax.htm.

80. Iris J. Lav, "The Final Tax Bill: Assessing the Long-Term Costs and the Distribution of Tax Benefits" (Center for Budget and Policy Priorities, August 1, 1997), pp. 3–4. http://www.cbpp.org/801tax.htm.

81. Lav, "Who Benefits from Specific Tax Cuts" (Center for Budget and Policy Priorities, August 1, 1997), p. 5. http://www.cbpp.org/801tax.htm.

82. Center on Budget and Policy Priorities, "Joint Tax Committee Distribution Table of the Roth Bill," p. 2, June 19, 1997.

83. Unpublished estimates provided by the Department of Treasury, September 30, 1997.

84. Clinton, remarks on Universal Savings Accounts.

85. Ibid.

86. William G. Gale, senior fellow, The Brookings Institution. "Public Policies toward Saving: Should We Expand Individual Retirement Accounts?" Hearings before the U.S. Senate Committee on Finance, March 6, 1997, p. 2. Available at www.brook.edu/views/testimony/gale/19770306.htm.

87. Ibid, p. 2.

88. Laurence S. Seidman, "Assets and the Tax Code," Ford Foundation Conference on the Benefits and Mechanisms for Spreading Asset Ownership, December 10–12, 1998 (New York University), p. i.

89. Seidman, "Assets and the Tax Code," p. 29.

90. Cynthia A. Glassman, "Consumer Finance: The Borrowing/Savings Dilemma," *Journal of Retail Banking Services,* vol. 28, no. 3 (Autumn 1996), p. 54.

91. John P. Caskey, *Beyond Cash and Carry: Financial Services, Financial Savings, and Low-Income Households in Two Communities* (Consumer Federation of America, December 1997), p. i.

92. Ibid.

93. Sondra Beverly, *How Can the Poor Save? Theory and Evidence on Saving in Low-Income Households,* Working Paper No. 97-3 (St. Louis: Washington University Center for Social Development, 1997), p. 25.

94. Ibid., pp. 14–15.

95. Data were provided by the U.S. Department of the Treasury from the 1993 Current Population Survey.

96. The White House, "Agenda Background Materials," prepared for the June 4–5, 1998 National Summit on Retirement Savings, p. 16.

97. Data were provided by the U.S. Department of the Treasury from 1996 Federal Thrift Investment Board statistics.

98. Data were provided by the U.S. Department of the Treasury from 1996 Federal Thrift Investment Board statistics.

99. Ibid.

100. Available research shows that companies with an automatic enrollment policy have participation rates of 90 percent, while the overall 401(k)-enrollment rate is 67 percent. The White House, "President Clinton: Preparing Americans for the Future," http://www.whitehouse.gov/WH/work?060498.htm, June 4, 1998.

101. Paul J. Yakoboski, *EBRI News* (Washington, D.C.: Employee Research Benefit Institute, March 1997), p. 1.

102. The literature suggests, for example, that frequent retirement education seminars are associated with higher 401(k) participation and contribution rates. See Michael Sherraden and Sondra Beverly, "Institutional Determinants of Saving: Implications for Low-Income Households," *Journal of Socio-Economics*, forthcoming, p. 11.

103. There is an extensive literature in this area. The quote is from Marguerite S. Robinson, "Savings Mobilization and Microenterprise Finance: The Indonesian Experience," in Maria Otero and Elisabeth Rhyne, eds., *The New World of Microenterprise Finance: Building Healthy Financial Institutions for the Poor* (Kumarian Press, 1994), p. 27.

104. Robinson, "Savings Mobilization and Microenterprise Finance," pp. 27–28.

105. Remarks of J. Brian Atwood, Inauguration of Bank Rakyat Indonesia International Visitor Program, Jakarta, Indonesia, June 26, 1996, p. 1. Text available at www.info.usaid.gov/press/spe_test/speech.416, last accessed on October 16, 1998.

106. Corporation for Enterprise Development, written comments on proposed rule for Management of Financial Agency Disbursements, 62 Federal Register 48,713, November 25, 1997 (letter from Robert E. Friedman et al. to Cynthia L. Johnson, Financial Management Service).

107. Rochelle L. Stanfield, "Capitalism for the Poor," *National Journal*, July 11, 1998, p. 1618.

108. The White House, *1998 National Summit on Retirement Savings, Summit Agenda* (June 4–5, 1998), p. 16. http://www.whitehouse.gov/WH/work?060498.htm.,

109. Jannett Highfill, Douglas Thorson, and William V. Weber, "Tax Overwithholding as a Response to Uncertainty, " *Public Finance Review*, vol. 26, no. 4 (July 1998), p. 8.

110. Jason DeParle, "On a Once Forlorn Avenue, Tax Preparers Now Flourish," p. 4.

111. Michael Sherraden, "IDAs in the Big Picture," *Assets: A Quarterly Update for Innovators* (Corporation for Enterprise Development, Summer 1998), p. 6.

112. Ibid.

113. Just as with social security—coverage was denied to agricultural workers and domestic servants under the 1935 Act, which included three-fifths of all southern black workers at the time, in order to secure the votes of southern Democrats—the transition to defined contribution plans also has racial implications. See Jill Quadagno, "Creating a Capital Investment Welfare State: The New American Exceptionalism: 1998 Presidential Address," *American Sociological Review*, vol. 64, issue 1 (February 1999), p. 3.

114. Jill Quadagno, "Creating a Capital Investment Welfare State," p. 3.

115. Gary Burtless and Barry Bosworth, "Social Security: The Troubling Tradeoffs," Policy Brief 14 (Brookings Institution, March 1997), p. 4.

Chapter Seven

1. "CRA: Revisiting Some Fundamentals," remarks by Ellen Seidman, director, Office of Thrift Supervision, at the Consumer Bankers' Association Annual Conference, Arlington, Va., April 26, 1999, p. 3.

2. "OCC Approves Local CRA Assessment Area for National Internet Bank," *CRA and Fair Lending News Service*, at www.cranewsservice.com, last accessed July 14, 1999.

3. "Gramm Says OTS 'Assessment Area' Policies Lack Statutory Authority," *CRA and Fair Lending News Service*, at www.cranewsservice.com, last accessed July 14, 1999.

4. "OCC Approves Local CRA Assessment Area for National Internet Bank," *CRA and Fair Lending News Service*, at www.cranewsservice.com, last accessed July 14, 1999.

5. Ibid., citing OCC.

6. John P. Caskey, *Fringe Banking: Check-Cashing Outlets, Pawnshops, and the Poor* (New York: Russell Sage Foundation, 1994), p. 149.

7. David L. G. Lidman, *Coupon Savings Account System*, United States Patent Number 5,471,669 (November 28, 1995).

8. Cheryl Wetzstein, "Welfare Reformers to Press Family Planning, Work Goals," *Washington Post*, December 30, 1998, p. A4; Al Kamen, "Clinton Touts Decline in Welfare Rolls, New Rules for States," *Washington Post*, April 11, 1999, p. A7.

9. Judith Haverman, "Drop in Food Stamp Rolls Is Worrying Officials," *Washington Post*, March 7, 1999, p. A2.

10. Jenifer Peterson, "Welfare with a Debit Card: States Look to Private Firms to Automate Delivery of Benefits," August 12, 1998. http://cnn.com/Allpolitics/1998/08/12/ebt.monopoly.

11. Weinberg & Vauthier Consulting, *EBT Watch*, Washington, D.C., December 4, 1998, p. 5.

12. Peterson, "Welfare with a Debit Card."

13. Robert E. Litan with Jonathan Rauch, *American Finance for the 21st Century* (U.S. Department of the Treasury, November 17, 1997), p. 146.

14. Stephen Brobeck, executive director of Consumer Federation of America, in *Financial Access in the 21st Century*, proceedings of a February 11, 1997, forum (Office of the Comptroller of the Currency), p. 27.

15. Message from Kirsten S. Moy, director of Community Development Financial Institutions Fund, in Community Development Financial Institutions Fund, *Annual Report Fiscal Year 1996* (U.S. Treasury Department, 1996), p. 1.

16. Paul J. Lim, "Your Money: Funds and 401(k)s, with Clinton Plan Education will be Crucial and Costly," *Los Angeles Times*, January 24, 1999, p. C1.

17. William G. Gale, "Public Policies toward Saving: Should We Expand Individual Retirement Accounts?" Testimony before the Senate Committee on Finance, March 6, 1997, pp. 9–10. (available at www.brook.edu.)

18. Many banks already offer no-cost/low-cost accounts, although it does not seem that they are heavily advertised and marketed. Currently, seven states—Illinois, Massachusetts, Minnesota, New Jersey, New York, Rhode Island, and Vermont—have lifeline banking laws that apply to state-regulated, but not federally chartered, financial institutions. Similarly, a recent survey by the Consumer Banking Association indicated that 80 percent of responding member banks offered no-frills checking accounts, as of December 1997. The average monthly service fee was $3.66, with a range of $2 to $7, and 24 percent of the banks surveyed did not charge any fees. Consumer Banking Association, Basic Banking Survey (December 1997), http://www.cbanet.org/Products/basic_banking_survey.htm. There is no empirical evidence, however, that lifeline banking per se significantly reduces the number of unbanked individuals in a state or community. Joseph J. Doyle, Jose A. Lopez, and Marc R. Saidenberg, "How Effective is Lifeline Banking in Assisting the Unbanked?" *Current Issues in Economics and Finance,* Federal Reserve Bank of New York, vol. 4, no. 6 (June 1998), p. 1.

19. Existing CRA policies with respect to IDAs discussed here are from Office of Thrift Supervision, *Individual Development Accounts (IDAs): Strategies for Asset Accumulation* (November 1998), p. 21.

20. "Activists: Regulate E-Banking Now," *The Regulatory Compliance Watch,* vol. 10, no. 17 (April 28, 1997), p. 1.

21. Robert Freedman, "Scores Rise with New CRA Exams, But Critics Charge Grade Inflation," *Affordable Housing Finance,* vol. 6, no. 6 (June/July 1998), p. 34.

22. Litan and Rauch, *American Finance for the 21st Century,* p. 145.

23. Office of the Comptroller of the Currency, "Interagency CRA Questions and Answers," 12 CFR 25.21-25, at http://www.occ.treas.gov/cra/craindx.htm.

24. Robert B. Avery and others, "Changes in the Distribution of Banking Offices," *Federal Reserve Bulletin,* vol. 83, no. 9 (September 1997), p. 11.

25. Office of the Comptroller of the Currency, "Interagency CRA Questions and Answers."

26. Glenn Canner and Wayne Passmore, "The Community Reinvestment Act and the Profitability of Mortgage-Oriented Banks," *Federal Reserve Board Paper 1997-7* (1997), abstract and p. 26.

27. E-mail to financial regulators from Marva E. Williams, senior project director, Woodstock Institute, Chicago, December 15, 1998.

28. Letter to Verne G. Istock, chairman, president and CEO, Chicago NBD Corporation, from Chicago CRA Coalition Steering Committee, August 6, 1998. The elements of the agreement are contained in this letter.

29. Details of this agreement can be found in two documents: Memorandum of Understanding between Action Alliance of Senior Citizens of Greater Philadelphia et al. and First Union National Bank, executed on July 19, 1998 (available from the law offices of Drinker, Biddle, and Reath, LLP, 1345 Chestnut Street, Philadelphia, 19107-3496); and memo from Jonathan Stein, general coun-

sel, CLS, George Gould, managing attorney, CLS, Irwin Trauss, staff attorney, Philadelphia Legal Assistance, to six partner organizations, July 15, 1998 (available from Community Legal Services, 1424 Chestnut Street, Philadelphia, PA 19102).

30. Caskey, *Fringe Banking*, p. 149.

31. Ibid.

32. National Consumer Law Center et al., *Comments to the Treasury on ANPRM 31 C.F.R. Chapter II, RIN 15055-AA74, Possible Regulation Regarding Access to Accounts at Financial Institutions through Payment Service Providers* (Washington, D.C.: no date), p. 4.

33. Ibid., p. 4.

34. Ibid., p. 3.

35. National Check Cashers Association, "NaCCA Announces New Debit Card Program," press release (January 11, 1999). Available at www.nacca.org/prb.htm.

36. National Consumer Law Center et al., *Comments to the Treasury*, p. 6.

37. Financial Management Service, "EFT'99, Commonly Asked Questions," Financial Management Service website, www.treas.gov/eft/index.html.

38. H.R.4311, "Electronic Funds Transfer Account Improvement and Recipient Protection Act." 105 Cong. 2 sess.

39. Caskey, *Fringe Banking*, p. 149.

40. David S. Neill, "Focus on ATMs, The ATM Surcharge Debate: Logical Fallacies and Antitrust Reality," *Bureau of National Affairs Daily Reporter*, vol. 71, no. 5 (August 3, 1998), p. 1.

41. Ibid., p. 1.

42. Title I, Section 101 (c) (2), S. 895, "Savings for Working Families Act." 106 Cong. 1 sess.

43. Quoted by Reverend James H. Daniel Jr., chairman/CEO of the East Fulton Street Group/21st Century Partnership, at hearings before the FDIC on electronic payment systems (Washington, D.C.: September 12, 1996).

44. Quoted in Joseph Radigan, "Will Electronic Banking Ignore the Poor?" *U.S. Banker*, vol. 106, no. 12 (December 1996), p. 68.

45. Rochelle L. Stanfield, "Capitalism for the Poor," *National Journal*, July 11, 1998, p. 1618.

46. "South Africans Push Smart Cards," *Smart Card Bulletin* (March 1995), p. IV; "SA Dwarfs Rest of Africa," *African Business* (October 1997), p. 11; "Banking for the Unbanked," *Bank Marketing International* (December 1994), p. 7; "E-Bank Meets the Unbanked Challenge," *Retail Banker International* (November 28, 1994), p. 14; "South African Banks Aim to Lure Black Savings," *Reuters Financial Service* (December 29, 1996); "Cashless South Africa a Step Nearer," *Financial Times*, London, November 25, 1997, p. 8.

47. Litan and Rauch, *American Finance for the 21st Century*, p. 135.

48. Attachment to letter to Donald V. Hammond, fiscal assistant secretary of Treasury, from attorneys general of the states of Arizona, California, Iowa, Maryland, Oklahoma, and Rhode Island, concerning the Advanced Notice of Proposed Rule M (ANPRM 31, Chapter II), January 8, 1999, p. 10. The quoted material is contained in footnote 29 of the attachment.

Index